WINDING ROADS

About the Author

Photo by Costa Hadjilambrinos

Diane Thiel is the author of seven books of poetry, nonfiction, and creative writing pedagogy. Her books include *Echolocations* (Nicholas Roerich Prize, 2000), *Writing Your Rhythm* (2001), *The White Horse: A Colombian Journey* (2004), *Resistance Fantasies* (2004), *Crossroads: Creative Writing Exercises in Four Genres* (Longman, 2005), and *Open Roads: Exercises in Writing Poetry* (Longman, 2005). Diane Thiel's translation (with co-translator Constantine Hadjilambrinos) of Greek author Alexis Stamatis's book, *American Fugue*, received a 2007 NEA International Literature Award, in conjunction with Etruscan Press. Thiel's work appears in the major journals *Poetry, The Hudson Review,* and *The Sewanee Review,* among numerous others, and is reprinted in more than thirty major anthologies, including *Best American Poetry 1999, Twentieth Century American Poetry, 180 More: Extraordinary Poems for Every Day,* and *Contemporary American Poetry.* Thiel received her BA and MFA from Brown University and has traveled and lived in various countries in Europe and South America. She has been a professor of creative writing for more than 15 years. A recipient of numerous awards, including the Robert Frost and Robinson Jeffers awards, and a recent Fulbright Scholar, she is Associate Professor of English and Creative Writing at the University of New Mexico.

WINDING ROADS

Exercises in Writing Creative Nonfiction

Diane Thiel
University of New Mexico

PEARSON
Longman

New York San Francisco Boston
London Toronto Sydney Tokyo Singapore Madrid
Mexico City Munich Paris Cape Town Hong Kong Montreal

Acquisitions Editor: Matthew Wright
Development Editor: Kristen Mellitt
Executive Marketing Manager: Joyce Nilson
Production Manager: Bob Ginsberg
Project Coordination, Text Design, and Electronic Page Makeup:
    Nesbitt Graphics, Inc.
Cover Design Manager and Cover Designer: Wendy Ann Fredericks
Cover Illustration: Franz Marc, *Two Horses,* 1911–1912. (Bildarchiv Preussischer
    Kulturbesitz/Art Resource, NY)
Senior Manufacturing Buyer: Dennis J. Para
Printer and Binder: RR Donnelley & Sons Company/Crawfordsville
Cover Printer: RR Donnelley & Sons Company/Crawfordsville.

For permission to use copyrighted material, grateful acknowledgment is made to the
copyright holders on pp. 293–294, which are hereby made part of this copyright
page.

Library of Congress Cataloging-in-Publication Data
Thiel, Diane, [1967–   ]
    Winding roads : exercises in writing creative nonfiction / Diane Thiel.
        p. cm.
    Includes bibliographical references and index.
    ISBN 0-321-42989-3 (alk. paper)
1. English language—Rhetoric. 2. Creative writing. 3. Essay—Authorship.
4. Reportage literature—Authorship. I. Title.
    PE1413.T449 2007
    808'.042—dc22
                                                                2007030833

Visit us at www.ablongman.com

ISBN-13: 978-0-321-42989-6
ISBN-10:   0-321-42989-3

1 2 3 4 5 6 7 8 9 10—DOC—10 09 08 07

For Aria and Christabel,
who both began their winding roads
during the writing of this book

Contents

PART THREE
Exercises for Exploring Revision,
Subgenres, and Frequent Concerns of
Creative Nonfiction 81

PART FOUR
A Collection of Creative
Nonfiction   125

PART FIVE
Writers About the Art of Creative Nonfiction   255

Preface

As teachers of creative writing, we face a unique challenge. The students in each of our courses have different talents and abilities. We must spark each student's creativity and help him or her develop the skills every competent writer must have. It is often said that creativity cannot be taught. It is my belief, however, that everyone possesses some innate creativity, and it is our task, as teachers, to nourish it and give each student the means to express his or her ideas effectively. The teacher of creative writing, and of creative nonfiction, in particular, faces a set of specific challenges and needs a variety of tools to meet the needs of his or her students. Over many years of teaching and via discussions with a multitude of other teachers, I arrived at a list of tools most useful to a classroom that focuses on writing creative nonfiction, tools that are featured in this book. The fundamental philosophy that this book embodies is that we learn by example and by practice. As writers, we are also readers, and we learn by emulating those writers who have most inspired us along the way. For this reason, the book includes an extensive selection of readings, and the exercises and discussions are designed to draw from and integrate with these readings.

Features of This Book

- Active lessons, with prompts to have the students writing something every day, or at least nearly every day.

- Exercises to address, individually, each element of writing creative nonfiction, while still building toward an understanding of all the elements that go into creating an effective piece of writing.

- Clear, concise discussions of particular techniques of creative nonfiction, followed by practice of these individual techniques.

- Potent, vital examples in an extensive selection of readings that will serve as models to our students.

Winding Roads: Exercises in Writing Creative Nonfiction addresses the varied needs of the teacher of creative nonfiction. The purpose of this book is to make the process of writing accessible and to help in the development of the necessary tools. The exercises identify and isolate the many elements of creative nonfiction, making them manageable in shape and size. Thus broken down and explored one at a time, they become easier to handle. Some can be extraordinarily useful as steps on the way to longer pieces.

Though the exercises are designed to cover and respond to the fundamentals of writing creative nonfiction, they are also motivating and fun. Even as established writers, in a way, we are always setting ourselves exercises. We study the techniques of other writers and often model a particular aspect of that writer's work (i.e., how the writer creates the rhythm in a piece; how the point of view shifts so fluidly in a particular scene).

I chose to write this particular book because there is a need for a creative nonfiction exercise book. At colleges and universities where I have had occasion to teach, visit, and give readings or where I have friends or contacts, teachers have expressed to me a desire for such a book. Several have commented that such a book would also be an exciting addition to texts they use in their composition classes, especially as an accompaniment to a rhetoric.

Certain readings in this text are chosen for their illustration of particular techniques of creative nonfiction and for the playful exercises they allow. Most of the selections in the book are from contemporary writers, although I do include a few classical pieces, primarily when they elucidate a particular point, but also because it is important for students to get a sense of the lineage of writers.

Organization: Ways to Use This Book

Winding Roads is divided into five main sections, with a number of subdivisions.

- Part One, Beginning: Points of Inspiration, offers exercises to get started, such as keeping a journal, working with photographs and objects as points of inspiration.

- Part Two, Developing Craft and Technique, addresses basic elements of writing creative nonfiction, with sub-sections such as voice, tone, perspective, figurative language, diction, selecting details, and creating tension.

- Part Three, Exercises for Exploring Revision, Subgenres, and Frequent Concerns of Creative Nonfiction, addresses the process of revision, the specific subgenres, and frequent concerns pertaining to creative nonfiction.

- Part Four, A Collection of Creative Nonfiction, contains an anthology of examples of creative nonfiction.

- Part Five, Writers About the Art of Creative Nonfiction, presents several writers writing about the art of creative nonfiction.

Exercises in Parts One, Two, and Three direct students to read particular works included in Parts Four and Five. This organization allows a particular piece of creative nonfiction to be used to illustrate a number of different elements of writing (as a piece of writing always does). A single piece of writing can illustrate a number of techniques and offer ideas for emulation. This organization also encourages students to "read as writers," to reread a piece with a particular filter, looking for its illustration of the particular technique.

You may choose to use the material in this book in the order of its appearance in the Contents, but the exercises can also be used as the issues arise in workshop. For instance, as discussions arise regarding voice or perspective, you can turn to the exercises, which address each particular concern and offer opportunities for practice.

Exercises and Anthology of Readings

As a professor of creative writing for the last fifteen years and as an author of books of nonfiction and poetry, I have developed hundreds of exercises which focus on particular elements of creative writing crucial for any writer's development (and crucial to writing creative nonfiction in particular). These include exercises addressing such concerns as establishing perspective, creating images and symbols, depicting culture and history, development of narrative, and an attention to form. I approach the essential tools of writing in ways that make each point relevant to the student's own experiences. For instance, in the section about perspective, I suggest tapping the perspective of an ancestor, inhabiting a period of history through that voice. In sections that discuss sense of place, I ask students to "revisit" their hometowns and explore the political, geographical, and historical dimensions of the place.

The exercises include opportunities to address specific, as well as more expansive, elements of writing. Some will work well as a 15-minute freewrite, whereas others can be used as inspiration for an assignment at home.

The exercises will motivate students, give teachers brief daily lessons for discussion, and offer hands-on exercises to follow. The book places strong emphasis on the process of revision as well. The revision exercises give ideas and present ways to approach revision and include a set of questions that can be used in any workshop of student work.

The readings in *Winding Roads* offer models of different types of creative nonfiction and represent writing in a number of different styles, from a number of different cultures and eras. A few selections defy classification in any genre and raise particularly intriguing questions about creative nonfiction. Fred D'Aguiar's "A Son in Shadow" for instance, acknowledges from the first line how much must be re-created (fictionalized, essentially) in writing about his parents' courtship: "I know nothing of how they meet." D'Aguiar's piece is also a strong piece to use in conjunction with exercises to practice metawriting, as he begins to question his reinvention of his parent's romance: "Am I going too fast on my father's behalf? Should there have been an immediate and cutting rebuttal from her and several days before another meeting?" As D'Aguiar's piece can be used to illustrate these two elements of writing, many of the works included in the text illuminate various concerns of creative nonfiction.

Included in the sections that follow are exercises I have found to be useful in the classroom as well as to my own creative development. As you travel through this book, either in the order of the table of contents or by moving around as the need in workshop arises, I hope you will be inspired to create additional exercises of your own and to find sources of inspiration for your own writing.

Acknowledgments

Many individuals offered suggestions for development and revision in the process of writing this book. I would like to thank my thousands of students and many colleagues over the years, as well as the many creative writing instructors who reviewed the manuscript in progress: Rita Ciresi, University of South Florida; Mary Christine Delea, Eastern Kentucky University; Sonya Huber Humes, Georgia Southern University; Ann McCutchan, University of North Texas; Michael W. Raymond, Stetson University; Lisa C. Roney, University of Central Florida; Linda H. Straubel, Embry-Riddle Aeronautical University; and Laura Valeri, Georgia Southern University. I am grateful to Joe Terry, Dana Gioia, Erika Berg, Kristen Mellitt, and Matthew Wright for their assistance at various stages in the process. Thanks to my mother (an inspiring teacher for 45 years) and all the members of my family. I am particularly grateful to my husband, Costa, for his support and generous assistance in the writing of this book. And special thanks to my three young children: Alexander, Aria, and Christabel, for the inspiration and new perspectives their presence has brought to me.

DIANE THIEL

WINDING ROADS

Introduction

If you have opened this book, even in curiosity, you have at least wondered about becoming a writer. The idea of writing to be read may be exciting, scary, or both. These feelings are natural, especially if you have not had much experience with it. Whether you have had much practice with writing or little, you should know that you are already a writer. You are a storyteller, even if you don't immediately think of yourself that way. When something exciting happens in your life, what is one of your first impulses? To tell someone else. This is true for every one of us. We tell stories all our lives and use them daily for entertainment, to give advice, to make community.

Creative nonfiction is a genre that particularly allows a writer to tap into his or her own stories and reflections. A number of subcategories exist, including memoir, personal essay, and literary journalism, among others. It is a genre that stretches back to the earliest writings, to classical essayists such as Plato and Aristotle, but the term *creative nonfiction* is a recent one, the term itself suggesting that the writing is essentially true, though there are a multitude of ways to render a story. We each find our own creative means of delivery.

Though the subgenres of creative nonfiction are generally thought of as distinct, several categories often overlap in a single piece. An essay might simultaneously include memoir, reflective writing, and personal opinion. It might be a piece that could be called a sense of place essay, while delving deeply enough into history to also be called a historical essay. Anthony Walton's *Mississippi: An American Journey*, for instance, is a book that could fit into any of these categories. The book fuses memoir, opinion, reflection, and history as Walton delves into his African American roots in Mississippi. Walton imparts vast amounts of information—historical, political, social—but does so using his own family history as a series of leaping-off points. His means of delivery make the politics, the history more real, more vital. As the writer Michael Harper says, "History is your own heartbeat."

As a storyteller, you are always looking and listening, consciously or unconsciously, for points of inspiration, and this attention becomes heightened when you start putting your ideas down on the page. It is usually this step, beginning to put your ideas on paper, that seems the most difficult to take. Beginning the process of writing, however, is easier than you may think. The first step is to keep a journal, and as the first exercise in this book shows, writing in your journal is really no more difficult than observing or imagining a few things that may later become points of departure for a piece.

While being a writer is as natural as being able to talk, to run, or to throw, being an *effective* writer is no different than being a singer or an athlete. You must sharpen and improve your natural abilities and reflexes. And there is no better way to do this than by reading widely and by trying out the techniques of writers you admire. Renowned 20th-century author F. Scott Fitzgerald says, "I want to be able to do anything with words: handle slashing, flaming descriptions like Wells, and use the paradox with the clarity of Samuel Butler, the breadth of Bernard Shaw and the wit of Oscar Wilde. . . . All that is by way of example. As a matter of fact I am a professional literary thief, hot after the best methods of every writer in my generation." Likewise, T. S. Eliot once commented (though he may have stolen it from Ezra Pound), "Good poets borrow. Great poets steal." The real art is in finding the way to emulate a technique so as to make it your own.

The tradition of writing stretches back to ancient times, and it can be inspiring to recognize ourselves as an extension of that rich and diverse lineage. This book will point out many roads you can take as a writer. It is an exciting process to see your writing as an extension of that ancient path, with a unique landscape of possibilities unfolding before you.

When we write, we tap into a wellspring that is the source of all the arts and that reflects the breadth of our human experience. In this book, we will explore different sources of inspiration, such as myth, history, and landscape, in the process of writing. If we look back in history to the early roots of writing, we can recognize the deep connections between our more recent divisions, such as story, poetry, and history. They all stem from the same source and once coexisted in our ancient texts. Creative nonfiction brings the different threads together, allowing narrative to coexist alongside expository writing.

One element vital to creative nonfiction, as opposed to other genres, is the requirement that the essay be true. We all remember things differently, however, so one person's truth can be quite different from another's. Creative nonfiction relies on facts and details but also recognizes that there can be many versions of a story. It is vital to find the "emotional truth" in rendering an account; this very term, now commonly associated with creative nonfiction, acknowledges these important issues about truth. It is also crucial, however, that you gain the trust of your readers. Even though you are writing *creative* nonfiction, it is still nonfiction, so making up stories and wildly embellishing details are not options. If you can't quite remember a situation, you might acknowledge that you can't, as Edwidge Danticat states in her essay "Westbury Court": "Even now, I question what I remember about the children. Did they really die? Or did their mother simply move away with them after the fire? Maybe they were not even boys at all. Maybe they were two girls." Similarly, Fred D'Aguiar states in a piece about his parents' first meeting, "I know nothing about how they meet," and yet goes on to reimagine in scene after scene. This form of acknowledgment can offer a kind of permission for reinvention.

As you collect and put on paper ideas for a piece of creative nonfiction, the question of what form the piece should take will arise. There is a good chance you have begun the process with a notion of the type of writer you would like to be. As you begin to develop your ideas, you may find that they "push" for a piece to take a form you may not have considered. Sometimes as you find the need for a different canvas, or to explore a different subject matter, another voice begins to emerge. Give yourself permission to explore, to experiment with a variety of forms of creative nonfiction, such as personal essay, memoir, or nature writing. Your experiments will be useful because the specifics of one form can teach you something about another.

You will find in this book numerous exercises that address the elements essential to all writing, as well as the specific needs of nonfiction. The exercises set simple tasks, the objectives of which are to help you practice your technique. They simultaneously provide inspiration and a delving into particular concerns of creative nonfiction.

Whether you are a beginning or experienced writer, it is important to begin each piece by breaking it down into a number of small explorations. This process of breaking down, or alternatively, of beginning with small pieces that you may later synthesize into a larger one, is useful because it both makes the task of writing easier to manage and helps you learn by isolating each element of your piece. As you focus your attention on each element, you are better able to determine how you can improve it. One of the greatest questions you will face as a writer is how you are going to *render*, cast, or shape your piece. The idea that sparks a work is important, of course, but, as Robert Frost writes, "how you say a thing" is what ultimately matters in writing.

Often a terrific idea can feel too huge to handle. Many extraordinary ideas remain, unfortunately, at the idea stage. The exercises in this book will help you break down the elements of writing into small ventures that will teach you about the art. All works, no matter how large, are composed in such pieces: a conversation, a scene, an extended metaphor, a line or a sentence. Poet and prose writer Annie Dillard's crucial question to a young person wanting to become a writer was simply, "Do you like sentences?" Likewise, as the writer Kate Braverman says, "All good writing is built one good line at a time. You build a novel the same way you do a pyramid. One word, one stone at a time." You always need to address each small component, however expansive the work might become.

The adage about activism applies in writing as well: "Think globally. Act locally." While it is always necessary that you maintain a "global" vision of the scope and purpose of your piece, this vision can be realized most effectively by paying close "local" attention to and carefully crafting, in turn, each word, sentence, and element of the piece.

All writers learn by reading and by setting themselves "exercises." Again this process of sharpening your tools and honing your techniques is necessary in the same way that ongoing training is necessary for an athlete, a musician, a visual artist. I encourage you to return to the exercises and the readings at different stages and to read widely beyond the sample of works included in the book. In fact, what you can learn from the exercises and readings grows and changes as your technique develops.

The art of writing, of course, as any art, is more than just "exercise." The poet Rainer Maria Rilke, in his "Letter to a Young Poet," refers to the true source of the art when he says, "I know of no other advice than this: Go within and scale the depths." While no formulas will assure you will write a great piece, you can develop and practice techniques that will help you truly "scale the depths."

PART ONE

Beginning:
Points of Inspiration

1
Keeping a Journal

Keeping a journal is an indispensable part of being a writer. In a sense, your memory is your journal. The point of both is to record things such as events, thoughts, sensations, and dreams. But as we all know, memory constantly discards details, and that is why it is good practice to keep a written journal. It may even be a good idea to keep more than one. Thoreau, for instance, kept different volumes for his scientific observations and his ideas for literary pieces but noted that it became increasingly difficult for him to keep things separate.

Though our technology has developed a multitude of machines to help us write, from recorders to computers to voice recognition systems, there is still no better way for you to begin than writing by hand. Use a journal of the traditional sort, a book with two covers and blank pages between. You can and should, of course, type things later, as you begin to revise, but it is important that you get started with your pen on paper. The immediate and direct physicality of forming words on the page cannot be substituted because it offers the closest connection between the writing process and its raw material, the word.

The shape and size of your journal are also important. It has to be small enough to carry in your purse or backpack, yet large enough to write comfortably and fluidly. You should be able to carry it with you conveniently everywhere you go. You might consider your journal as your enhanced memory and write in it everything which can conceivably be of use to you later. And considering that you never know ahead of time what will be useful, the category of things you write in your journal could be very broad: dreams, quotations, overheard bits of dialogue.

Then be prepared to "throw away" 95 percent of your writing (or rather, let it go no further than your journal). You will often write ten lines to get a single good one. Think of the journal as a no-pressure situation. There is never a "blank page" to face because your hand keeps moving.

Of course, journal entries are far from final pieces. Writers often walk around with an idea for many years—a great idea that hasn't quite found its form, or its connecting force. *Freewriting* (keeping the hand moving without censoring or revising for the moment) in a journal can help you find these connections, as you record the ebb and flow of your thoughts. Practically speaking, the journal is a convenient way of keeping thoughts and ideas organized and safe from being lost.

When you are feeling somewhat uninspired, you can turn to the pages in your journal for instantaneous sparks of creativity. You will hardly remember writing some of the things that make it into the pages.

Suggestions for Writing

1. If you don't already have a journal, begin one and record in it such things as

   your dream last night;

   quotations from things you are reading;

   overheard snippets of conversation;

   intriguing scientific facts;

   something unusual you saw on the way home.

2. If you have been keeping a journal for a while, revisit some old entries. Open it at a random place and read a few pages. Pick a thought, an idea, an image, and explore it from your current perspective. Write a new entry that revisits an old theme.

2
Family Stories: History as Heartbeat

Read/Revisit

Leslie Marmon Silko, "Landscape, History, and the Pueblo Imagination" (see page 224)
Philip Brady, "Myth and Uncertainty" (see page 148)

Researching history can be a way to access the past and connect it to the present and the future. But the research has to mean something. It has to become personal. "History is your own heartbeat," as the poet Michael S. Harper says. History, especially your personal history, is a fundamental source and shaper of your ideas. So go ahead and mine it.

Suggestions for Writing

1. Choose an ancestor who has always interested you and do some research on events that took place during his or her life. Do some personal research. "Interview" your family members about family history. Record what you hear in your journal. You may find that the story you are seeking has always been at your fingertips.

2. Start with a single incident. It might be hard to get started if you think you have to tell a whole life story. So just start with one story: a story the family still tells, the one that has survived via the oral tradition. This might be a defining moment in the ancestor's life, or a story he or she might tell (or have told) you.

3. Write a three- to five-page biography of this family member, again using a few specific stories that have become family lore. Begin by making a list of the most important details to include in this sketch. Many of these details could later grow into longer pieces.

9

3
Memory and Imagination

Read/Revisit

Edwidge Danticat, "Westbury Court" (see page 171)
Joy Harjo, "The Flying Man" (see page 202)

Memory is the source of imagination. After all, what we think of, regardless of how imaginative or whimsical, is in one way or another based on what we know. The inventive use of memory is an integral aspect of the creative process. We all remember things differently, so the very act of reconstructing the past is always a creative one. The details we include and the details we exclude help to form our own personal version of events.

Suggestions for Writing

1. Note how Edwidge Danticat questions her memory: "Even now, I question what I remember about the children. Did they really die? Or did their mother simply move away with them after the fire? Maybe they were not even boys at all. Maybe they were two girls." She includes this at the end of her piece, but try getting into a piece by beginning: "Even now, I question what I remember about. . . ."

2. Think of your earliest memory. As you write about it, try to inhabit the voice of the child. You might incorporate nonsense words to enhance the effect of the particular age. Try to incorporate details that help capture a child's perspective (e.g., the doorknobs were eye level).

3. Write a memory of something you couldn't possibly remember, at least not on a conscious level: your birth, your great-grandparents' wedding, the creation of the earth. Try beginning with the words: "On some level, I know . . ." Or emulate Joy Harjo, in her more direct approach, as in the opening paragraph of her essay "The Flying Man":

   > As I was being born I fought my mother to escape, all the way out to the breathing world, until I was pulled abruptly by the doctor who was later credited with saving both my mother and me. I dangled there from his hands, a reluctant acrobat caught in flight. I took note there was a rush with the release, with flying free, and like an addict I flew whenever I could, from crib bars to jungle gyms and once the roof of the garage.

4
Telling Lies to Tell the Truth

Read/Revisit

Tracy Kidder, "Making the Truth Believable" (see page 267)

As children, we are all told not to lie, and yet in truth, much of our lives we end up telling lies: tiny harmless "white" lies, perhaps, but lies nonetheless. In telling "white" lies, though, we often deny our true selves. In creative nonfiction, we are writing "truth" and making a kind of pact with the reader. We want the reader to trust our words. And yet in telling the same story, several people might each remember a different "truth."

It could be said that all figurative language is, in a sense, a lie, because it presents one thing as something else. And yet it so often has the effect of getting closer to the truth. (See the section "Figurative Language" for more specifics.)

Suggestions for Writing

1. The following exercise is a good one to access the true events of your life that are strange enough to sound like lies: Write three short statements or anecdotes about yourself—-two lies and one truth, with the same level of believability. In a workshop, it can be fun to read your responses aloud and let others guess which is the truth.

2. Write about 50 words telling an absolute lie that somehow is true to the way you feel. For instance, a student once wrote about her Spanish teacher vanishing into thin air. Perhaps the student was wishing her away, or perhaps she was just for the moment turning to magic realism (where reality suddenly becomes fantastic). Since you are writing creative nonfiction, acknowledge the invention, and it gives you license.

5

Making the
Old Story New

Read/Revisit

Sherman Alexie, "Superman and Me" (see page 128)
Philip Brady, "Myth and Uncertainty" (see page 148)
Jonathan Swift, "A Modest Proposal" (see page 234)

Our stories never change. They simply take on different forms. Once we learn to recognize archetypes (patterns or models present in the unconscious as well as in our heritage of art), we can often see them at work in our own lives.

Countless sources are available today to show how archetypes can be used to understand various aspects of our lives—from psychology, to relationships, to job-related issues. The works of psychologist Carl Jung and mythologist Northrop Frye are classic sources. A rather accessible source as an introduction to archetype is Joseph Campbell. His *Hero with a Thousand Faces* draws on the idea of the same stories existing in different cultures, with the heroes and dragons wearing different faces but undergoing similar journeys, trials, and revelations. ("The Hero's Adventure," in particular, in a series of videotaped interviews with Campbell called *The Power of Myth* provides an excellent introduction.)

Of course, there can be a danger in being too aware of archetypes as we re-create them. And one can say this about any kind of art—that on some level it is good not to be too aware. Sometimes the first conscious efforts at using myth or archetype can yield rather clunky results. Nonetheless, it is good practice to let the mind connect story to story, to become familiar with recurring themes, symbols, and sequences of action: the battle, the cycle of life, the forest, the flood, the fountain, the journey, etc. Then they will begin to wander your writing with more fluidity.

All works of art can be explored for archetypal ideas. Certain works themselves have become patterns after which so many other pieces are modeled. Some works declare the influence of such a text in the very title: James Joyce's *Ulysses* or Derek Walcott's *The Odyssey* or *Omeros*, for example, establish the connection with Homer's *Odyssey* and the archetype of the journey.

Many writers use other works of literature, from ancient texts to fairy tales, as explicit points of departure. They might use means such as exploring a particular character or sequence of action, or add an ironic twist or ending. American humorist James Thurber retells the story of "Little Red

Riding Hood," a classic example of the archetypal encounter in the dark forest. Thurber's version, however, ends with the girl pulling a revolver out of her basket and shooting the wolf dead. The moral that ends the parody is "little girls aren't as foolish as they used to be."

Suggestions for Writing

1. Choose a myth, fairy tale, or other well-known story and use the general motif or plot to reflect on a real-life situation. You might also change the tale somewhat for comic purposes, as in James Thurber's version of "Little Red Riding Hood," mentioned above. If you like, the symbols or patterns of action in the fairy tale or myth might provide more subtle undercurrents for your piece, rather than a retelling.

2. Find folk tales or myths from different cultures: Native American, African, Chinese, etc. Note any connections to stories with which you are familiar. Write a piece that explores an archetypal theme or symbol in the stories: creation, a flood, transformation, etc. Perhaps use a line from the tale as an epigraph. (Your response might have a contemporary slant. For instance, write about a flood in your hometown.) Note how Philip Brady in "Myth and Uncertainty" incorporates myth into his own family history.

3. Respond to a well-known work of art, emulating the shape and progression of the piece. For instance, use Jonathan Swift's *A Modest Proposal* as a model for your own modest proposal about an issue in contemporary society.

6

A Picture Brings Forth a Thousand Words

Read/Revisit

Jamaica Kincaid, "Biography of a Dress" (see page 209)

Looking at photographs can be inspiring—old photographs of relatives, pictures from childhood. You can find many layers of stories in the moments of your family's history captured on film. Note the way Jamaica Kincaid's "Biography of a Dress" is inspired by an old photograph. This is clear from the opening sentence: "The dress I am wearing in this black-and-white photograph, taken when I was two years old, was a yellow dress made of cotton poplin. . . ."

Choose a family photograph to do the exercises below. For some of the exercises, you might use a photo of a family member you know little about. When doing these exercises, you need not be constrained by the photograph. Your response does not have to make reference to the photograph or be limited to the moment or events surrounding the taking of the picture. The following exercises also contain a few excerpts from in-class responses, some of which inspired longer pieces.

1. Describe the setting in your photo. Who are the people? What is the relationship? Could you convey this relationship through remembered/reimagined dialogue?

2. Kincaid incorporates the memory of the photo being taken. Write a scene that describes the moment of your own photograph being taken.

3. Take your photograph to a workshop. After everyone writes about their own photographs, a fun and evocative exercise might be to scramble photographs among participants. Writing about someone else's photographs might yield particularly interesting results, because you will have fewer preconceptions. Begin your piece by acknowledging what you don't know. For example, "I don't know for sure, but the little girl seems sad in the picture." Or "I hold in my hands this black and white photograph. The people have long since passed on, so I don't know for sure, but they seem tense together."

4. Describe the photograph using heightened visual imagery:

> Red, blue, and gold, she stands barefoot in the sand. Hands raised to a clear sky. A floating crimson scarf rides the breeze above her head . . .
>
> —CRIS FARINAS, STUDENT

5. Write a dramatic monologue from the perspective of your younger self in the photograph. Include the setting somehow.

> . . . I mean, the alligator farm is cool, kind of scary, but boring after half an hour. I hope we get to go to Universal Studios later and see some really cool stuff . . . My Dad—look at him. He loves taking pictures of us. Probably so that when we grow up, he can bring out the old pictures and embarrass us.
>
> —JOSÉ TORRES, STUDENT

6. What is happening outside the frame of the photo?

> Upon the sight of the formation of the tornado, the actors began shrieking and running towards safety. Cars stopped on the highway. Storm chasers were seeking every possible route to get as close as possible, while clicking their cameras at every conceivable angle. . .
>
> —BETH CHIOFALO, STUDENT

7. Write about an inanimate object in the picture: This might provide a new thought or bring back a story that may have nothing to do with the picture.

> Looking at this ornate, heirloom bridal gown, it's hard to believe that it carries the dreaded Klotchnick family curse. Three generations that descended from that Ukrainian matchmaker and part-time psychic, Kvech Klotchnick, have suffered public humiliation when wearing the gown. Perhaps the problem is with Kvech's genes and not the sequined satin outfit itself. Legend has it that marauding Cossacks retreated in disarray when beholding Kvech and her sisters.
>
> As an amateurish psychic, Kvech stubbornly supported Czar during the October Revolution. She narrowly escaped the Bolsheviks with her life, emigrating to the New World disguised as the Czarina.
>
> Klotchnick descendants have come and gone. Mysteriously, the lace-appliqued outfit hasn't aged one day. Kvech unintentionally passed it on to her daughter, Sharon. Sharon passed it on to her daughter, Elissa. The pearl-studded dress with its streaming rosette-speckled train has the supernatural power of diverting well-intentioned grooms away from their marriage vows at the last moment.
>
> —FRED SHERMAN, STUDENT

8. You might also construct a narrative combining elements from the results of all of these exercises.

7
Object Lessons

Read/Revisit

Jamaica Kincaid, "Biography of a Dress" (see page 209)

Jamaica Kincaid's "Biography of a Dress" is a piece built entirely around an object, a yellow cotton poplin dress, made for her by her mother. The dress becomes a vehicle for moving through scenes and developing characterizations that make important revelations about and comment on the author, her family, and social issues of the time. For instance, one scene describes her mother buying material from one of the Harneys stores: "Someone named Harney did not wait on my mother, but someone named Miss Verna did and she was very nice still . . ." As discussed in the previous section, Kincaid builds a scene around a photo being taken of her as a little girl in the dress and then elaborately describes that day. Later in her piece, she describes what ultimately happened to the dress:

> It was carefully put aside, saved for me to wear to another special occasion; but by the time another special occasion came (I could say quite clearly then what the special occasion was and can say quite clearly now what the special occasion was but I do not want to), the dress could no longer fit me, I had grown too big for it.

Kincaid's style often involves juxtaposing the ordinary detail with a sudden and striking revelation. She describes her mother as possibly

> . . . just exhausted by this whole process, celebrating my second birthday, commemorating an event, my birth, that she may not have wished to occur in the first place and may have tried repeatedly to prevent, and then finally, in trying to find some beauty in it, ended up with a yard and a half of yellow poplin being shaped into a dress . . ."

The dress has a vital role in the piece. In this biography of a particular dress, Kincaid is able to speak about her own childhood and her relationship with her mother. It is their biography as well. Using the dress to tell the story allows a visual, visceral way into the piece and perhaps allows the writer to get even closer to the heart of the matter, because she has the yard and a half of yellow poplin as a motif.

Suggestions for Writing

1. Choose an object from your childhood that has a particular resonance for you. Maybe you still own this object. Maybe it is present in a photograph. Freewrite about the object. (You might also choose an object from your current life for the exercise.)

2. Extend the previous exercise and even further emulate Kincaid's approach. Write a biography of the object. Who made it or gave it to you? When did you see it or use it? What happened to it? Do you know? For instance, was it put away, never to appear again?

3. Choose an object that is a family heirloom. Imagine a biography for the object before you were born. Who owned it then? Imagine a day's journey of the object; for instance, the journey of the pocket watch in your great-grandfather's coat pocket.

PART TWO

Exercises for Developing Craft and Technique

8
Voice and Style

Finding Your True Subjects

Read/Revisit

> Fred D'Aguiar, "A Son in Shadow" (see page 160)
> Bruce Chatwin, from *In Patagonia* (see page 151)

The term *voice,* when it refers to the writer, is sometimes confused with the term *style.* After all, writers often have both a distinctive voice and style. However, while style refers specifically to a writer's technique, a writer's unique voice includes elements of a writer's work that are less tangible than technique. Raymond Carver, in "On Writing," says that voice is "akin to style," but it isn't style alone. "It is the writer's particular and unmistakable signature on everything he writes. It is his world and no other. This is one of the things that distinguishes one writer from another. Not talent. There's plenty of that around. But a writer who has some special way of looking at things and who gives artistic expression to that way of looking: that writer may be around for a time."

What does it mean to find your voice? What is a writer's voice? While developing your voice includes learning and using effectively elements of style and tone, it also refers to the stories that are your own and the particular insights and worldview that your telling of your stories reveals. So your choice (or discovery) of subjects is one factor that will begin to define your voice. Often our true subjects may very well be the wounds or difficulties we have undergone. In a way, your subject chooses you. You may not want a certain subject matter, but it is yours anyway, because it is something you may need to work through for a period of time, or even for the rest of your life.

Writer Tim O'Brien's period of service in Vietnam was a catalyst for his finding his subject matter. He returns to this particular setting and the series of external and internal conflicts in many of his works. One of Bruce Chatwin's recurring concerns is the wandering life. He begins to explore the tendency of humans to be on the road in his first book, *In Patagonia,* and then goes on to refer to this idea in his later books, among them, *The Songlines,* which deals with the Australian aboriginal dream tracks on which descendants travel. Chatwin was an incessant traveler, and this is reflected not only in his choice of the travel memoir as a genre, but also his dealing with the ideas of *wanderlust,* or a desire to be on the road.

Suggestions for Writing

1. Look through your journals. Are there any subjects that appear again and again? Has someone ever pointed out to you that you talk about the same thing? Often the word *obsession* has negative connotations, but for writers, obsessions can be the mark of having found a true subject.

2. Keep a dream journal. A true subject might be revealed by the frequency with which you dream about it. Record your dreams for a few weeks. Write down what you remember immediately on waking.

3. Experiment with refrains in your prose. Try returning to a subject via a particular line or idea. Fred D'Aguiar, in "A Son in Shadow," continually emphasizes that he knows nothing about his parents' meeting, that so much is of the story is in shadow. He states this several times in the essay, as a kind of refrain.

A Question of Style

Read/Revisit

> Rudolfo Anaya, "Why I Love Tourists: Confessions of a Dharma Bum"
> (see page 131)
> Jamaica Kincaid, "Biography of a Dress" (see page 209)

Style is the way in which a piece of literature is written. As was mentioned before, the term *style* refers to the techniques a writer uses to render a piece. Style reflects the choice of words (diction), sentence structure (syntax), grammatical framework (choice of tense, person, etc.), density (use of figurative or symbolic language), and narrative mode (which includes dialogue, action, inner reflections, and background). Thus, style is the result of the writer's many conscious and unconscious decisions in rendering a piece.

Style is shaped, to some extent, by the age in which we live—the language of a work written in an earlier century will not be the same as the language of a contemporary piece. However, style is also very much a result of the author's choice and inclination. Thus, a writer may develop an individual style that is rather uniform throughout his or her body of work. For example, Ernest Hemingway has an easily identifiable personal style that stamps his writings. On the other hand, a writer may choose to vary his or her style in order to render a piece most effectively.

Suggestions for Writing

1. Study the styles of Anaya and Kincaid. How does gender figure into their styles? Select a paragraph, or paragraphs, from Anaya and rewrite the sentences using the parenthetical style of Kincaid's "Biography of a Dress." Now try writing a paragraph from Kincaid using Anaya's conversational style. Does it work as well, in your opinion?

Conditional Voice

Read/Revisit

> Leslie Marmon Silko, "Landscape, History, and the Pueblo Imagination" (see page 224)

Sometimes voice refers to the grammar of a piece of writing. The conditional voice is a seldom-used construction, but some writers have turned it to their advantage. Leslie Marmon Silko, in an essay called "Landscape, History, and the Pueblo Imagination," uses techniques such as the conditional voice to inhabit the world of her ancestors and bring it to life. Study the following paragraph from the essay. Notice the way her re-creation of the past is articulated with constructions such as "I imagine," "there might have been," and "the surprise attack would have cancelled. . . ."

> I imagine the last afternoon of my distant ancestors as warm and sunny for late September. They might have been traveling slowly, bringing the sheep closer to Laguna in preparation for the approach of colder weather . . . There might have been comfort in the warmth and the sight of the sheep fattening on good pasture which lulled my ancestors into their fatal inattention. They might have had a rifle, whereas the Apaches had only bows and arrows. But there would have been four or five Apache raiders, and the surprise attack would have canceled any advantage the rifles gave them.

One of my favorite books, Marilynne Robinson's *Housekeeping*, frequently returns to the conditional voice to speak about the past. The effect is a kind of dreamlike quality, a drifting between past and present:

> Looking out at the lake one could believe that the Flood had never ended. If one is lost on the water, any hill is Ararat. And below is always the accumulated past, which vanishes but does not vanish, which perishes and remains. If we imagine that Noah's wife when she was old found somewhere a remnant of the Deluge, she might have walked into it till her widow's dress floated above her head and the water loosened her plaited hair. And she would have left it to her sons to tell the tedious tale of generations. She was a nameless woman, and so at home among all those who were never found and never missed, who were uncommemorated, whose deaths were not remarked, nor their begettings.

Suggestions for Writing

1. Using the excerpts from Silko and Robinson as models, try writing about an ancestor or a historical figure using the conditional voice. (Try using constructions like "My grandmother would have said . . . ," "My great-grandmother would have gone . . . .") See if it helps create the same dreamlike effect.

2. Try reading your favorite piece with grammar-discerning eyes. See how the writer uses, bends, or breaks the rules of grammar for any rhythmic or connotative purposes. Take a paragraph or series of lines and emulate the writer's particular choice of grammar in the passage.

Breaking the Rules

In *The Writing Life*, Annie Dillard tells a story of a university student who asked her, "Do you think I could be a writer?" Dillard responded by asking, "Do you like sentences?" The student in Dillard's account was surprised and somewhat dismayed by the response. "Sentences? Do I like sentences? I am twenty years old, do I like sentences?"

Dillard's classic story addresses the need to take pleasure in the individual components of the art. Good writing has attention to such elements as rhythm, syntax, diction, smooth or startling arrangements, juxtaposition of images, compression and development of narrative (all discussed later in this book).

Even grammar can make for exciting revelations. It is important to study the way a writer uses particular techniques of grammar to achieve certain purposes. Tom Wolfe, for instance, in the essay "O Rotten Gotham," breaks many rules of grammar on purpose. He uses a run-on sentence half a page long, for instance, to convey the feel of the subject he discusses: overcrowding. The sentence itself is overcrowded. He uses the present participle to show the never-ending nature of the congestion:

> In everyday life in New York—just the usual, getting to work, working in massively congested areas like 42nd Street between Fifth Avenue and Lexington, especially now that the Pan-Am Building is set there, working in cubicles such as those in the editorial offices at Time-Life, Inc., which Dr. Hall cites as typical of New York's poor handling of space, working in cubicles with low ceilings and, often, no access to a window, while construction crews all over Manhattan drive everybody up the Masonite wall with air-pressure generators with noises up to the boil-a-brain decibel levels, then rushing to get home, piling into subways and trains, fighting for time and space, the usual day in New York—the whole now-normal thing keeps shooting jolts of adrenaline into the body, breaking down the body's defenses and winding up with the work-a-daddy human animal stroked out at the breakfast table with his head apoplexed like a cauliflower out of his $6.95 semispread Pima-cotton shirt and nosed over into a plate of No-Kloresto egg substitute, signing off with the black thrombosis, cancer, kidney, liver, or stomach failure, and the adrenals ooze to a halt, the size of eggplants in July.

Suggestions for Writing

1. Using Tom Wolfe's above sentence as a model, write a run-on sentence about the hectic quality of a single day, using the present participle to suggest the ongoing nature of responsibilities.

9
Perspective and Point of View

How You See It; How You Don't:
Defining Perspective and Point
of View

Read/Revisit

Sherman Alexie, "Superman and Me" (see page 128)
Tracy Kidder, "Making the Truth Believable" (see page 267)

Some years back, I had the opportunity to take a canoe trip through South Florida's swamp cypress forest with some friends, among them a botanist and an ornithologist. To the botanist, the trip was an exciting exploration of the overabundant plant life of the area. Her eye sought the epiphytes growing on the limbs of the tall trees, the vines fighting their way over almost every stump, and the flowers proclaiming the presence of both rare and common species. Not only was she able to identify each plant, but her training allowed her to use clues such as their relative abundance and position to "see" the state of the ecosystem as we passed through it. To the ornithologist, on the other hand, the forest we were passing through consisted primarily of sounds. He was able to identify the birds, which were mostly hidden in the branches, through their calls. He could even interpret the calls: mating song, cry of alarm, and so on. Were both to be asked to describe the trip, each would come up with a very different account—each description shaped by the education, experience, and interests of the narrator. The differences in their *perspectives* would give rise to two very different accounts.

The perspective from which you choose to tell a story is an essential element of the narrative because it determines what you can reveal about the situation and the action, what position you take regarding these things, which details you will focus on and which you will omit, and so on. Perspective is such an integral part of the story that very often it is absolutely clear whose story this is, so there really is no choice to be made about it. Nevertheless, it is always useful to maintain a critical attitude about all elements of the narrative. By challenging even as fundamental an aspect as perspective, by trying out different alternatives, you can be sure that

27

you do not miss an opportunity to strengthen your piece by, for example, choosing a perspective that could offer an unexpected insight.

Point of View

Perspective and point of view are terms that are often used interchangeably. However, while perspective particularly relates to *whose* eyes we see the story through, point of view generally is understood to refer, as well, to *how* the story is told. Following is a list of the several points of view often used in writing creative nonfiction, with brief discussions of their relative merits:

First Person

Choosing first person point of view has the important advantage of immediately engaging the reader. When the narrator is the story's main character, a sense of immediacy is created. Using the first person point of view can make it difficult to introduce insights into what others might be thinking—even the narrator, for constructions such as "I thought . . ." tend to become tedious when repeated too often.

Second Person

This point of view invites the reader to pretend that he or she is the narrator. It is not uncommon in nonfiction (particularly the essay), probably because the assumption in these genres tends to be that the author is relating personal experiences. Using the *you* in either its specific sense (where the writer addresses the audience directly) or its general sense (where the *you* is equivalent to *one*) creates a conversational tone and tends to make universal the thoughts and experiences the writer describes.

First Person Plural

The use and usefulness of this point of view is very similar to that of the second person. The primary objective of the use of the pronoun *we* is to create the impression of a bond between the writer and the reader and to emphasize the commonality of thought, feeling, and experience.

Complete Objectivity

The completely objective point of view places the narrator, and the reader, outside the events described—in the position of simple spectator. The author describes only what can be seen and heard directly, cannot provide any commentary, and is limited in revealing the thoughts and intentions of characters to only what they would speak out loud. It is sometimes used in nonfiction because of the "documentary" atmosphere it can create. By refusing to comment on what clearly requires a reaction, the author can evoke strong reactions in the reader.

Suggestions for Writing

1. In an earlier exercise, you wrote about your earliest memory. Now take that memory and tell the same story from a variety of different perspectives (imagine how your mother might have seen it; your older sibling). Acknowledge to the reader that you are imagining.

2. You wrote the earliest memory using first person point of view. Now write the same memory (or a different one) using third person (refer to yourself as "he" or "she"). Sherman Alexie, in his essay "Superman and Me," switches from first person and begins talking about himself in the third person: "But he is an Indian boy living on the reservation and is simply an oddity. He grows into a man who often speaks of his childhood in the third person, as if it will somehow dull the pain . . . ."

3. Now try the less-common second person point of view. Think of a point in your life when you had to obey someone or follow his or her instructions and advice for much of your day (the army, your childhood home, a classroom, a sports team). Describe an incident or a day using only a list of instructions, orders, or admonitions.

A Communal Story: Using Multiple Perspectives

Read/Revisit

Gregory Martin, "Other People's Memories" (see page 277)

Some writers have found a conventional use of first person point of view too confining when writing memoir. Greg Martin, in "Other People's Memories," for instance, writes about the challenges of writing a memoir about his family in Mountain City, Nevada. One solution he found was to use multiple points of view. In his essay, he offers an example of shifting from a first person point of view to a third person point of view when telling a story from the perspective of his grandfather.

Using a multitude of perspectives can be especially useful in historical accounts (whether as part of a memoir or not) and in biographies, where the perspectives of participants or witnesses (other than the author) to events can provide important information, challenge assumptions, bring events or people to life, etc. Interviews, letters, other people's diaries or memoirs, even the writer's recollection of conversations with others can bring multiple perspectives into a piece.

In "How to Tell a True War Story" (a work of fiction, but one that is very similar to a memoir), Tim O'Brien weaves the perspectives of several characters together in a story that is narrated from the first person point of view. The changes in perspective are integral to the story because the author's point is that there is no such thing as a "true" war story because of the subjective nature of each experience. O'Brien comments in the piece that "a true war story is never moral. It does not instruct, nor encourage virtue, nor suggest models of proper human behavior, nor restrain men from doing the things men have always done." In his story, O'Brien accomplishes transitions in perspective smoothly by having a character tell a story to the narrator:

> In other cases you can't even tell a true war story. Sometimes it's just beyond telling.
>
> I heard this one, for example, from Mitchell Sanders . . . The occasion was right for a good story.
>
> "God's truth," Mitchell Sanders said. "A six-man patrol goes up into the mountains on a basic listening-post operation. The idea's to spend a week up there, just lie low and listen for enemy movement . . .

Suggestions for Writing

1. Take an event in which you were a participant (an occasion when you got in serious trouble with your parents, the first time you met your significant other, your or a friend or family member's wedding). Write an account of the event, presenting, first, your

memories about it, and then, what others had to say about it. You may want to conclude by discussing any differences that emerge.

2. Take a historical event in which you were *not* a participant. Do some research. Find at least three accounts of the event by three different people. Write a description of the event using quotes from *all* of your sources.

3. After reading Greg Martin's essay "Other People's Memories," think of a family story that you know very well, a story your grandfather has told you a number of times, for instance, and try writing the story from that family member's perspective. Try using a change in point of view (for instance, first person to third person) to indicate the change in perspective. For example, in the following passage, Greg Martin shifts from first person to third person when he enters his grandfather Oliver's story:

> The day begins before dawn. The sky is dark and shadowed with clouds as Oliver takes the bucket to the pump, where he will draw water from the well. He is six. He is small and wiry, his hair blonde and uncombed and curly. He is dressed in patched jeans and shortsleeves, though it is not yet 5 a.m. He knows what cold is like and this is not cold . . . It is the Fourth of July, 1919, and today the Tremewan Family will travel north to Mountain City for the celebration.

Innocent Perspective

A "newcomer" in a society has a unique perspective because of an unfamiliarity with certain linguistic and social conventions. He or she has to deduce meaning from what is observable. We can learn much by looking at familiar things with a new perspective. This innocent view has the power to illuminate something obvious but hidden to most observers. Children, for instance, in their naïveté, are often the ones who reveal that the emperor has no clothes.

Writing from a perspective other than one's own can be mind broadening. This technique is particularly effective in revealing and challenging aspects of our lives and cultures that are taken for granted. For this reason, it is well suited to the essay, where it can inject creativity and often humor to make an effective argument. It can also, however, be useful in the other subgenres of creative nonfiction—memoir, biography, historical essay, etc., especially when used in combination with the conditional voice. (See the earlier section "Conditional Voice.") What would an outsider make of a family interaction? What would someone from the past or a different culture make of a current practice? What would someone from the present make of a custom in a particular historical setting?

Of course, the most challenging aspect of utilizing the innocent perspective is to truly shed our own preconceptions. We need to realize that our daily rituals, as common as they are to us, would seem bizarre to another culture, just as other cultures' rituals often strike us as strange. We have all opened *National Geographic* and been fascinated by the "necks wound round and round with wire," as Elizabeth Bishop says in her poem "In the Waiting Room." But how would our own daily rituals seem to an outsider: acts as common as shaving or applying makeup? What might other cultures think of plastic surgery? It is certainly no less bizarre as a cultural practice than the scarification rituals of certain African tribes that shock us when we see them depicted in magazines or on television.

We have seen this use of an innocent or *limited* perspective in mainstream media, in popular TV shows like *Third Rock from the Sun* or *The Wonder Years*, or in movies like *Crocodile Dundee* or *Look Who's Talking*. I have a favorite moment in the movie *Starman*, when the alien has observed and quickly assessed the rules of driving. He says, "I understand. Red means stop. Green means go. Yellow means go very very fast." He misunderstands the rules but reveals a truth we all recognize.

Suggestions for Writing

1. Writing from an alien perspective is the type of exercise that will allow satire of many different aspects of human society. You could focus on a bar, a nuclear waste disposal site, a landfill, a school, a jail, a factory, a strip club, a battlefield. It is a useful way to shake up your own notions about the society in which you live, to look

at it with new eyes: the eyes of an outsider who may misunderstand, and in doing so, reveal a deeper truth.

2. Explore various aspects of 20th-century America through the perspective of an alien. Construct a narrative or consider writing an analytical piece, a report on your findings.

3. The following is a variation on the above exercise, as it brings up the assumptions archaeologists make about past cultures: You arrive on a desolate, uninhabited Earth in some future year. Write through the perspective of an archaeologist digging up the objects of our everyday lives. Focus on the symbolic value of the objects you find. What do they suggest about the culture that lived here? What assumptions can you make about a society that leaves behind the golden arches of McDonald's and a landfill full of Styrofoam? What might a high-heeled shoe, makeup, and a bikini say about the society? Write an assessment of some aspect(s) of 20th-century America based on the items that you find. This variation of the exercise works well to fulfill essay assignments in particular.

4. Use limited perspective to tap into your own perspective as a child. Think of an incident from your childhood. Try to inhabit that 7- (or 8- or 9-, etc.) year-old voice. Make a list of what you do know at 7 years old. Make a list of what you don't know about the matter.

Using Biography

Read/Revisit

> Leslie Marmon Silko, "Landscape, History, and the Pueblo Imagination" (see page 224)
> Philip Brady, "Myth and Uncertainty" (see page 148)

Suggestions for Writing

1. In an earlier exercise, you wrote a brief biography of a family member or an ancestor. Now choose a single incident to describe more fully. Don't take on too much at once. Choose one dramatic moment of this person's life as a focal point of the narration.

   Try to imagine your ancestor's perspective at the time, as Philip Brady does in "Myth and Uncertainty." This will allow you to include solid details: sights, sounds, smells that you might not otherwise have considered using.

2. Narrate a historical event and imagine your ancestor's life and actions during the event, as Silko does in "Landscape, History and the Pueblo Imagination."

3. Write a letter to an ancestor. Or if you have any actual old correspondence, use it as a source of inspiration, as in Hart Crane's "My Grandmother's Love Letters":

   > . . . There is even room enough
   > For the letters of my mother's mother,
   > Elizabeth,
   > That have been pressed so long
   > Into a corner of the roof . . .
   >
   > And I ask myself:
   > Are your fingers long enough to play
   > Old keys that are but echoes . . .

10
Detail, Image, and Symbol

Detailing a Narrative

Read/Revisit

Shirley Geok-Lin Lim, "Splendor and Squalor" (see page 178)
Joy Harjo, "The Flying Man" (see page 202)

As the saying goes, the devil is in the details, and it's true. Think of the world as made up of countless little pieces, the details our senses perceive. There are just too many to include when we describe something in writing. So when we write, we must choose which details are most crucial to the story we are trying to tell or the scene we are trying to depict. We must choose carefully and deliberately, because the choice of what we include and what we omit establishes the mood, tone, and direction of our piece. Shirley Geok-Lin Lim's selection of details establishes rich depictions of place and contributes to the tone of the piece.

Suggestions for Writing

1. Describe a person (a parent or sibling, perhaps) by the things in his or her purse, briefcase, desk, office. Let these details reveal something about the character.

2. Establish a setting or character. List every detail you can come up with. Now try to select from the list. Which details might have symbolic value and function on more than one level (e.g., a heat wave, which might also imply passion or anger brimming beneath the surface)? Which details help reveal something about the character or setting without stating it directly (e.g., a fur coat and diamonds)?

Turning Abstractions into Images and Action

Read/Revisit

Naomi Shihab Nye, "Three Pokes of a Thistle" (see page 215)

One old adage of writing bears repeating: Show, don't just tell. A little "telling" (or expository discussion about the matter) is sometimes essential, as long as it doesn't merely restate or replace the image and is kept in balance with the "showing" (the vivid details). Specificity can actually have a far greater power of universality than vague abstractions. If you write, for instance, about one very specific loss and inhabit the experience with vivid, descriptive language, it will have more far-reaching effects than if you speak about loss in the abstract.

Suggestions for Writing

1. Use an earlier piece of class writing to find examples of abstractions that could be made concrete. Or write down several abstract words, such as emotions (anger, happiness, etc.) or any word ending in *-ism*. Then use an image or series of images to convey the abstraction. For example: for anger, one might depict a red face or a muscle in the temple twitching. If you are in a workshop, you could scramble and exchange your abstract words with other participants.

2. Write down an abstract idea, such as "loss." Then make a list of specific details that might convey the abstract idea.

3. List a few abstract concepts (e.g., domesticity, longing, love). Now replace them with a common household object. Write a short piece with the common object as its focus. Don't state the abstract concept in your response.

4. Write a short piece about an emotion, using the emotion as a one-word title. The speaker or main character in your piece feels this emotion but wants to keep it secret.

   a. What kind of weather could reflect or intensify this emotion? List a few images.

   b. What actions by other people would intensify this emotion? List three or four such actions.

   c. What actions by the main character or speaker would subtly betray this emotion? Again, list three or four.

   d. What images or details about a person's appearance could indicate the emotion?

Make a list and review it to remove any of the details that would "shout" the emotion—anything that seems too obvious as you review it. Construct your piece using the four sets of images and actions.

Using All of Your Senses

Read/Revisit

Diane Ackerman, "The Truth About Truffles" (see page 127)
Judith Ortiz Cofer, "Silent Dancing" (see page 154)

All good creative writing is based on sensory experience. We often think of images as being visual, but they are also auditory, tactile, olfactory, and gustatory. Good imagery reveals something with new eyes and ears and hands and turns it around for examination, as in Diane Ackerman's words from "The Truth About Truffles": "The Greeks believed truffles were the outcome of thunder, reversed somehow and turned to root in the ground." Judith Ortiz Cofer, in "Silent Dancing" explores the memories of her childhood, with descriptions such as the following:

> Even the home movie cannot fill in the sensory details such as a gathering left imprinted in a child's brain. The thick sweetness of women's perfume mixing with the ever-present smells of food cooking in the kitchen: meat and plantain *pasteles*, the ubiquitous rice dish made special with pigeon peas—*gandules*—and seasoned with the precious *sofrito* sent up from the island by somebody's mother or smuggled in by a recent traveler. *Sofrito* was one of the items that women hoarded, since it was hardly ever in stock at la Bodega. It was the flavor of Puerto Rico.

Suggestions for Writing

1. Try writing a few descriptive paragraphs about a place, selecting details that appeal to senses other than vision. What difference is created by the detail of the scent of roses, as opposed to the visual description of a rosebush? Describe, for instance, the kitchen of the home you grew up in, emulating Judith Ortiz Cofer's specificity about smells and tastes.

2. The paragraph that opens T. C. Boyle's story "Greasy Lake" is rich in imagery appealing to all of the senses. Read the paragraph below.

   > There was a time when courtesy and winning ways went out of style, when it was good to be bad, when you cultivated decadence like a taste. We were all dangerous characters then. We wore torn-up leather jackets, slouched around with toothpicks in our mouths, sniffed glue and ether and what somebody claimed was cocaine. When we wheeled our parents' whining station wagons out onto the street we left a patch of rubber half a block long. We drank gin and grape juice, Tango, Thunderbird and Bali Hai. We were nineteen. We were bad.

   Make a list of the images in the paragraph and the different senses to which they appeal. Now emulate the paragraph. Write a paragraph describing yourself (current self or younger self) and incorporate imagery that appeals to each of the five senses.

3. Diane Ackerman's "The Truth About Truffles" is creative nonfiction, but what elements of poetry and fiction do you notice in her essay? Notice, for instance, the imagined scenario that ends the piece, with the truffle farmer and his sow. Choose a scientific subject, perhaps one from biology (such as the mating rituals of hyenas, for a wild example). Do some research on the subject. Write a page of research information. Now create an imagined narrative using the research information. Use imagery that appeals to a number of the senses.

Writing from Art

All forms of art essentially do the same thing: they explore the nuances of the human experience. It is not surprising, then, that artists working in one form often find inspiration from works of art in other forms. The connections between literature and painting are particularly strong, perhaps because of the vivid imagery both art forms must employ.

Almost every occasion and aspect of the human condition has been elaborated upon by great painting, and so parallels can often be drawn and insights gained by writing from art. Consider, for instance, the truths about the "new" shock-and-awe approach to war revealed by Picasso's *Guernica*. Or consider the insights into your family's background that the art (original or reproduction) hanging on your living room wall can provide. Art can be the source of both inspiration and revelation. In addition, writing from art, known as ekphrastic writing, is a great way to hone your sense of the image.

Suggestions for Writing

1. Visit a museum or an art gallery or spend some time in a library or bookstore looking through some books with photographs of works of art. Write a response to a work of art that moves you because of its subject or imagery. When you travel and visit museums, make it a point to carry your journal with you. Wandering through a gallery usually fills you with rich images and inspiration.

2. Riff on the art. What does the painting make you think about? Where does it send you? Write a piece that focuses on a seemingly obscure detail in the piece of art—a cat on the windowsill in the background, for instance.

Symbols, Not Cymbals

Read/Revisit

Joy Harjo, "The Flying Man" (see page 202)

Invariably, when we talk about symbols in workshops, someone will ask a question like "Isn't a car ever just a car?" The question recalls Sigmund Freud's famous answer that "sometimes a cigar is just a cigar." Whether something has symbolic value, of course, depends on the context. A car that is used for a getaway, an "accessory" made necessary by the plot, may be just a car, for instance, but your first car usually carries great meaning and symbolism. A symbol asks the reader to ascribe a concept or idea (like freedom) to something tangible (like a car).

Symbols vary from culture to culture, depending on religion, history, landscape, and other elements. However, because they also arise out of our unconscious, there are many similarities between symbols in different cultures. These "universal" symbols or models, such as a flood, a forest, or a fire are known as archetypes and often carry a duality of meaning. A flood is both restorative and destructive, a forest is a place of natural beauty but also danger, and fire gives warmth but has great power to destroy. Symbols often enter one's writing on their own, and only later may the writer realize what has happened on the page. They may carry many layers of meaning.

A piece of writing might be overt about its symbolism, or the symbolism might exist more subtly. An *allegory* is the simplest form of symbolism—a piece in which it is obvious that the elements stand for something. In Nathaniel Hawthorne's classic story "Young Goodman Brown," for instance, the character named Faith is clearly symbolic. In longer allegorical works such as Dante's *Divine Comedy*, there are often many layers of meaning and interpretation. Because allegory lends itself especially to didactic writing (work that attempts to teach ethical, moral, or religious values), in the wrong hands it can feel like a sledgehammer to the reader. Overt symbols can easily become loud cymbals if the rest of the music is not kept in balance.

We live in an elaborate symbolic matrix. No one can deny it. We can see the evidence on the average drive to work. Deliberately invented symbols in our society such as words, flags, and road signs are usually referred to by scholars as *signs*. We also have *traditional* or *conventional* symbols, such as flowers or religious icons that have a certain meaning in society and that might appear in a writer's work. Writers might also use *private* or contextual symbols that develop throughout a single piece (such as the whale in *Moby Dick*) or ones that recur in different works.

Even people might take on a legendary or symbolic quality in a culture (Attila the Hun, Socrates, Mother Teresa, Elvis, John F. Kennedy). Actions are also sometimes symbolic—in real life and on the page. Actions tell a great deal about a person's character.

Suggestions for Writing

1. In a workshop, look among your possessions for symbolic items. Take out your wallet or purse. What symbolic items do you have in your possession at the moment? Money is a sign for something, of course, but it also functions on a symbolic level. Pictures? A driver's license? Unmentionables? Do you have a piece of jewelry, clothing, a tattoo that is symbolic? Write a short piece that makes the symbolism of the item clear, but subtle. (You might also use symbolic items in your vicinity—a tree, a blackboard, a painting.)

2. Choose a symbolic object, or action, as Joy Harjo does with "flight" in "The Flying Man." Sketch out the various times in your life when this object or action figured prominently. Note how Harjo turns her very birth into an image of "a reluctant acrobat caught in flight." And later heavy with unexpected teenage pregnancy and numerous other difficulties, she says, "There was no way I could fly." Emulate Harjo's return to this idea of flight as a motif for discussing various periods of her life. Sketch out all the times a particular motif resurfaced in your own life.

11
Figurative Language

What you say is important, of course, but *how* you say it often makes the difference. As Robert Frost says, "All the fun's in how you say a thing."

The "how" is made up of a great variety of elements operating simultaneously, some of which have been discussed in other sections: *diction* (word choice), *syntax* (the arrangement of words), figurative language, form. Each of these elements contributes to the *tone* (the stance or attitude) of the piece. Titles might be used to set up the tone from the beginning.

The following is a brief review of types of figurative language, with examples of prose and poetry. Most of the terms derive from the Greek (which gives them their unwieldy quality in English). The technique is the essential element, not the terms themselves, although you will probably also learn the terms as you try your hand at them.

personification: giving human characteristics to something nonhuman (an animal, inanimate object, abstract idea, etc.)

The great crane still swung its black arm from Oxford Street to above their heads.

—DORIS LESSING (B. 1919)

A tattered coat upon a stick, unless
Soul clap its hands and sing, and louder sing
For every tatter in its mortal dress . . .

—WILLIAM BUTLER YEATS (1865–1939)

synesthesia: (from the Greek, "blended feeling") the association of an image perceived by one of the senses with one perceived by another. For instance,

And taste the music of that vision pale

—JOHN KEATS (1795–1821)

Perfumes there are as sweet as the oboe's sound
Green as prairies, fresh as a child's caress

—CHARLES BAUDELAIRE (1826–1867)

hyperbole: (from the Greek, throwing beyond) exaggeration

And from far up, ringing from peak to peak of the summits over us, came a cry of such unutterable and ecstatic joy that it sounds down across the years and tingles among the cups of my quiet breakfast table.

—LOREN EISELEY (1907–1977)

understatement: something phrased in a restrained way

. . . for destruction ice
Is also great
and would suffice

—ROBERT FROST (1874–1963)

metonymy: referring to something by using the name of something associated with it (the Church, the Crown, the White House, the silver screen). There are many categories of metonymy, such as using the name of the place for the institution: "Wall Street is jittery"; or the object for the user: "the factories are on strike." Note how scepter, crown, scythe, and spade represent social classes in the following passage:

Scepter and crown must tumble down
And in the dust be equal made
With the poor crooked scythe and spade.

—JAMES SHIRLEY (1596–1666)

synecdoche: (from the Greek, taking whole) a type of metonymy, in which a part refers to the whole

The hand that signed the paper felled a city.

—DYLAN THOMAS (1914–1953)

Every day brings a ship,
Every ship brings a word;
Well for those who have no fear,
Looking seaward well assured
That the word the vessel brings
Is the word they wish to hear.

—RALPH WALDO EMERSON (1803–1882)

paradox: (from the Greek, "contrary to expectation") a statement that seems like a contradiction but reveals another layer of truth. Shakespeare's poetry is filled with paradox.

When most I wink, then do mine eyes best see . . .
All days are nights to see till I see thee.

When my love swears she is made of truth
I do believe her, though I know she lies

—WILLIAM SHAKESPEARE (1564–1616)

Sylvie did not want to lose me. She did not want me to grow gigantic and multiple, so that I seemed to fill the whole house.

And below is always the accumulated past, which vanishes but does not vanish, which perishes and remains.

—MARILYNNE ROBINSON (B. 1944)

Twenty men crossing a bridge,
Into a village

Are twenty men crossing twenty bridges,
Into twenty villages,
Or one man
Crossing a single bridge into a village.

—WALLACE STEVENS (1879–1955)

oxymoron: compressed paradox, like "jumbo shrimp" or "sweet sorrow"

Parting is such sweet sorrow.

—WILLIAM SHAKESPEARE (1564–1616)

allusion: reference to another literary work, history, art, event, etc. An allusion might be direct or subtle. Sometimes a work declares an influence directly, such as the quotation from Dante that opens T. S. Eliot's "Love Song of J. Alfred Prufrock." Names are another method of creating allusion, such as Melville's choice of the biblical tyrant Ahab for the captain in *Moby Dick*.

An allusion might also be more subtle, such as the use of a quotation or a paraphrase from another author within the piece. Sometimes the allusion has an archetypal quality about it that recalls an age-old story, such as the reference to the Flood in Alice Munro's short story "The Found Boat":

At the end of Bell Street, McKay Street, Mayo Street, there was the Flood. It was the Wawanash River, which every spring overflowed its banks . . . Light reflected off the water made everything bright and cold, as it is in a lakeside town, and woke or revived in people certain vague hopes of disaster . . . There were always things floating around in the Flood—branches, fence-rails, logs, road signs, old lumber; sometimes boilers, washtubs, pots and pans, or even a car seat or stuffed chair, as if somewhere the Flood had got into a dump.

—ALICE MUNRO (B. 1931)

metaphor: a comparison in which something is directly described as being something else

I dangled there from his hands, a reluctant acrobat caught in flight.

JOY HARJO (B. 1951)

Then he turned on the bumblebee of himself and I was the hapless flower of his attentions.

FRED D'AGUIAR (B. 1960)

extended metaphor: a metaphor that expands on an original comparison. Many poems operate on this principle, as do many prose passages, sometimes extensive works.

I dangled there from his hands, a reluctant acrobat caught in flight. I took note there was a rush with the release, with flying free, and like an addict I flew whenever I could, from crib bars to jungle gyms and once the roof of the garage. Later it was anything dangerous, like smoking cigarettes in the bathroom of the church, or jumping off a cliff into the lake after drinking illegal beer. And then the plain stupid: I leaped from the house of the proverbial cruel stepfather to the arms of a young dancer I met at Indian school who could not love me.

—JOY HARJO (B. 1951)

That wasp on the windowpane nibbling up and down the glass for a pore to exit through, back into the air and heat, tries to sting what it can feel but cannot see. My father is the window. I am the wasp. Sometimes a helping hand comes along and lifts the window, and the wasp slides out. Other times a shadow descends, there is a displacement of air, and it is the last thing the wasp knows. Which of those times is this? I want to know. I don't want to know. I am not nibbling nor trying to sting.

—FRED D'AGUIAR (B. 1960)

simile: a type of metaphor using such words as *like, as, seems, appears*

There is a snatch of a lyric that has stuck in my mind like a needle on a worn groove.

The beauty mark on her cheek as big as a hill on the lunar landscape of her face

—JUDITH ORTIZ COFER (B. 1952)

For the letters of my mother's mother
. . . are brown and soft
and liable to melt as snow.

—HART CRANE (1899–1932)

implied metaphor: uses neither a connective such as *like* or a form of the verb "to be"

In Mississippi I wandered among some of the ghosts and bones, and it is my great lesson to have learned to stop trying to evade and forget what I have seen and heard and understood and now must know, but rather to embrace the ghosts and cradle the bones and call them my own.

—ANTHONY WALTON (B. 1960)

. . . telephones crouch, getting ready to ring
In locked up offices.

—PHILIP LARKIN (1922–1985)

analogy: a kind of reasoning (used in the sciences, math, history, and other disciplines) that is based on metaphor and crucial to our process of thinking and making connections
     Terry Tempest Williams uses analogy and extended metaphor, as well as other figurative language, in "Peregrine Falcon" from *Refuge*:

Our urban wastelands are becoming wildlife's last stand. The great frontier. We've moved them out of town like all other low-income tenants . . . I like to sit on the piles of unbroken Hefties, black bubbles of sanitation . . . The starlings gorge themselves, bumping into each other like drunks. They are not discretionary. They'll eat anything, just like us . . . Perhaps we project on to starlings that which we deplore in ourselves: our numbers, our aggression, our greed, and our cruelty. Like starlings, we are taking over the world.

—TERRY TEMPEST WILLIAMS (B. 1955)

Writers often use many figures of speech within a single passage, as in the following familiar soliloquy from Shakespeare's Macbeth (Act V, Scene v), which uses nearly all of them:

> Tomorrow, and tomorrow, and tomorrow
> Creeps in this petty pace from day to day
> To the last syllable of recorded time;
> And all our yesterdays have lighted fools
> The way to dusty death. Out, out, brief candle!
> Life 's but a walking shadow, a poor player,
> That struts and frets his hour upon the stage,
> And then is heard no more. It is a tale
> Told by an idiot, full of sound and fury,
> Signifying nothing.

Aristotle (384–322 BCE) believed that metaphor (the word is sometimes used to mean all figurative language) was the most important skill of an educated person. He wrote:

> By far the greatest thing is to be a master of metaphor. It is the one thing that cannot be learned from others. It is a sign of genius, for a good metaphor implies an intuitive perception of similarity among dissimilars.

Although Aristotle may have been right in suggesting that mastery of metaphor cannot be learned from others, we all use metaphor in our daily language. Practicing the different means of making figurative language is a way to understand its use, bring it into our own writing and speech, and exercise our ability to draw connections in the world. By consciously practicing, we can improve our use of figurative language and become masters of metaphor.

(Using too much figurative language in a piece of writing, of course, might also weigh it down or cause confusion. Some combinations of metaphor might be useful to create a surreal effect, but be wary of creating unintentional *mixed* or *warring* metaphors such as "language is the river that opens doors" or "the curves on the road unfolded.")

Suggestions for Writing

1. Look at the passage above from *Macbeth*. How many figures of speech can you identify?
2. A fun way to practice these techniques (and simultaneously generate ideas) is to write the terms defined and discussed above on scraps of paper. Now pick three out of a hat. Write a short paragraph containing all three elements.

12
Diction

Origins of Words

Word choice in English can be particularly daunting, probably because English derives from so many languages. Following is a list of words that derive from Germanic/Anglo-Saxon roots and a corresponding list of words with the same or similar meaning that derive from Greco-Latin roots. Words of Anglo-Saxon origin are often monosyllabic, which makes them particularly useful to poets using metrical verse, or for achieving the effect of a sparse style.

Germanic/Anglo-Saxon	*Greco/Latin*
house	domicile
woods	forest
dark	obscure
mad	insane
eat	consume
speak	discourse
sorrow	anguish

Suggestions for Writing

1. Write a short piece, first incorporating only words from the first column. Then write the same piece incorporating only words from the second column. Do you notice any difference in the tone?
2. Now try writing the piece using words from both origins.

Foreign Flavor

Read/Revisit

Rhina P. Espaillat, "Bilingual/Bilingüe" (see page 175)
Amy Tan, "Mother Tongue" (see page 241)
Guillermo Gómez-Peña, "Documented/Undocumented (see page 201)

Sometimes the use of a word or words in another language seems essential to conveying aspects of a particular setting. If you grew up with a second language, you may have memories of events that took place in another language. Or you might be writing about a travel experience that would benefit from the occasional foreign word. The challenge is to let the words add flavor to the rendering in English without overburdening the piece.

Notice how Rhina P. Espaillat uses the register of two languages to write about the conflict of generations. Amy Tan also uses the register of different languages to write about her family history. In "Mother Tongue," she discusses her experience as a first-generation American and the "different Englishes" she grew up with.

Suggestions for Writing

1. Write a piece in which you substitute certain words with their equivalent in another language. This probably works best if you are bilingual, but if you are not, you might think of the words you do know in another language. Why do you remember them? Is there a story behind the words or phrases—how they planted themselves in your brain? Use one of these words or phrases as the impetus for a piece. Some words struck me as extraordinarily memorable the first time I heard them because of their musicality, their root, or their meaning. The Spanish *sueño* feels dreamlike to me. I've always liked the French *plume* because of the feather and pen connection. *Besuchen,* German for *visit,* contains the word *suchen,* to seek.

2. Write a bit of dialogue between two people, one of whom speaks only in English while the other mixes a word or phrase from another language with English. Write the dialogue so the context of the situation and the action of the speakers make it clear what the non-English words mean.

3. Guillermo Gómez-Peña, in "Documented/Undocumented," discusses a number of names that have been used to categorize him: *chilango, norteño,* etc. Write a short essay that discusses the perceptions others have or have had of you; you might mention names and labels that have been used. You might also try emulating Gómez-Peña's tongue-in-cheek tone.

Simplify

Although some exercises in this section suggest ways to use words in fresh, innovative, sometimes surreal arrangements, diction certainly need not be difficult or bizarre to have a powerful effect.

In Paule Marshall's essay "Poets in the Kitchen," she reveals that her relatives talking around the kitchen table were a major influence on her writing life:

> It's all a matter of exposure and a training of the ear for the would-be writer in those early years of apprenticeship. And this training, the best of it, often takes place in as unglamorous a setting as the kitchen . . . I grew up among poets. Now they didn't look like poets—whatever that breed is supposed to look like. Nothing about them suggested that poetry was their calling.

She speaks about the value of "common speech and the plain workaday words" that are the "stock in trade" of some of the writers. The richness of her family's idiomatic expressions from Barbados found their way into her work. She learned more from them than from the established writers she could name as influences.

Suggestions for Writing

1. Think of your own history, your earliest memories of language, your introduction to your own identity. What "poets" do you recall (of the kitchen, the pool hall, the corner of Fifth and Main, etc.)? Focus on one person or one group that was somehow crucial to your language, your views, your voice.

2. Take some cryptic lines from your journal and think about what stories they are concealing. Have the courage to just "tell it straight." Use simple diction and a straightforward manner of narration.

Tell-tale Dialect

Read/Revisit

Fred D'Aguiar, "A Son in Shadow" (see page 160)

Dialect is a difficult element to master in writing, particularly if you are using a dialect with which you are not completely comfortable. If so, writers often work with linguists or natives of a region to make sure that their characters' speech sounds authentic. The exercise below will get you thinking about the way using a different dialect can entirely change a piece of writing.

Suggestions for Writing

"Translate" a famous passage into a different form of English. You might try this alone or as a group activity. For instance, use the opening paragraph of Edgar Allan Poe's "The Tell-Tale Heart" and have the murderer use a different dialect: from the deep South, a Brooklyn youth, Spanglish, etc.

> True!—nervous—very, very dreadfully nervous I had been and am; but why *will* you say that I am mad? The disease had sharpened my senses—not destroyed—not dulled them. Above all was the sense of hearing acute. I heard all things in the heaven and in the earth. I heard many things in hell. How, then, am I mad? Hearken! and observe how healthily—how calmly I can tell you the whole story.
>
> It is impossible to say how first the idea entered my brain; but, once conceived, it haunted me day and night. Object there was none. Passion there was none. I loved the old man. He had never wronged me. He had never given me insult. For his gold I had no desire. I think it was his eye!—yes, it was this! He had the eye of a vulture—a pale blue eye, with a film over it. Whenever it fell upon me, my blood ran cold; and so, by degrees—very gradually—I made up my mind to take the life of the old man, and thus rid myself of the eye forever.
>
> —EDGAR ALLAN POE

> Word!—nervous—I was mad scared, yo! But why you got to be say I'm trippin', you know? The disease woke me up—I ain't sleepin'. My ears was on fire with knowledge! I heard things in da heaven above and da earth, and all the way down to Hell. How am I nuts? Peep this! 'Cuz I got a story to tell
>
> I don't know how it got in my head, yo, but once it was there, yo boom—it haunted me day and night. There was no beef, no hype, 'cuz I had mad love for the old geezer! I ain't got no reason, ain't got no rhyme. He never dissed me. I wasn't trying to take his paper. But he had this nasty ol' lookin' eye. He had eyes like a vulture, blue, all glazed and all! Whenever he peeped me, my blood ran cold, and so over time, I decided to cap him before he got me.
>
> —MICHELLE BYNUM, JEREMY GOLDSMITH,
> JENNIFER PEARSON, STUDENTS

You could, of course, use any of many well-known works for this exercise. The passage is a good, albeit eerie, choice because of the urgent voice: the madman who tries to convince us of his sanity. It also contains several archaic words, such as *hearken*, which offer opportunity for humorous translations.

13
Setting

Setting with Personality

Read/Revisit

> Edwidge Danticat, "Westbury Court" (see page 171)
> Wendell Berry, "An Entrance to the Woods" (see page 139)

An important question for the writer to answer early on is "where are we, and when?" This is because readers generally need the details of a concrete setting in order to "enter" the story and imagine themselves in it. Sometimes, particularly in shorter pieces and especially in poetry, the title helps to place the narrative in space and time. Maxine Kumin says that titles are "geography, chronology, or furniture."

Though in most creative nonfiction the setting is concrete (i.e., represents a specific time and place), in some cases the setting might describe purely a state of mind—thoughts or emotions. Other times, the setting might even be a dream world. In all these cases, however, the setting is both specific and an essential element of the narrative.

Suggestions for Writing

1. Choose a limited setting. Try to select an area or a place that might have symbolic resonance on a number of levels (a church, your grandmother's attic, a cabin in the woods). In a workshop, you might also all come up with ideas for evocative settings and then decide on a single one.

2. Each person should then write an opening paragraph using the same setting. It would be interesting to read these aloud and hear how much they differ in tone—or perhaps don't, depending on the setting selected and the different contexts.

3. Write a piece that takes place in a dream or an essay about a dream you hope could become real. Describe how the world would be if your dream were realized.

4. Sometimes in creative nonfiction, or in fiction as well, the setting can be so significant it almost becomes a character in the story. In the movie *The Money Pit,* for example, the story is about everything that can go wrong in restoring an old house. In this case, the old house is a character in the story. In a setting with oppressive

heat, the heat might take on a life of its own. Think of a real-life scenario and describe the aspects of your setting in terms of a character. Try not to use a cliché like "the angry sea," although you may certainly describe the ways in which the sea is angry.

Setting from Family History

Read/Revisit

Fred D'Aguiar, "A Son in Shadow" (see page 160)
Bruce Chatwin, excerpt from *In Patagonia* (see page 151)

Bruce Chatwin's travel narrative *In Patagonia* opens with the memory of a piece of brontosaurus skin in his grandmother's dining room cabinet. This memory from childhood sparked an interest in Patagonia, which was where this particular brontosaurus had supposedly lived. Chatwin uses this image to establish a personal link to the region of Patagonia, as he begins to introduce the setting of the narrative.

A travel narrative is, by its very nature, largely concerned with setting and sense of place. Chatwin's personal connection with Patagonia through family history and the recounting of his early memories of the piece of brontosaurus skin creates a charge that has the effect of drawing the reader into the narrative.

In Fred D'Aguiar's "A Son in Shadow," D'Aguiar imagines his father and mother meeting in mid-fifties Guyana. His reconstruction of their courtship is assisted by his keen sense of the location and time in which the event took place:

> Georgetown's two-lane streets with trenches on either side mean a mostly single-file walk, she in front probably looking over her shoulder when he says something worthy of a glance, or a cut-eye look if his suggestions about her body or what he will do with it if given half a chance exceed the decorum of the day—which is what, in mid-Fifties Guyana? From my grandmother it's, "Don't talk to a man unless you think you're a big woman. Man will bring you trouble. Man want just one thing from you. Don't listen to he. Don't get ruined for he. A young lady must cork her ears and keep her eye straight in front of she when these men start to flock around . . . ."

Suggestions for Writing

1. Reimagine a family story using details of place to help re-create the past, as in D'Aguiar's use of Georgetown's two-lane streets.
2. Write about a place where you have traveled or would like to travel. Try Chatwin's approach of linking the place to a family story or personal memory that will entice the reader to join you on the adventure.
3. Choose a natural setting from your family history and use it to make a comment about a personal or societal issue. For instance, is there a part of your town you feel has been ruined? How does it connect with your own personal history? The history of the country?

4. Choose a place or a building that has evocative memories for you. Let your piece stay focused on the place as a "container" for memories.

Setting Your Hometown

Read/Revisit

Shirley Geok-Lin Lim, "Splendor and Squalor" (see page 178)

How much do you really know about your hometown? What questions might you want to ask about it? When was it founded and by whom? Are there any political incidents that you think define it? How are they connected with the geography, the climate? Approaching your hometown from these different angles will let you see it both as a specific entity and a place that represents the connections and tensions between nature and culture around the world.

Your memories and questions are likely to lead you toward further research, into archives. Start with what you do know about your hometown. You will be surprised how many of your preconceptions get shaken up. Look for original sources. It can be very exciting to hold first editions and letters in your hand. A letter has an immediacy that can be very inspiring. Consider Ernest Hemingway's account of the 1935 hurricane in Key West, which took so many lives. He wrote it first as a letter and then as an article, revealing the combination of failures in particular, that led to the death of a large number of World War I veterans—the failure of the Weather Bureau to issue a proper warning and of the people in charge of the veterans who failed to take the precaution of sending a train early enough to move them out of the area:

> We were the first in to Camp Five of the veterans who were working on the highway construction. Out of 187 only 8 survived . . .
>
> The veterans in those camps were practically murdered . . .
>
> What I know and can swear to is this; that while the storm was at its height on Matecumbe and most of the people already dead the Miami bureau sent a warning of winds of gale strength on the keys from Key Largo to Key West and of hurricane intensity in the Florida straights [straits] below Key West. They lost the storm completely.

Hemingway's eyewitness testimony has a distinctive energy of its own.

Suggestions for Writing

1. Return to your hometown, even if you have never left. Try to see it as you have never seen it before. Visit the natural regions of your hometown. Describe what you see. Look up the geological, natural, and human history. Focus on the names of places. Research their origin. Do you find any ironies in them? Have any natural phenomena defined the place: floods, hurricanes, droughts? Have you experienced them? What images do you remember?

2. Think about how landscape helps to shape identity. Do you consider more than one place home? Write about how the places you have lived have influenced who you are. Focus on elements such as climate, culture, history, etc.

14
Creating Tension

Foundations of Tension

Read/Revisit

Edwidge Danticat, "Westbury Court" (see page 171)

Plot

The term *plot* is often used interchangeably with the terms *story* and *action*. In the language of creative writing, however, the three terms are not equivalent, and a great deal can be learned by understanding the distinction between them.

Story usually refers to the whole piece, whether it be, in nonfiction, an essay or a book-length work. Thus the term has a broad meaning that encompasses more than what happens. It also includes the *point of view*, the *setting*, the *characters*—in short it refers to all the elements of a work of creative writing. A term that can be used interchangeably with *story* is *narrative*.

Action refers to everything that happens in a story. This includes everything that happens in the characters' minds (*internal action*) as well as everything that is done by or to the characters (*external action*). In Edwidge Danticat's piece "Westbury Court," much of the action essential to the essay is external, with the dramatic effect of a fire in her childhood building. However, a great deal of energy exists in the internal action, the replaying of the event from the perspective of many years later.

The action can be categorized in terms of its importance to the development of the story. *Significant action* is essential to the story's development. *Incidental* or *peripheral action* is not essential to the story's development but is useful because it can enhance the realistic feel of the story: characters must be shown to perform at least some routine functions such as sleep or eat. Background action can provide context for the significant action. Events happening to characters totally unrelated to the main characters or to the significant action can be used to illustrate the broader effects of the significant action, etc.

Plot refers to the arrangement of the significant action in a story. One can think of plot as the skeleton of the story—the layout of each significant action in sequence.

Each sequence of significant action in a story reveals information that is important for the development of the story. When outlining a plot, the writer must decide when it is most effective to reveal certain information. Withholding information from the reader until just the right moment increases the tension in the plot and makes the story more effective.

It is important to remember, however, that the plot of a story or play is only the skeleton and has to be fleshed out into the complete story by adding the other basic elements, such as setting, definition of characters, dialogue, and peripheral action.

Suggestions for Writing

1. A fundamental plot underlying many pieces of literature is that of a hero setting out on a journey to obtain something of vital importance and then meeting and overcoming obstacles on the way. Write an outline, following this simple but effective model. For your hero, since you are writing nonfiction, choose a real person. (You might choose yourself or a person in your family—your grandfather, for instance.) Choose an objective this person had that could be attained only by traveling somewhere. Think of three obstacles that the person encountered on his or her path: another character, a natural obstacle (weather, a natural disaster, a mountain, etc.) and a situation (airline strike, car crash, family demands, etc.) After you have sketched out an outline, write a short narrative about how your hero overcame these obstacles.

2. Write a short narrative in which an important detail is concealed until the story is well under way.

A Spell of Trouble:
Conflict and Tension

Read/Revisit

Rudolfo Anaya, "Why I Love Tourists: Confessions of a Dharma Bum"
  (see page 131)
Rhina P. Espaillat, "Bilingual/Bilingüe" (see page 175)
Amy Tan, "Mother Tongue" (see page 241)

Trouble makes an interesting story. While a perfect day at the beach with the sun shining, the water calm and just the right temperature, and a nice tan with no sunburn as the outcome is very pleasant and desirable in real life, it is uneventful and thus does not make an interesting story to tell others. Consequently, most effective stories follow pretty much the same fundamental path of development—the *narrative arc of conflict* (and its complications), *crisis*, and *resolution* (often the crisis is followed by *falling action* before the resolution is achieved). The way a writer renders a story—and his or her focus on the conflict and highlighting tension—is what often makes a story *creative* nonfiction. The selection of details helps build this tension.

Conflict is the beating heart of the narrative. It provides the dramatic tension that keeps the story alive. So a crucial task of every author is to weave conflict into the story in a way that is natural and appropriate. To do this, it is important to note that the source of all conflict is the *desires* of the characters that populate the story. Conflict results from obstacles the characters encounter in the pursuit of fulfilling their desires. Such obstacles can come only from a limited set of sources: other characters, society at large, nature, and from within each character. Even though this means that there are only four basic types of conflict (with people, with society, with nature, and internal conflict), the possibilities within each category are virtually unlimited.

Categorizing types of conflict is useful in analyzing the structure of story plot, but it also holds the danger of making it appear as if the conflict should be simple and direct—between hero and villain, or hero and society, etc. The concept of "hero" tends to tempt writers, especially beginning writers, to see characters as isolated entities, struggling alone to overcome the obstacles in their path. In fact, stories that explore relationships between characters are richer and more interesting. This is true even when there is an overarching conflict between a person and some force placing obstacles in his or her path. It is, therefore, important to understand that relationships entail conflict between characters, and the narrative arc can be conceived as a set of conflicts leading to a variety of crises. It is also important to note that for each conflict to be able to provide enough tension in the story to hold the reader's attention, the two sides of the conflict must be closely balanced so that the outcome of the conflict is in question.

Suggestions for Writing

1. Describe a character (yourself, a friend, a relative, etc.), a desire he or she has, and an obstacle to this desire that is imposed by society. Repeat this with an obstacle imposed by nature and an obstacle imposed by the character.

2. Begin with one character and her desire (for instance, she wants to have the perfect wedding). Make a list of ten obstacles: obstacles presented by people, society, nature, and the character herself. Each of these obstacles is the foundation of a conflict. How well did the character overcome each obstacle and prevail in the conflict? Order the conflicts with those whose outcome was most in doubt at the top. Write an outline for a narrative that utilizes the top five conflicts on this list.

Reversing the Action

Our universe is expanding, with the galaxies speeding away from each other. One of the fundamental questions of cosmology is what the universe's ultimate fate will be. Several theories have been proposed. One of these asserts that the expansion will eventually stop, and the universe will begin to collapse. The physicist Stephen Hawking has suggested that if this theory is correct, the arrows of time will not point in the same direction for the whole history of the cosmos. At the point the universe begins to contract, time as we know it will move backward.

Martin Amis's book *Time's Arrow* uses Hawking's idea to explore questions of time. He narrates an imagined life story backward, with a soul trying to make sense of a backward world. In doing so, he comments satirically about society—from the weighty and grave to the comic and irreverent. The following passage describes rain, lightning, and earthquakes from a backward perspective:

> I know I live on a fierce and magical planet, which sheds or surrenders rain or even flings it off in whipstroke after whipstroke, which fires out bolts of electric gold into the firmament at 186,000 miles per second, which with a single shrug of its tectonic plates can erect a city in half an hour. Creation . . . is easy, is quick.

The conversations in the book, too, are backward:

> "Don't go—please."
> "Goodbye, Tod."
> "Don't go."
> "It's no good."
> "Please."
> "There's no future for us."
> Which I greet, I confess, with a silent "Yeah, yeah." Tod resumes:
> "Elsa," he says, or Rosemary or Juanita or Betty Jean. "You're very special to me."
> "Like hell."
> "But I love you."
> "I can't look you in the eye."
> I have noticed in the past, of course that most conversations would make much
> better sense if you ran them backward. But with this man-woman stuff, you could run
> them any way you liked—and still get no further forward.

While recent discoveries provide support for the competing theory that the universe will continue to expand forever, reversing the flow of time in the plot remains a useful literary device. One task for which it is particularly useful is for uncovering the true magnitude of events or actions.

W. S. Merwin's "Unchopping a Tree" uses the reversal of time to achieve this effect. This can be quite an intriguing technique for expository pieces. In Merwin's description of the mammals, the nests, the insects that would have to be returned, the splintered trunk reconnected, one senses the enormity of the destruction in the felling of a single tree. In describing the process backward, he makes a comment about the intricate balance of nature, which, once destroyed, is impossible to restore:

> With spider's webs you must simply do the best you can. We do not have the spider's weaving equipment, nor any substitute for the leaf's living bond with its point of attachment and nourishment.

Suggestions for Writing

1. Describe something backward. Create your reverse-time version in order to make a comment about something that has been done and might be better undone (e.g., undevelop a new development, unpollute a river).

Trading Characters, Settings, and Conflicts

The mind searches for ways to make sense of disparate elements, to make narrative. Although the following exercise might not always yield the best story, it is a good challenge. The combinations that arise can be kernels of later, more substantial pieces.

Suggestions for Writing

1. Have each person write down a character, a place, and an event on three separate scraps of paper. Each person should choose details that are common enough that everyone would have a story spring to mind (e.g., a father, a car, a fight). Collect them in piles. Then each participant will select one from each pile. Construct a short narrative using the three elements you have chosen. Try to use each of the elements in an equally significant way. Note the following student example:

   > (a student, a cabin, devious plans):
   > The school had called a snow day, and Tom had been hunting all day down in the state forest. When he came back to the house, he had no idea where Billy was or what he was up to. He saw the diffuse glow of a single hanging lightbulb coming from the guest cabin located in the far end of the field behind their house. As he brushed through the overgrown reeds in his rubber boots, he saw tiny fireworks bursting sporadically in one of the broken out windows. Billy was doing something with the scraps from the rusted out brick wagon. Tom crept closer. Little glints of light flew, and as Tom felt along the splintery wood walls, it became obvious to him what his brother was doing. The mildewed map of the world was dangling on the wall. The little flags were posted precariously. Billy was at it again.
   >
   > —EMILY BUSCH, STUDENT

2. Assign each other titles, based perhaps on heritage and inclinations. The titles might send you where you otherwise would not have gone. Or try a different approach and use them randomly. In a workshop, come up with titles and then scramble them. Write a piece with the title you receive.

Reverberating Closure

Read/Revisit

> Amy Tan, "Mother Tongue" (see page 241)
> Guillermo Gómez-Peña, "Documented/Undocumented" (see page 201)

Robert Frost says, "Anyone can get into a poem. It takes a poet to get out of one." W. B. Yeats believed good closure occurred when a poem would "come shut with a click, like a closing box." What gives a piece of writing that click? It is hard to identify, but we know it when we see or hear it. An essay or a chapter with strong closure will both shut like a door at the end and yet also echo into the next chapter, or in the reader's consciousness. Good closure will reverberate. Some writers favor the ironic ending, which usually has to be set up from the beginning. One prepares the reader for one kind of story and then delivers an unexpected result.

A poignant or startling event, scene, image, or moment can make for good closure in prose or poetry. An essay by Alice Walker, "Am I Blue," ends with a poignant, life-changing decision. The essay describes Walker's connection with a horse, Blue, and links his experience to her own. The essay ends with the speaker spitting out "misery":

> And so Blue remained, a beautiful part of our landscape, very peaceful to look at from the window, white against the grass. Once a friend came to visit and said, looking out on the soothing view: "And it *would* have to be a *white* horse; the very image of freedom." And I thought, yes, the animals are forced to become for us merely "images" of what they once so beautifully expressed. And we are used to drinking milk from containers showing "contented" cows, whose real lives we want to hear nothing about, eating eggs and drumsticks from: "happy" hens, and munching hamburgers advertised by bulls of integrity who seem to command their fate.
>
> As we talked of freedom and justice one day for all, we sat down to steaks. I am eating misery, I thought, as I took the first bite. And spit it out.

Closure often reemphasizes an important point of the essay, sometimes with an additional piece of information or a humorous detail. Amy Tan's "Mother Tongue," for instance, ends with a reference to Tan's mother commenting on her book *The Joy Luck Club*. Throughout the essay, Tan has described her mother's broken English and how this affected her relationship with her mother, as well as her mother's opportunities as an immigrant. The essay's final sentence reemphasizes Tan's issues with her mother's English and, finally, the way Tan decided to envision a reader for her work: "Apart from what the critics had to say about my writing, I knew I had succeeded where it counted when my mother finished reading my book and gave me her verdict: 'So easy to read.'"

There is an old German proverb regarding closure: "Beginning and end shake hands with each other." Sometimes we know when we have reached the end, and it happens naturally, perhaps with an organic, circular structure that contains elements of the opening. Other times we have an idea, but it takes a while to find the right words. And sometimes a piece does not seem to find an end. Try not to force it. It might be telling you to continue down that road.

Suggestions for Writing

1. Try writing a piece with an ironic closure, one that surprises the reader because the opposite of what is expected takes place. Play the trickster. Some real-life stories have a natural irony when they occur, with a clear closure, a line of dialogue, perhaps.

2. Look at the closure of a piece you have written with new eyes. Are there any other ways your piece could end? Write an alternative closure and compare the two. Discussions about closure should be an important aspect of a workshop. Often, as writers, we don't know when to stop; a natural closure might already exist in the piece. Other sets of eyes can help identify what is missing or what can be cut.

15
Rhythm

Finding Your Rhythm:
Poetry in Prose

Rhythm is an organic part of our everyday lives—in the tides, crickets in the night, our heartbeats. What makes rhythm in a piece of writing? Rhythm is defined as a systematic variation in the flow of sound. It is sometimes based on the unit of breath. Good prose can learn much from poetic technique as well.

Consider the following passage from Marilynne Robinson's *Housekeeping*:

> Looking out at the lake one could believe that the Flood had never ended. If one is lost on the water, any hill is Ararat. And below is always the accumulated past, which vanishes but does not vanish, which perishes and remains. If we imagine that Noah's wife when she was old found somewhere a remnant of the Deluge, she might have walked into it till her widow's dress floated above her head and the water loosened her plaited hair. And she would have left it to her sons to tell the tedious tale of generations. She was a nameless woman, and so at home among all those who were never found and never missed, who were uncommemorated, whose deaths were not remarked, nor their begettings.

Robinson's choice of language is a beautiful example of poetry within prose. If you read the above passage aloud, you will notice the rhythm of the sentences, the near-iambic lines such as "If one is lost on the water, any hill is Ararat," "If we imagine that Noah's wife when she was old . . ." or ". . . whose deaths were not remarked nor their begettings." She even uses internal assonance (such as *past* and *vanish* or *tale* and *hair)* and alliteration (such as *tedious tale)*. There are parallel structures such as "which vanishes but does not vanish, which perishes and remains" and "who were never found and never missed, who were uncommemorated, whose deaths were not remarked . . . ." Notice also the variation of sentence length and structure. Much of the music of this type of passage is best heard, however, when read aloud.

President Lincoln, in his Gettysburg Address, employed poetic techniques so effectively that the speech has been often called a poem and is one of the very few speeches (and perhaps the only presidential address) to be considered a piece of literature. Phrases such as "we cannot dedicate—we cannot consecrate—we cannot hallow this ground" employ repetition and variation to full rhythmical effect. Certain portions of the speech even employ meter: "The world will little note nor long remember what we say" is in perfect iambs.

> Four score and seven years ago our fathers brought forth upon this continent a new nation conceived in Liberty, and dedicated to the proposition that all men are created equal.
>
> Now we are engaged in a great civil war, testing whether that nation or any nation so conceived and so dedicated can long endure. We are met on a great battlefield of that war. We are met to dedicate a portion of it as the final resting place of those who here gave their lives that that nation might live. It is altogether fitting and proper that we should do this.
>
> But in a larger sense we cannot dedicate—we cannot consecrate—we cannot hallow this ground. The brave men living and dead who struggled here have consecrated it far above our poor power to add or detract. The world will little note nor long remember what we say here, but it can never forget what they did here. It is for us, the living, rather to be dedicated here to the unfinished work that they have thus far so nobly carried on. It is rather for us to be here dedicated to the great task remaining before us—that from these honored dead we take Increased devotion to that cause for which they here gave the last full measure of devotion—that we here highly resolve that the dead shall not have died in vain—that the nation shall, under God, have a new birth of freedom—and that governments of the people, by the people, and for the people, shall not perish from the earth.

Suggestions for Writing

1. Try to discover what your natural rhythm might be. Take a passage of your writing and study various elements. For instance, what is the ratio of short to long sentences? What repetition of sentence structure do you see? Do you notice any repetitions of words?

2. Take a favorite passage of prose that has an evocative rhythm. Look at it closely and examine what elements contribute to that rhythm. What poetic techniques can you identify in the passage?

3. Write a short prose piece using a parallel structure to emphasize your point and give the passage a certain rhythm.

Song and Story

Music, of course, is a great source of inspiration and has been closely linked to literature throughout ages and cultures, such as the traditional ballads of Ireland or the operas and ballets that have set many great works of literature to music. We all have powerful associations with particular tunes or lyrics, which can be used as points of inspiration for writing. We can use music to inspire the rhythm or subject matter of a particular piece.

Suggestions for Writing

1. In a workshop, have each person bring in a favorite song, preferably one that will be relatively familiar to others. Play one of the songs in class. Now have everyone freewrite in response. Does the song trigger any specific memories? Can you remember the first time you heard it? Perhaps use a line from the song as an epigraph. Read a few of the responses aloud.

2. Imitate the rhythm of different kinds of music with your lines or sentences. Let the rhythm of your lines or sentences reflect the influence of the beat.

3. Listen to songs in a language you don't know. Can you tell the tone of the song—longing, joy, reverence? "Translate" the song via the tone.

4. Listen to classical music. Try writing as you listen. Try Beethoven's Sixth Symphony, for instance, the "Storm Passage" created by violins and cellos. (If you introduce it to others who do not know the piece, you might withhold the name, at first, to see what kind of "stormy" feelings get evoked and appear beneath the pen.)

Listening to Nature

Read/Revisit

> Wendell Berry, "An Entrance to the Woods" (see page 139)
> Henry David Thoreau, "Walking" (see page 249)

The natural world is filled with songs. We can learn a great deal about the rhythms of nature by just listening. Go to the ocean, a waterfall, a river near your home. Listen for a while. Then try writing as you listen. How does it affect your rhythm?

Go into the woods and listen to the trees. Listen to the wind in the trees. Stay very still and listen to bird calls for a while. Then write. What might they be saying? Can you tell the tone of their songs? Do you hear the scolding shriek of a blue jay, the wild laugh of a loon, or the lyrical song of a warbler? Do they sound like anything you know?

You might also be able to discern certain rhythms with your eyes. A good example is a lizard's dewlap. I have sat mesmerized by the hypnotic beat of the dewlap concealed in the throat, revealing itself again and again.

Think about your own voice. What physical realities make the sounds and words emerge? Why do people have accents when they speak other languages? Do we train our mouths to move in a certain way? A favorite novel of mine, David Malouf's *An Imaginary Life*, contains a passage where the Roman poet Ovid is teaching a wild boy to speak. The boy can imitate all the birds and animals of the woods, but rather than merely mimicking, he seems to become the creature:

> His whole face is contorted differently as he assumes each creature's voice. If he were to speak always as frog or hawk or wolf, the muscles of his throat and jaw might grow to fit the sound, so intimately are the creatures and the sounds they make connected, so deeply are they one . . . I have begun to understand him. In imitating the birds, he is not, like our mimics, copying something that is outside him and revealing the accuracy of his ear or the virtuosity of his speech organs. He is being the bird. He is allowing it to speak out of him.

Try making the sounds you hear. What new muscles do you use? One interesting and easy exercise to do in the wild will attract many birds to you. Conceal yourself well and make repeated *psh psh psh* sounds. The sounds imitate the scolding calls of many birds. It can also be a meditative experience to remain still and call like that. Listen to the responses you get. Are there rhythms, repetitions? Imagine yourself as an arriving bird. What are you hearing? What are you thinking as you respond?

In Malouf's book, as Ovid learns more about the wild boy, he realizes how deeply the boy is connected to the universe. If he is to understand the child, he needs to "think as he must: I am raining. I am thundering."

Suggestions for Writing

1. Imitate the rhythm of a sound you hear—a bird call, the ocean. Let your form reflect something in the natural world.

2. You might also listen for the rhythms of something other than the natural world. Let the rhythms of everyday speech find their way into your writing. You might also try to capture the pace of the city—the positives or the negatives. (See Tom Wolfe's use of the chaotic run-on sentence to depict this pace in the section "Breaking the Rules.")

3. Some words seem to have sounds as their origin—crunch, growl, splash, hum. They are known as *onomatopoeia*, from the Greek, meaning name making. As you listen to sounds around you, repeat the sounds, listening to your own voice for the words they bring to mind. Keep a list of such words. Incorporate them in a piece of writing.

16
Character and Dialogue

Populating a Piece

Read/Revisit

Jamaica Kincaid, "Biography of a Dress" (see page 209)
Leslie Marmon Silko, "Landscape, History, and the Pueblo Imagination" (see page 224)

Just as the real world is populated by living things, literature is populated by characters. The term *living things* is used here deliberately, to emphasize that a nonhuman character might also figure prominently, even in nonfiction. In Silko's "Landscape, History and the Pueblo Imagination," for instance, the wide, deep arroyo on the reservation borderline is decribed as "ravenous," having devoured many vehicles: "The big arroyo has a wide mouth. Its existence needs no explanation. People in the area regard the arroyo much as they might regard a living being, which has a certain character and personality."

Characters in literature can be described via a number of literary devices. While some of these devices may be specific to a genre, three are common to all four genres: description, dialogue (direct or indirect), and thoughts. The process of "populating" a piece with characters is called *characterization*. In nonfiction, characters are real people; in a first person narration, the writer herself is a character.

Characters can be presented in varying detail or *depth*. When little detail is provided, the character is superficial or two dimensional—*flat*. When the characterization provides more details, the character is more realistic or three dimensional. Typically, it is the secondary characters in a piece that are flat, but there are important exceptions. The lack of depth in characterization tends to produce characters that are stereotypes: the tall, dark, handsome lover, the ugly, crude villain, etc. Consequently, flat characterization of main characters is particularly appropriate for parody, allegory, or a lighter piece that is intended purely to amuse.

Suggestions for Writing

1. Describe an interesting stranger you came across in the street (or the park, airport, etc.). Focus your description exclusively on appearance and what it conveys about the character.

2. Create a nonhuman character and a human character and write an essay about a special relationship that develops between them. Endow the nonhuman character with human characteristics. You might also take the relationship further and imagine a fantastic relationship, one that can never happen in reality. But since this is nonfiction, you need to acknowledge this "magically real" element to your reader.

Inside a Character's Mind

Dialogue or a character's response to a setting or situation can tell a great deal more about her personality than straight physical description or abstract words. Another way of revealing character is via the workings of that character's mind. If you are writing a personal narrative, this is a natural task, but if you are trying to explore how another person felt, it can be a difficult endeavor. One never really knows exactly what another thought or felt. If one has been told, this is dialogue and can be taken only at face value. You may have to acknowledge what you don't know, as an observer. You could imagine how someone else felt, as long as your reader understands that you are trying to reimagine something. This can be a particularly useful approach when writing about an ancestor or historical figure. You will be writing nonfiction, but you could state what you don't know to your reader. This can give you a kind of permission for invention.

Novelists such as James Joyce and Virginia Woolf bring us into the twists and turns of a character's mind via a *stream-of-consciousness* approach. The following passage of Virginia Woolf's *The Waves*, for instance, shows the character Bernard in turmoil about writing a letter to the girl he loves. The layers of character development are numerous here, as Bernard admits to creating another persona for the letter:

> Yes, all is propitious. I am now in the mood. I can write the letter straight off which I have begun ever so many times. I have just come in; I have flung down my hat and my stick; I am writing the first thing that comes into my head without troubling to put the paper straight. It is going to be a brilliant sketch which, she must think, was written without a pause, without an erasure. Look how unformed the letters are—there is a careless blot. All must be sacrificed to speed and carelessness. I will write a quick, running small hand, exaggerating the down stroke of the "y" and crossing the "t" thus—with a dash. The date shall be only Tuesday, the 17th, and then a question mark. But also I must give her the impression that though he—for this is not myself—is writing in such an offhand, such a slapdash way, there is some subtle suggestion of intimacy and respect. I must allude to talks we have had together—bring back some remembered scene. But I must seem to her (this is very important) to be passing from thing to thing with the greatest ease in the world . . . I want her to say as she brushes her hair or puts out the candle, "Where did I read that? Oh, in Bernard's letter." It is the speed, the hot, molten effect, the lava flow of sentence into sentence that I need. Who am I thinking of? Byron, of course. I am, in some ways, like Byron. Perhaps a sip of Byron will help to put me in the vein. Let me read a page. No; this is dull; this is scrappy. This is rather too formal. Now I am getting the hang of it. Now I am getting his beat into my brain (the rhythm is the main thing in writing). Now, without pausing I will begin, on the very lilt of the stroke—
>
> Yet it falls flat. It peters out. I cannot get up steam enough to carry me over the transition. My true self breaks off from my assumed. And if I begin to rewrite it, she will feel, "Bernard is posing as a literary man;

Bernard is thinking of his biographer" (which is true). No, I will write the letter tomorrow directly after breakfast.

Suggestions for Writing

1. Freewriting, in effect, reveals our own stream of consciousness. Try getting "in character." First, acknowledge to your reader that you don't know, so you imagine. Now try freewriting as this other person, in order to create the mental wanderings of the character's mind. (One caution: Go deeply into your character but leave more than a trail of bread crumbs to find your way back.)

2. Use dialogue or a sequence of action to reveal a character's personality.

3. Write a description of a character's physical qualities, using details such as bumping one's head on the doorway or wearing shoe-lifts, or causing a stir when he or she walks into the room.

Compelling Characters

Read/Revisit

Hilda Raz, "Looking at Aaron" (see page 218)
Philip Brady, "Myth and Uncertainty" (see page 148)

As pointed out in "Populating a Piece," populating your piece with compelling characters is of primary importance. Unless you are writing a piece such as satire, where there is a good reason for presenting *flat* characters, you must bring your characters to life and make the reader care about what happens to them.

Effective *characterization* (i.e., building a character) is a process very similar to getting to know someone in real life. We first perceive people through our senses: we see them and hear them, and to a lesser extent, smell them, feel them through touch, and even taste them. It is, therefore, important to give some physical details about our character. Be careful not to overburden the reader with such details—be judicious in selecting those details that are relevant to the piece. Do let the reader feel (or feel along with) the character through some of the less frequently used senses if possible—such details give unexpected, subtle brushes to the character's portrait.

Give your character a distinctive voice. Note, for example, the way Hilda Raz in "Looking at Aaron" gives each of the speakers a distinctive voice. They are characters within her essay, and hearing their actual voices gives the essay substance.

Finally, as we become intimate with someone, we begin to understand why they act in particular ways. To build a fully rounded character, you must help the reader understand what the character thinks and wants in any given situation. You can give this information to the reader directly, by using a narrator who can reveal such intimate details, or you can use dialogue, nonverbal cues, and action to let the reader uncover your character's motivation. While the former approach gives you more latitude, the latter may be more effective in bringing the reader closer to the character.

Suggestions for Writing

1. Describe a person using one attribute from each of the four categories below:
   a. Physical appearance (height, weight, hair color, age, etc.)
   b. Voice (sound, tone, accent, etc.)
   c. Smell, feel, taste
   d. Accessories (clothes, jewelry, objects carried, etc.)
2. Think of a situation between two people that you took part in, or observed, in which one person speaks while the other responds nonverbally. Do not reveal your thoughts. Build a scene that allows

the dialogue and nonverbal responses to establish the character of the participants.

3. Write a short dialogue in which you reveal a character through dialogue with another character. Hilda Raz creates a compelling conversation in "Looking at Aaron," a selection from the new memoir *What Becomes You*.

4. Tape one of your own conversations at a café or a bar and then transcribe it. Then select the most distinctive portions that would work well in a story. How much of the actual conversation can be discarded? What elements might be kept to convey a certain rhythm of the conversation, even if they aren't information rich?

5. Interestingly, dialogue can often be most revealing through what is not said. Think of an incident in which someone had something to conceal. Place him or her in a controversial conversation. Now re-create the scene, allowing the person to say a great deal with what he or she chooses not to say.

Dialogue Dropping from the Eaves

Read/Revisit

John McNally, "Humor Incarnate" (see page 279)

We all have a natural curiosity about other people's lives. If we didn't, storytelling would have no place in our world. Tuning in to other people's lives, particularly in places where we are anonymous, can offer inspiration. Of course, many people today eavesdrop in chatrooms on the Internet, which can be an interesting experience in itself. But people don't tend to tell elaborate stories on the Internet; the over*heard* story can give a richness and reality to your listening, and later, to your writing.

Eavesdropping—the word itself is like a talisman, like the words dropping magically from the eaves into your own writing.

Suggestions for Writing

1. Here is your license to eavesdrop. Go to a public space (a café, the beach, a bus, a train—anyplace where you might mingle with people from many walks of life). Give yourself different "listening" exercises. Try to catch some dialogue, intonation. Transcribe the actual words people say. (But be as discreet as possible. People tend to sense an ear bending toward them to hear better.)

   . . . Hallelujahs mask oh-no-she-didn'ts. She didn't invite *who* to the wedding? Guess who's not invited to the mother's banquet. Deacon Wiley's sleeping with *who*? No wonder she hasn't been to choir practice . . . Sister Jones is testifying once again, going on about how the Lord brought her a Lexus.

   —MICHELLE BYNUM, STUDENT

2. Use the eavesdropping to create a *dramatic monologue*. Let the character's speech create a dramatic scene.

3. As John McNally does in "Humor Incarnate," record a conversation overheard in some public setting or in the media, an even more public setting. We have all happened upon conversations that seem too impossible to be real. Mine one of these for its potential for humor.

PART THREE

Exercises for Exploring Revision, Subgenres, and Frequent Concerns of Creative Nonfiction

17
Revision

_____

Rereading, Reimagining, Reshaping

Read/Revisit

Tracy Kidder, "Making the Truth Believable" (see page 267)

So, you have finished the first draft of your piece. Reward yourself with something and get ready for the next stage of writing: revising.

Begin by reading your piece. Be critical. Evaluate both the parts and the whole. Try asking yourself why anyone would want to read this piece—what are its meaning and purpose? A writer rarely begins a piece knowing what its meaning will be, and even when he or she does, can be sure that the intended meaning will change in the process of writing. In creative writing, meaning and purpose emerge organically, as the piece is shaped—as Joan Didion said, "I write to find out what I'm thinking." What your piece is truly about becomes clearer as you are completing it. Identifying and articulating your intentions can be an iterative process that helps you reimagine, reorganize, and reshape your piece until it is finished.

Suggestions for Rewriting

1. Read your piece carefully, slowly. Then write down what is at stake in it. The longer your answer, the more likely the stakes are not well defined and not high enough. Pare down your answer to one or two sentences. Make sure that what is at stake is compelling enough. If the meaning and purpose of your piece are not very compelling, restate them so they are

2. Reimagine your piece. What do you need to change in it—what scenes, images, statements do you need to delete, insert, or revise—to achieve the revised meaning and purpose?

3. Repeat the process described in the first prompt until you can reveal the central idea of your piece in a single short, concise sentence. Now reduce the main idea of this sentence to a short list of words (as few as one and no more than five). Express each

word in your list in an image, a statement, or a short dialogue. Insert these in your piece and read it again. Does the added material strengthen your piece? Does it clarify the piece's meaning and purpose?

What's in a Name:
Finding a Title

Read/Revisit

> Lee Gutkind, "The Creative Nonfiction Police" (see page 261)
> Sherman Alexie, "Superman and Me" (see page 128)

An important aspect of revision can be finding a title for your work. Maxine Kumin says that titles are "geography, chronology, or furniture." By furniture, she means some element present in the piece that becomes the title. Lee Gutkind's title "The Creative Nonfiction Police" helps set up the tone for the essay. We hear the wry voice but underlying seriousness from the very title. Sherman Alexie's title "Superman and Me" has a similar effect. It appeals to the child in all of us and draws on our own childhood associations with Superman, even before we begin reading.

Sometimes a title arrives early in the process. But more often the selection of titles can make for a good story in itself. The title of James M. Cain's famous novel *The Postman Always Rings Twice* (adapted for two movies, a play, and an opera) has an intriguing story. Cain gave two different accounts as to the origin of the title. He said that while he was working on the novel, the postman would ring twice if the mail carried bills and once if a personal letter. The arrival of bills every day drove the writer into a state of frustration as he worked on his novel. But in Cain's other account of the title's genesis, he says that the postman would ring twice if he carried rejection letters and once if an acceptance letter. When Cain's novel was accepted, and the doorbell rang once, he celebrated by giving the novel its name.

Suggestions for Writing

1. Take a piece of writing that has, in your opinion or others', a mediocre working title. Apply Kumin's concept of "geography, chronology, or furniture." Give the piece a title that places us somewhere. Now find the "furniture"; look for an extraordinary line or image already present in the writing that might work as the title. If you do use it as the title, you might consider removing it from the text.

2. Try a symbolic title. Can you identify a particular element in the piece that has resonance on both a literal level, as well as a symbolic one?

Revision: Beyond the Frame

Read/Revisit

> Tracy Kidder, "Making the Truth Believable" (see page 267)
> Margaret Atwood, "Nine Beginnings" (see page 257)

Sometimes what is necessary in the process of revision is to reimagine various aspects of the piece. In nonfiction in particular, the selection of details is crucial to the telling of the story. It is important to recognize that the choice of details creates a particular kind of "truth" in the account, as does the omission of certain details.

Think of the natural storytellers you know. The way they select details has a great deal to do with why people ask them to recount stories, saying that they "tell it better." Some writers include far too many details to get to the point, boring the reader (or listener) in the process with twice as many details as necessary. Others tell too little, leaving out the background information or atmosphere that might make the piece more poignant.

Looking at a piece of writing with fresh eyes and a willingness to move far outside the frame of the original shape can be an essential part of the revision process. Writers need to be willing to expand both from the outside as well as internally.

Suggestions for Rewriting

1. Write one or more scenes describing events that happened before the beginning of your story. Do any of these add something important to the narrative? Do the same with the end of the story. Again, do scenes describing events that happened after the end of the narrative add something important?

2. Adding elements to the narrative might make your piece longer than you first intended. Look at your piece of writing and underline all the specific details. Is there any nonessential information that might be cut? Also, are there any points that might be shortened if you move beyond the frame? Perhaps these could be replaced with the use of a subtle flashback or flashforward in time.

3. In an expository piece, examine the details both within and outside the frame of the discussion. Sketch out the main points you want to get across. Add the sequence of information, thoughts, and arguments you use to make each point. Are any superfluous? Are you missing something? Is the sequence logical? Can some of the main points be combined into one? Are they what you intended to argue when you began the piece?

Revision: Reimagining
Character and Conflict

As was already discussed, a fundamental element of effective characterization is character motivation: what do your characters want? In evaluating your story you need to review what your characters are willing to risk in order to get what they want. If your characters do not care enough to risk something important, neither will the reader. The stakes must be high enough to keep the reader engaged. On the other hand, if the stakes are too high, the story and the characters may not be believable, however true the events might be.

Sometimes the resolution of the conflict might seem too obvious. We have all been frustrated by films and novels that spell out their resolutions long before we reach them. One solution might be to pace events differently. Withhold some of the information so that the reader is convinced to continue reading. Consider the variety of ways the action and intensity might reach their peak.

Suggestions for Rewriting

1. Take your piece apart. Are there places where the story is thin? Are some characters too flat? Are there places where the action lags? Does the sequence of scenes or chapters work? Do you get the feeling something might be missing? Does the story feel unfinished? Make notes of your criticisms in the margins or in a notebook.

Creating Scenes:
A Revision Narrative

Read/Revisit

> Diane Thiel, "Crossing the Border" from *The White Horse: A Colombian Journey* (see page 245)

We all have a wealth of stories from our lives that we tell and retell to family, friends, new acquaintances. The process of retelling a story is, in itself, a process of revision. Even in the oral rendering we search each time for the most effective means of narration and the most evocative way of describing details and building scenes. Rendering the story as a piece of writing involves yet another level of revision, and in draft after written draft, we are often able to see the story with new eyes and envision different ways of rendering the narrative, detail by detail, scene by scene. "Revision" has this idea of a fresh outlook in its very term.

On pages 91–94, a very early draft of "Crossing the Border" (excerpted from *The White Horse: A Colombian Journey*), has been reproduced. The final version of the chapter is included in the anthology section of this book. It is not the very first draft (I write everything initially by hand) but the first typed draft. One of my readers for the manuscript was Anthony Walton, author of the nonfiction book *Mississippi: An American Journey*. Walton was a keen reader of the manuscript, noting crucial possibilities for revision, such as passages that needed to become scenes, as well as various missed opportunities for raising issues vital to the book. Walton makes a vital suggestion in the margin at the end of this draft, to move the discussion about the passport officials to "real time." In subsequent drafts, building the scene with the passport officials increases the tension in a crucial part of the book while also injecting a measure of humor. In the book, my Colombian friend Ana Maria and I are traveling alone doing environmental work in Panama and Colombia. The narrative arc of the book is dramatically affected by chapters such as this one, which emphasize what it was like to be two women on the road alone in Latin America, and the somewhat dangerous (albeit also humorous) encounters along the way. The chapter stands at the crossing of an important real, as well as symbolic and emotional, frontier: from the "known" of our technology-dominated society into the "unknown" of a setting in which nature still has a dominant role in human existence.

In the early draft, I make only a quick comment at the end of the chapter: "The passport officials in Jaqué had flirted fiercely with us, commenting on our pictures, asking about our marital status. I had already learned to say that I was 'prometida,' engaged, in order to avoid complications. As we left Jaqué had the official gave me back my passport, he opened it and kissed my picture . . . ." In the final version, this afterthought has developed into the central scene in the chapter, with a page of dialogue between us and the officials, including the following:

> "And why are you two going to Colombia?" the slicked-back man asked.
> "To spend Christmas with a friend," said Ana Maria. I just smiled.
> He had Ana Maria's passport open, admired her picture, and asked flirtatiously if she was married: "*Casada o soltera?*"
> "*Prometida*," she lied, saying that she was engaged.
> He motioned at me: "Does she speak Spanish?"
> "*Sí*," I answered.
> He smiled. "*Casada o soltera?*" he opened my passport.
> "*Prometida*," I answered, following Ana Maria's lead.
> "Too bad," he said. "But you must have crazy fiancés to send you out to the jungle alone. And on Christmas!" He shook head gravely at the foolishness of our imaginary men. "When are you returning?"

Building the scene in "real time" also encouraged me to further develop the setting and describe the room in detail. In a later section of this textbook, "Mapping Your Memory," I describe how "mapping" the room in my memory made me think of the fan that kept blowing the calendar off the wall and the bullet hole that would reappear each time. Adding the scene, the dialogue, and details such as the bullet hole had a significant effect on building the tension in the chapter as well as an effect on enhancing tension in the entire book.

In examining this earlier draft, I note several other significant moments that had initially fallen somewhat flat. For instance, during the incident of the passport officials examining our papers, I state simply that "they began discussing whether the tiny village of Punta Ardita was Panama or Colombia. They were in disagreement as to whether we were actually leaving the country." In later drafts, I found it necessary to convey the actual conversation in order to enhance the symbolic and emotive significance of this frontier, and in order to tap the opportunities it offered for injecting humor. The final version is much more dramatic, with the dialogue between the officials replacing the mere expository statement.

Another passage that needed significant elaboration was the later conversation with Nigel on the boat. In the early draft, the scene is underdeveloped: "He and I talked the whole way. Unfortunately, by the end of the five-hour trip, Nigel was proposing marriage, or at least that we should go out with him to the bar that night." The final version is much more dramatic, with more than a page of dialogue in an elaborated scene on the windy boat ride with Nigel, offering details such as the following:

> "You know, I've been feeling that I'd like to settle down soon" was another sentence I caught completely.
> "It's good to settle down," I agreed innocuously, or so I thought.

There were a few sentences I didn't catch in the wind, so I just smiled and nodded.

Finally, he said something and looked at me so intensely that I knew I had to get him to repeat it.

"I said," he moved close to my ear, "that I've been looking for the right woman to float by." He paused. "I'm so glad you'll be in Jurado tonight for the disco."

I instantly stopped smiling and nodding. I wondered what else I had agreed to.

A number of other changes flesh out the chapter further. In its final version, the chapter is nearly twice as long, and it heightens the sense of embarking even further toward the unknown. The various scenes developed from the draft become the essence of the chapter and have a greater impact on building the tension and sense of danger in the book as a whole.

Suggestions for Writing

1. Look at a short piece of your nonfiction (from your journal or perhaps a more developed piece). What details are most crucial to creating the tone(s) of the piece? Are there any important details you can identify that need further elaboration?

2. Write your own revision narrative. An important aspect of revision involves knowing when to stop, an issue which often troubles both beginning and established writers. Save drafts of each essay and number them. You may find yourself returning to earlier drafts, or at least sections of earlier drafts. It is useful to put your writing aside for a while before revising. Take a particular essay that has several drafts, and write a short piece of prose describing what your revision process has been with the piece. You might begin to notice your own patterns of revision.

3. Take a first or early draft of a piece and look for details that are mere statements at present. Build a dramatic scene from one of these statements, using dialogue and paying close attention to the setting.

The White Horse   59

20

at the Torres house,
at Rosita's,
(and the children)
etc.

We asked about the boat at least ten times the next morning. People didn't seem

to know the answer. Some said it would come in the afternoon. Some said no more boats

until after Christmas. The boat had actually been there when we arrived a few days

no one

before, but, for whatever reason, ~~people~~ had ~~not~~ told us about it. So we kept walking

down to the dock to check.

whims of the

It was a new feeling, this helplessness, a reliance on the tides and a single boat and ✓

I was used to Miami time + the way in the States you can

its captain. Ana Maria really wanted to be in Colombia for Christmas, and it was already

get

everything

the 23rd. Her friend Ricardo was planning to meet us at the port in Punta Ardita, to take

you

us down the coast to his piece of land to camp for a week on the ocean. In one way, it

want

when

was a good thing that we missed the boat the day we arrived in Jaque, because we ended

you

want,

up speaking to various town officials about the ongoing environmental project in Punta

provided

you

Ardita, Colombia, about how we would like to start a similar program in Jaque, to

have

the

improve the water conditions, to promote crafts for sale, to clean up the beaches, and

$.

other plans. We were told that the town council allots land and that we should write a

request to set up an environmental station there; we wrote it immediately and were told

we would find out the response in a few weeks, on the way back. So we saw our delay

in Jaque as an unplanned blessing, but we really didn't want to miss the next

boat.

First typed draft of Diane Thiel's "Crossing the Border," from The White Horse:
A Colombian Journey.

continued

The White Horse   60

To our relief,

¿It finally arrived with the tide in the late morning, and we went to pay and reserve

our places, and to fill out the proper paperwork to leave the country. As the officials

Create a scene & the more actual dialogue here.

looked at our papers and heard where we were headed, they began discussing whether the

tiny village of Punta Ardita was Panama or Colombia. ~~They were in disagreement as to~~

whether we were actually leaving the country. Jaque and Jurado were the two border

towns, but Punta Ardita and Ricardo's place sat somewhere between them. They finally

decided to stamp our passports as leaving the country.

At first, I thought it strange that they didn't know where the country ended and the

new one began. But then I thought about the imaginary lines which make such

demarkations, and the fact that Panama was part of Colombia until the turn of the century,

when the Canal made Panama such valuable territory to foreign interests. This tiny

checkpoint felt like a huge border, a significant frontier rich with history, the edge of the

other continent.

B

Move the paragraph from the end here — & elaborate on "prometida" + kissing my passport!

The boat which would take us over the edge was a tiny motorboat, almost a

dinghy, the captain a young Colombian boy, who introduced himself as Archangel. I was

surprised by the name, and when he walked away for a moment, Ana Maria whispered to

me that his father, Momento, had named all of his sons for saints. "Let's see," she said,

"there's Santo, and Lazaro, and Archangel, and I forget the others right now. We were

interrupted by Archangel's return; for some reason, he had seemed unsure he could take

us, but then agreed, after a short discussion with some officials.

'the frontera'

Also describe the room: detail of bullet holes in the wall!

continued

His uncertainty ?.

~~It became clear~~ *what the problem was* When the plane arrived that afternoon, ~~the~~

children who had been our shadows suddenly disappeared, and a half hour later, a party

of ten or so arrived to board the boat. The mayor of Jurado, the Colombian village close

to Punta Ardita was in the party with his family and entourage and about fourteen huge

bags of Panama City Christmas purchases. There was no way we would all fit in that

boat.

We did. Somehow, they loaded every bag into the boat and then everybody. We

were tightly packed. Ana Maria sat me down next to a young man, whispering to me,

"It's the mayor's son, Nigel. Talk to him." She wanted me to tell him about our plans

for Punta Ardita, the plans we would be proposing as alternatives to cutting trees.

The tide had come in, and it was finally high enough to leave Jaque. The waves

were huge, especially when first heading out into the ocean. The boat climbed up each

wave, reached a crest, and then slammed down into the water. My body rose off the seat

and slammed down with it. It happened about ten times before we were far enough out

in the ocean, beyond the breaking waves. Nigel commented that it was a pretty calm day, *as the boat gathered speed.* Made

that it was usually much worse than this. He and I talked the whole way. Unfortunately, *its*

(after about half an hour) by the end of the five hour trip, Nigel was proposing marriage, or at least that we should *way towards*

go out with him to the bar that night. *the* "border"

It was one of many such proposals on the trip. I was speaking to Nigel in a frank,

matter-of-fact way about the environmental state of the world, but with the open manner

of my American upbringing. But in his culture, my behavior might be viewed as

use the conversation . today" lunch "It's pretty calm as I tried to keep my down .

continued

The White Horse   62

flirtation, invitation. I quickly began undoing the web I had inadvertently woven on the ride.

I have encountered sexism throughout my life, but there is an obvious set of rules here that is even more pronounced. The passport officials in Jaque had flirted fiercely with us, commenting on our pictures, asking about our marital status. I had already learned to say that I was "prometida," engaged, in order to avoid complications. As we left Jacque and the official gave me back my passport, he opened it and kissed my picture, then handed it to me and said to ask for him when I was returning, to make everything go smoothly.

In the United States, I don't like to go to bars alone, but I could if I wanted to. Here, I began to realize that just being an unescorted woman could cause a great deal of trouble and miscommunication. As we stepped off the boat in Punta Ardita, I was thanking Nigel, but declining the disco and the marriage.

[Handwritten margin annotations: "MAYBE move THIS n EARLIER to 'REAL TIME'"; "B"; "x 2"; "60."; "r"; "was"; "my"; "By the time"; "would be"; "more subtly,"; "?"; "o"]

Workshop: Thirteen
Ways of Looking for Revision

Writers often have a hard time evaluating their own pieces for the purpose of revising—especially pieces they have recently been working on. Workshopping offers the opportunity to get another perspective on your work, to get feedback from your potential audience. If you do not have the opportunity to participate in a formal workshop, you could still ask a peer to read your piece critically. The reader of your piece can use the following questions to obtain insights into how the piece might be revised so it can become more effective. You may even use these questions yourself, but it would be best to attain some "distance" from your piece, perhaps by putting it aside for a period of time, before you review it.

Suggestions/Questions for Revising

1. What effect does the title have on the piece? Does it add anything? Could you think of something else that would serve a functional or symbolic purpose?

2. Is the opening effective? Is there another scene or image in the piece that might serve as a stronger way to begin?

3. Does the piece work best in its current form? Can you imagine another possibility for rendering it?

4. Does the chosen perspective present the piece most effectively? How would the piece work told from someone else's perspective?

5. How does the setting work for this piece? How soon, as readers, do we know where (and when) we are? How does the writer give us this information? Could it be more subtle? Direct? If the setting is generic on purpose, does this work?

6. Does the piece hold your interest throughout? What creates the dramatic tension in the piece, and is there enough of it? Does the tension drop at any points? What might be done to maintain the intensity?

7. Is the language general or specific? Is it abstract or concrete? Note any abstract words that could be replaced with fresh images. Can you suggest any images? Does every word, sentence, scene have a purpose? What can be cut?

8. Is the voice (and/or dialogue) of the speaker(s) or character(s) believable? Is there consistency? What creates inconsistencies? How might this be refined? If there is intentional inconsistency, is that working?

9. Read a passage aloud. Does the language of the piece have rhythm? How might the piece be made more rhythmical?

10. How is the piece structured? Does the series of scenes or images work effectively? Can you think of another arrangement that might work better?

11. Is there anything that may confuse the reader unnecessarily? How might the confusing passage be clarified?

12. Does the closure reverberate? Does it effectively give an ending without restating too much? Does it leave the reader thinking? Is this piece really finished, or could you envision a different, more effective ending? Does the piece go on beyond what might be a more effective closure?

13. Finally, but perhaps most crucial, what is "at stake" in the essay? What is the purpose of this piece of writing? How are all the above-named elements working for or against the achievement of what seems to be at stake? Perhaps the essay sets out with one thing in mind, but something more vital has revealed itself in this draft. This could be an important point for discussion.

18
Exploring the Subgenres of Creative Nonfiction

From Memory to Memoir

Read/Revisit

Naomi Shihab Nye, "Three Pokes of a Thistle" (see page 215)
Dana Gioia, "Lonely Impulse of Delight: One Reader's Childhood" (see page 196)
Bret Lott, "Toward a Definition of Creative Nonfiction" (see page 270)

In a sense, all creative writing springs from personal experience. However, when the focus of a piece is on relating personal experiences as truthfully and accurately as possible, the piece is a *memoir* or *autobiography*. Usually an autobiography is a book-length piece that describes the events of the author's life in their entirety (or, at least, over a long period) up to the point that the piece is written. A memoir, on the other hand, tends to focus more on a specific event or events that took place at a specific location. Of course, the boundaries between autobiography and memoir are not very precise, and neither are those between memoir and other types of nonfiction such as the travel narrative and the historical account.

This is where your memory (the word *memoir,* after all, springs from the same root) and your journal, which is an extension of your memory, are of crucial importance. You will need to mine them for topics. What you write about need not be earthshaking or exotic. It does need to capture the interest of your readers, but it is often the experiences we have in common that we find compelling. One thing you must keep in mind, however, when you are relating personal experiences is that you must be honest about your feelings. Insincerity is very difficult to hide, and there is nothing like it for turning a reader off.

Suggestions for Writing

1. Think of a special occasion you were a part of (Christmas, wedding, Thanksgiving dinner, graduation, etc.) when not everything went as planned—when something unexpected, either good or bad, happened. Why is the occasion one you still remember? Write a short piece describing what happened, what you felt, and what you think other participants felt about the situation.

2. Make a list of memorable moments in your life: when you were the happiest, saddest, angriest, most afraid. Pick one and write a short piece describing the events that led up to the moment. Discuss how these events affected you. How did you resolve your feelings? Did the situation change you in some way?

3. Personal experience and growth are almost synonymous. The experiences that help you mature are, therefore, natural topics for personal narratives. Recount an important experience that led to significant personal growth. Was a relationship with another person instrumental in this situation? How did your experience affect relationships with parents, siblings, friends?

4. In "Lonely Impulse of Delight: One Reader's Childhood," Dana Gioia writes about growing up in a working-class Latin family and about the impact of reading on his life. His mother's brother, Ted Ortiz, had left the family a significant library of books, which Gioia began reading as a child and which contributed to his becoming a passionate reader. Write a short piece about a single book or author that had an impact on your life.

5. Emulate Naomi Shihab Nye's style in "Three Pokes of a Thistle" and write a short piece about a very specific memory. Perhaps focus on a specific object as symbolic of something, like the first bra in "Bra Strap." Is there a related piece that might work as another "poke of the thistle"?

Researching a Life:
Biographical Sketch

Read/Revisit

Fred D'Aguiar, "A Son in Shadow" (see page 160)
Judith Ortiz Cofer, "Silent Dancing" (see page 154)

Some of the most popular and powerful works of creative nonfiction are biographies. Works such as Walter Isaacson's biography of Benjamin Franklin and David McCullough's biography of John Adams are best sellers. Some, like Sylvia Nasar's biography of mathematician John Nash, *A Beautiful Mind,* have become successful major motion pictures. But just as you don't need to be famous to produce an interesting memoir or autobiography, you don't need a famous subject to produce a compelling biography. In fact, if you don't have much experience in biographical writing, it is best that you begin with the people and subjects that are most familiar to you: your family, immediate or extended. And since who your family is has much to do with who you are, a biographical sketch may well be an interesting and important component of a more personal piece such as a memoir.

Biographical writing, like much of creative nonfiction, requires a research effort. Characterization is crucial in writing an effective biography or even biographical sketch. You have to bring your subject to life and make him or her compelling to the reader, just as in a good piece of fiction. Only in this case, the details about the character have to be true. Think of your subject as a puzzle whose pieces you must find before you can put them together.

Judith Ortiz Cofer, in an essay, "Silent Dancing," re-creates her family's past via a home movie of a party. She returns several times in the piece to this movie, which becomes a leaping-off point for her imagination about the relatives and family friends involved:

> The movie opens with a sweep of the living room. It is "typical" immigrant Puerto Rican decor for the time: the sofa and chairs are square and hard-looking, upholstered in bright colors (blue and yellow in this instance, and covered in the transparent plastic) that furniture salesmen then were adept at making women buy. The linoleum on the floor is light blue, and if it was subjected to the spike heels as it was in most places, there were dime-sized indentations all over it that cannot be seen in this movie. The room is full of people dressed in mainly two colors: dark suits for the men, red dresses for the women. I have asked my mother why most of the women are in red that night, and she shrugs, "I don't remember. Just a coincidence." She doesn't have my obsession for assigning symbolism to everything.

Sometimes one has only the tiny fragments of a biography and must reimagine the rest. Fred D'Aguiar's "A Son in Shadow" (discussed more fully in "Finding the Emotional Truth" later in this section) works with the idea of what the writer knows about his father, as well as what he doesn't.

Suggestions for Writing

1. Interview a member of your family. Grandparents and great-aunts and -uncles would be good choices because they are more likely to surprise you with information you did not know. They are also more likely to open up to you than your parents or siblings. Record the interview or keep extensive notes. Choose five events or thoughts you find particularly compelling and develop a biographical sketch around them.

2. Try Judith Ortiz Cofer's approach of creating a "home movie" about your family home. Describe a few scenes the movie would capture. Now go back in time, and perhaps place (another city or country, perhaps). What scenes would the movie capture before you were "in the picture"?

3. Choose a historical figure you admire. Research your subject's life. Get a volume of his or her correspondence and read it. Write a short piece about the relationship between your subject and one or more of the correspondents. How did the relationship(s) influence your subject's life?

Personal Opinion: Taking a Stand

Read/Revisit

> Jonathan Swift, *A Modest Proposal* (see page 234)
> Anthony Walton, from *Mississippi: An American Journey* (see page 251)

The most familiar form of personal opinion piece is the newspaper editorial. However, this type of writing is often not considered *creative* writing because it often does not pay the close attention to the language that is the mark of a literary work. Because the distinguishing characteristic of the literary essay is the *style* of the writing, the best way to understand this form is to read and compare essays written by several different authors.

Conventional and literary opinion essays share a common goal: in both types of piece, the author argues a particular position on a specific issue. The value of the literary opinion piece is that the argument is structured in terms of concrete images rather than abstract concepts. This distinctly creative approach has the potential to make a powerful argument because it addresses the reader on both the intellectual and emotional levels. Swift in *A Modest Proposal*, for example, never states explicitly what his point is. Instead, he makes a forceful argument on the need for a civilized society to care for its less fortunate members by constructing an absurd argument in which he proposes the extreme opposite.

Everything you write is, ultimately, shaped by your feelings, opinions, and beliefs about the world. Consequently, every piece of writing is a "personal opinion" piece in some respect. The personal opinion essay can be distinguished by the fact that the author makes it clear that the piece's intent is to argue an opinion (even when the opinion itself is not stated directly). You can always identify the author's central position by summarizing the theme of the essay in a single sentence that begins with "the author believes (or thinks) that . . ." (although these words will likely be edited out as your essay develops). It is always a good idea to write down your thesis before you begin working on your essay.

Alice Walker, in an essay, "Am I Blue?" uses a personal narrative to express her opinion about an issue. She tells a story of her experience with a horse, Blue, and how his grief over his mate being removed makes her think about slavery. She looks at the penned horse through the window and likens his life to the experience of her ancestors. Blue is crazed at the loss of his mate and looks so human to Walker's eyes. His grief makes her move through history, through beliefs people have held at different times. The essay courses through history to arrive at a statement about choices of what we will tolerate, what we will support with our actions. Walker reads the message clearly reflected in Blue's eyes: "Everything you do to us will happen to you; we are your teachers, as you are ours. We are one lesson."

One of the powers of a good story is its ability to strengthen an argument. A narrative can be one of the best ways to convince a reader. In essays in particular, the modes of discourse often get divided—expository, narrative, descriptive writing. But try bringing these elements closer together.

In *Mississippi: An American Journey*, Anthony Walton expertly weaves together the narrative of his journey to a Southern plantation with descriptive and expository elements. The descriptions of a restored quarter house (slave cabin) and of the plantation founder's will in which he disposes of his "goods and worldly effects," placing the slaves on par with field animals—oxen, cows, horses, and sheep—splitting families with a stroke of his pen, validate and strengthen Walton's central argument—that slavery bears a heavy responsibility for the social disarray that plagues the African American community to this day. Though this argument is presented in a paragraph that is purely expository, the narrative and descriptive elements of the piece elicit an emotional response in the reader that complements and reinforces the rationality and logic of Walton's argument.

Suggestions for Writing

1. Begin by writing down a thesis. Outline your essay by selecting details that will support your thesis: personal experiences, what you like and dislike, what your interest and emotional investment in the world is.

2. Write out the theme for a personal opinion essay. Choose something you are passionate about. Now emulate Swift and structure an argument (a "modest proposal") for an opposite position that is so extreme and unacceptable that it implicitly supports your thesis.

3. Think of a story from your life that you might use to create a convincing argument. Try writing the piece as an argumentative essay. Then write your personal story. Which one makes the more compelling argument? You might find that the two join together at some natural point. Perhaps the argument will begin to reveal itself as an extension of the story.

Living Sources: Gathering and Using Information

Read/Revisit

Diane Ackerman, "The Truth About Truffles" (see page 127)
Anthony Walton, from *Mississippi: An American Journey* (see page 251)

Research is not something you do only for a class project—or, necessarily, only for a project of any kind. You collect and analyze information every moment you are awake (and, some claim, even while you sleep): everything you see, hear, smell, taste, or touch gives you information about your surroundings. You may not think of this process as "research" because the collection and analysis of the information is mostly not conscious, but there are still many occasions in your everyday life when the process is conscious (for example, each time you make a conscious decision).

Becoming aware of all of the information you collect every moment of your life, and of the ways you use it, can give you important insights about what research really means. Research is a natural process. You do research when you collect and use information. The collection of information is not necessarily a "formal" process—information is not found only in the library or online. What you see, feel, and think is also information, and this type of information is especially important in creative writing. Think of your poetry and fiction—of the way in which you communicate your feelings, perceptions, and ideas about the world. This type of communication is also very important in creative nonfiction, in pieces such as Ackerman's "The Truth About Truffles" and Walton's excerpt from *Mississippi: An American Journey*. These rather different pieces are designed to present information about and discuss specific topics and, therefore, offer some "hard" data (information from authoritative sources). Ackerman's piece uses primarily scientific information but presents it in a poetic and humorous way, having the reader enter the piece by imagining the feelings of the sow searching for truffles. Walton uses direct observation and experience as well as historical research and personal insight. The use of both "hard" data and creative techniques in each of these pieces makes them particularly effective.

Suggestions for Writing

1. Think of the decisions you've had to make recently: buying a car or a stereo, choosing a college, a major, getting a job, moving, etc. Pick one decision that entailed a major commitment from you. How did you make your decision? You can detail your decision-making process by making two lists. Title the first list "Personal Experience" and in it include things you did or thought about that led you to your decision. For example, if the decision you are analyzing is your choice of college, include in this list things like a visit to this and

other colleges, your thoughts about location, cost, etc., and whether, perhaps, you've always wanted to go to this school. Title the second list "Outside Sources" and in it include information you obtained from sources other than your own personal experience. Here you would include things such as information on college rankings, student/faculty ratio, job placement of graduates, etc., that you got from catalogs, your high school counselor, magazines, and other sources. Note that some of the information may be hard to categorize: should you list your talking about the school with someone who is enrolled in it or graduated from it under "Personal Experience" or under "Outside Sources"? If what you got from your discussions was only a sense of what you might like, list them under "Personal Experience." If, on the other hand, you got concrete information or advice, list it under "Outside Sources." If you got both, list them in both categories. When you are done with your lists (be exhaustive), go over them and decide whether you relied mostly on personal experience or outside sources in making your decision. Explain why you chose as you did (relying on one type of information more than the other) in a few sentences. Now look only at the list of outside sources. Did you trust some sources more than others? Write a few sentences explaining why. Finally, write a few sentences about what additional information (of both types) you would have liked to have in making your decision and discuss why that information would have been useful to you.

2. Think of a topic you are interested in and write it down as a title. Do a ten-minute freewrite, putting on paper anything that comes to mind about this topic: facts, questions, beliefs, etc. Read what you wrote and begin to organize it. Group together those things that seem to be connected. Write one sentence for each group, stating an idea that the group seems to represent. Are some of these ideas connected? If yes, join those that are. Which of the ideas do you think it would be practical to research? Choose one and phrase it as a question. Break this main question into as many smaller questions as you can (when you answer all of these subquestions, you will have answered the main question). Use each of these subquestions as a heading, and under it list all of the information you will need to have in order to answer it. Also list where you believe you will be able to find this information.

Reflective Writing:
Reflecting on the World

Read/Revisit

Diane Ackerman, "The Truth About Truffles" (see page 127)

The basic difference between a reflective piece and an essay is style. Reflective pieces tend to convey the tone of introspective monologue, weaving and turning, usually moving from image to image. Annie Dillard's "Seeing," in the spirit of the classical essay, meanders through personal story, collected narratives, and factual information to make her point about perception—how we all have different perceptual filters through which we view the world.

"The lover can see, and the knowledgeable," Dillard points out, calling nature a "now-you-see-it, now you don't affair":

> It's all a matter of keeping my eyes open. Nature is like one of those line drawings of a tree that are puzzles for children: Can you find hidden in the leaves a duck, a house, a boy, a bucket, a zebra, and a boot? Specialists can find the most incredibly well-hidden things. A book I read when I was young recommended an easy way to find caterpillars to rear: you simply find some fresh caterpillar droppings, look up, and there's your caterpillar.

In "The Truth About Truffles," from *A Natural History of the Senses*, Diane Ackerman, in writing about the "world's homeliest vegetable," uses biology, chemistry, history, and poetic narrative to reflect on her subject. Consider her final paragraph and the bizarre narrative she creates for the truffle farmer and his sow, who (confused by the similarity of truffle smell to male pig) digs furiously in the earth, trying to reach the "sexiest boar she's ever encountered in her life, only for some reason he appears to be underground."

While the tone of the reflective piece is introspective, it generally conveys more than the personal thoughts of the author—it is more than a piece from the author's personal journal. It presents information, often from solid scholarly research, but unlike a research report, it integrates that information with the author's personal experience. This method brings the information down to earth, presenting it through the lens of personal understanding and ultimately making it more accessible to the reader.

Suggestions for Writing

1. Choose a topic you are interested in but know relatively little about. Research the topic. Make note of interesting images that illustrate important aspects of your topic. Write a reflection piece in which you present your topic primarily by listing these images.

2. Dillard's "Seeing" discusses more than the sense of vision—it addresses some of the fundamental ways in which people relate to the world around them. Write a reflective piece about one of the senses other than vision (i.e., hearing, touch, smell, and taste) and the ways in which it helps us relate to the world. Use an equal measure of research data and personal experiences to make your argument.

Writing About Place

Read/Revisit

> Bruce Chatwin, excerpt from *In Patagonia* (see page 151)
> Leslie Marmon Silko, "Landscape, History, and the Pueblo Imagination" (see page 224)
> Henry David Thoreau, "Walking" (see page 249)

From the Ancient Greek writer Pausanias to the articles in the travel sections of every modern major newspaper, travel narrative has a particularly long and continuous history and popularity. This should not be surprising in light of the fact that "the journey" is one of the fundamental, archetypal themes of literature. By definition, the travel narrative takes the reader along for the ride. What distinguishes the *literary* narrative from its cousins that every week grace the pages of countless newspapers is that the literary travel narrative also guides the reader through an internal journey of the author—one of mental, spiritual, or emotional change.

Bruce Chatwin's travel narrative, *In Patagonia*, is an intriguing blend of memoir, history, and natural history. The book is composed of a series of short vignettes that present different aspects of Patagonia and effectively allow us to experience the place. Sometimes the place is depicted through encounters with particular people Chatwin meets on his journey:

> The poet lived along a lonely stretch of river, in overgrown orchards of apricots, alone in a two-roomed hut. He had been a teacher of literature in Buenos Aires. He came down to Patagonia forty years back and stayed.
>
> I knocked on the door and he woke. It was drizzling and while he dressed I sheltered under the porch and watched his colony of pet toads.
>
> His fingers gripped my arm. He fixed me with an intense and luminous stare. 'Patagonia!' he cried. 'She is a hard mistress. She casts her spell. An enchantress! She folds you in her arms and never lets go.'

The travel narrative, however, is only one category of writing about place (which, in turn, is one category of the personal narrative). Another important aspect of this type of writing is the piece that relates the special significance of a particular place for the writer. Silko's "Landscape, History, and the Pueblo Imagination" relates the significance of place not only for the author but for her ancestral Laguna Pueblo culture as well.

Suggestions for Writing

1. Write a short piece about a place you have traveled to. Begin by making a long list of details about the place. Pay attention to all of your senses—write not only about the sights but also about the smells, the sounds, etc. Make another list of events that happened during your trip there or back, and during your stay. Make a third list about the feelings the place or the events surrounding it evoked.

Be sure to include negative and mixed, as well as positive feelings. Look through your lists to identify unique or particularly interesting aspects of the place and your experiences. Structure your piece around these elements.

2. Write a piece in which you describe your connection with the land. What particular landscape do you find compelling? This could be an urban landscape, but if this is the case, also discuss your feelings about the nature the urban landscape is located within. Describe your connection at the physical, emotional, and spiritual levels.

A Piece of History

Read/Revisit

Anthony Walton, from *Mississippi: An American Journey* (see page 251)

History is a great source for both fiction and nonfiction. The historical novel is a well-established and popular form, one that sits at the end of the spectrum opposite the "academic" history. Historical creative (or literary) nonfiction sits between them. While the historical novel introduces fictional characters in a real, well-researched historical setting, the creative nonfiction piece sticks to real people. And while the nonliterary history is primarily concerned with completeness, accuracy, and documentation, the literary piece is primarily concerned with bringing a historical period or event to life, and therefore pays close attention to the use of language and style.

Of course, the lines dividing these categories are not always very clear. The further back the historical period and the more obscure the event, the less is likely to be known about it and the more the writer will have to fill in with guesses, supposition, or imagination. Also, the better the writer of the "academic" history, the more likely he or she is to write vividly and bring the period she is writing about to life. The earliest histories we have, written by Herodotus, Thucydides, and other Ancient Greek and Roman writers, are to a large extent accounts of events that were directly witnessed by the authors or that happened during their lifetimes. Thus, they take the form of personal accounts, and because the authors were also talented writers, these histories are regarded as classic works of literature.

The one thing that all forms of historical writing share is the need for attention to detail and aptitude for research on the part of the author. This is so, even if the piece is an account of the writer's personal experiences within a historical event or setting, such as O'Brien's "Alpha Company" from *If I Die in a Combat Zone, Box Me Up and Ship Me Home*. Details in this book remain as essential as in O'Brien's well-known fiction piece "The Things They Carried," and the author's story is enriched with information he learned only after he came to Vietnam—information that was given to him by his comrades:

> During the first month, I learned that FNG meant "fuckin' new guy," and that I would be one until the Combat Center's next shipment arrived. I learned that GI's in the field can be as lazy and careless and stupid as GI's anywhere. They don't wear helmets and armored vests unless an officer insists; they fall asleep on guard, and for the most part, no one really cares; they throw away or bury ammunition if it gets heavy and hot. I learned that REMF means "rear echelon motherfucker"; that a man is getting "Short" after his third or fourth month; that a hand grenade is really a "frag"; that one bullet is all it takes and that "you never hear the shot that gets you"; that no one in Alpha Company knows or cares about the cause or purpose of their war: it is about "dinks and slopes," and the idea is simply to kill them or avoid them. Except that in Alpha you don't kill a man, you "waste" him. You don't get mangled by a mine, you get

fucked up. You don't call a man by his first name—he's the Kid or the Water Buffalo, Buddy Wolf or Buddy Barker or Buddy Barney, or if the fellow is bland or disliked, he's just Smith or Jones or Rodriguez . . . . You can go through a year in Vietnam and live with a platoon of sixty or seventy people, some going and some coming, and you can leave without knowing more than a dozen complete names, not that it matters.

While O'Brien's piece overlaps the categories of memoir and opinion essay, it is primarily a historical account because the author's objective is to bring the reader into a particular historical period. *If I Die in a Combat Zone, Box Me Up and Ship Me Home* represents the *personal* approach to historical narrative as contrasted to the *objective* approach, which considers the general history of a period or event rather than the author's personal involvement with it.

Anthony Walton, in his book *Mississippi: An American Journey*, includes quotations and descriptions of slave life from 18th- and 19th-century Mississippi, as well as details such as tax returns listing the revenue from sales of slaves and typical advertisements for the slave market. This kind of real data grounds the book and gives the reader a sense of the grim realities of daily life at the time. After giving us this foundation in history, Walton then moves into the personal. For instance, following a discussion of early 18th-century cotton picking, in which after a grueling day "the overseer meets all hands at the scales, with the lamp, slate and whip," Walton reflects on his personal connection with the history. His transition is evocative:

> In search of a true plantation (lamp, slate, whip), I drove thirty minutes through dense, almost tropical kudzu, willow and live oak trees, hanging vines, swamps, cotton bean fields and pine forests. Sometimes the lush vegetation came right to the edge of the road. I drove North of Natchez to the large white door of Springfield, a working plantation that has been maintained in historically accurate eighteenth-century detail since its establishment in 1786 by Thomas Marston Green.

Walton's movement from the purely historical to the personal narrative, and then back to the historical, allows the reader to experience the material in a more visceral way.

Suggestions for Writing

1. Choose a historical person and an important or interesting event this figure participated in. Research both the person and the event. Write a story about the role of the person in the event.

2. Make a list of current or recent events about which your family, friends, schoolmates, teachers, or community have different opinions. Choose the event that seems to you to incite the widest and strongest conflicting opinions. Interview at least six people, three on one side of the opinion divide and three on the other. Write a story about the event and about the reactions it elicited in people.

3. Try a piece that opens with a purely historical account. Use real data such as a newspaper article, a bill of sale, a list of casualties. After revealing the factual details, allow the piece to become more personal. How does your own life's journey fit into the journey back in time?

19
Exploring Frequent Concerns of Creative Nonfiction

Finding the Emotional Truth

Read/Revisit

> Fred D'Aguiar, "A Son in Shadow" (see page 160)
> Lee Gutkind, "The Creative Nonfiction Police" (see page 261)
> Bret Lott, "Toward a Definition of Creative Nonfiction" (see page 270)
> Tracy Kidder, "Making the Truth Believable" (see page 267)

Writers of memoir (as well as several other genres of creative nonfiction) are presented with a unique challenge. On the one hand, a writer of memoir is writing nonfiction and thus wants to stay as close as possible to the truth. On the other hand, the "truth" must always be an individual affair. We all have varying accounts of the same reality. Have you ever found yourself recounting a family story only to have a sibling insist that it didn't happen that way? Her memory had stored her own "truth."

Interesting arguments arise among memoir writers about what constitutes "fictionalizing" a piece. Most memoir writers use techniques of fiction in the way they construct the intensity of the narrative and in their selection of details. Some writers have argued that too much fictionalizing goes on in the memoir.

As a memoir writer myself, I recognize that in the process of writing a nonfiction narrative, the most essential thing is to find the "emotional truth," a phrase now commonly associated with memoir. Perhaps a detail is slightly changed for the purpose of the story, but the feeling of the experience (the emotional truth) remains. As writers, we are always creating our own versions of the truth—by the details we decide to include as well as by the details we leave out, and by the way we shape the narrative.

In Tim O'Brien's well-known short story "How to Tell a True War Story," the author makes the point that one cannot tell a true war story because in the fog of war perceptions are altered, and so much of the account is based on the perceptions of the people involved. However, one could argue that the "emotional" truth is still being realized in such "stories."

Fred D'Aguiar, in "A Son in Shadow," his piece about his father's meeting his mother, acknowledges from the first sentence what he doesn't know: "I know nothing about how they meet." As he invites the reader to join him on the process of discovery, he reimagines aspects of their lives together but often returns to the refrain of what he doesn't know: "Most of the puzzle is missing." And later: "I try to fill the gaps, piece together the father I never knew. I imagine everything where there is little or nothing to go on."

The result is a vital, intriguing piece that uses techniques of nonfiction, fiction, and metawriting (writing about the process of his own invention). It is the missing fragments that intrigue us most as readers, perhaps because we all have family stories like this, particularly from our childhood, stories in which we can only reimagine the "truth."

Suggestions for Writing

1. Imagine a significant moment in your parents' lives that occurred before you were born or before you were old enough to remember. Sketch out the details you have heard them recount. What details do you need to invent?

2. Now try D'Aguiar's method of acknowledging what he does not know about the past. Make this awareness of invention part of your process as you write the piece about your parents.

Writing Between the Lines: Subtext

Read/Revisit

> Jamaica Kincaid, "Biography of a Dress" (see page 209)
> John McNally, "Humor Incarnate" (see page 279)

Do you always say everything that comes to your mind? It is not very likely that you do—none of us really do, because if we always said exactly what we thought we would likely have no friends. Communication, however, takes place at levels other than the verbal. Gestures, body position, facial expressions, etc., make up what is often referred to as "body language." Body language and other nonverbal cues such as tone of voice, heart rate (and its consequences such as flushing), and eye movement, are not as easy to control as our words. When we try to hide something, often we are betrayed by our body language.

This subtle level of communication (the nonverbal) is not as easy to present in writing, but it is well worth the trouble because it enlivens our stories—it increases the subtlety and richness of our writing. The easiest way to reveal that a character's words do not express true feelings is by revealing his or her thoughts. However, this can become cumbersome if used too much, and it lacks subtlety. When it comes to describing the thoughts of characters, a good rule of thumb is to reveal the absolute minimum amount necessary.

A good story means more than it says; therefore, it has both *text* (what is stated in a situation) and *subtext* (what remains unsaid but is implied or otherwise communicated). The subtext operates at a deeper level than the action and dialogue of our story. Jamaica Kincaid's "Biography of a Dress" is a good example of the importance of subtext. Much of the story is left unsaid: what it was like to be a girl in the Antigua of Kincaid's childhood; what the status of women was, and how it affected her upbringing.

Suggestions for Writing

1. Describe an event from the perspectives of two people. Focus your description on actions rather than thoughts. The two people are related in some way (parent-child, husband-wife, etc.). Each character remembers the event differently (one may hardly remember it at all). Let the differences reveal something important about the relationship.

2. Write a short scene involving you and one other person. In the scene, you are not able to reveal everything you feel. Reveal your feelings through your thoughts. Now try revealing your feelings through the description of nonverbal cues.

3. Subtext in dialogue can offer numerous possibilities for humor. Read John McNally's "Humor Incarnate" for ideas about making your writing more humorous. Note the account that opens McNally's essay. Write a scene that depicts a memory of an interview of your own (or an embarrassing moment that you consider quite funny in retrospect). Try to incorporate the subtext of the dialogue and/or certain interview questions and answers.

Time Lines and the
Larger Context

Read/Revisit

Shirley Geok-Lin Lim, "Splendor and Squalor" (see page 178)

When writing a memoir or personal essay in particular, it can be particularly useful to find a way to tie in the personal with broader societal issues or questions. Think back to particularly memorable moments in your life. Your time line might become a very long one, from which you could harvest a number of essays. This kind of longer time line could be used for general inspiration and to help access your memory.

You might also make a time line that traces a particular theme (such as losses in your life). This could be a much more specific, elaborate time line (dealing with one particular subject) to help you gather precise memories and details for an essay or longer piece that is already developing around a theme.

A time line can therefore be useful in both the early stages of a draft and in later revisions of a piece. By identifying societal events that coincide with the years of your memory, you also gain a sense of what was taking place in the world at the time. This can work as inspiration for a piece and also for intriguing juxtapositions: for example, some kind of violence you experienced in your personal life juxtaposed with a larger conflict somewhere in the world.

Suggestions for Writing

1. Sketch out a longer time line of particularly memorable events in your life, using three main columns:

   First column: year, your age, family/local event

   Second column: personal/emotional impact

   Third column: world event at the time

2. As discussed above, your time line might also reflect events that all deal with a specific theme. For instance, sketch a time line that deals with one of these subjects:

   a. your relationship with a childhood friend

   b. losses you experienced

   c. childhood travel experiences

   d. early experiences/perceptions of violence, in your own life or overheard in discussion, etc.

The Passage of Time

Read/Revisit

Diane Thiel, "Crossing the Border" from *The White Horse: A Colombian Journey* (see page 245)

The passage of time is the most fundamental underpinning of the telling of a story. Every narrative, from beginning to end, moves through time—most often forward. The *way* in which it moves through time is the most basic element of the structure of the plot. Plot is a term most often associated with fiction, but a strong plot is vital to a nonfiction narrative as well.

Because a narrative is just a small piece of a larger reality, it must discard those elements of reality (objects, people, events, etc., that would have been part of the situation had the story been actually happening in the real world) that are not essential to the story. Consequently, a story almost never moves through time at an even and steady pace. Alice Munro comments about her nonlinear process of writing:

> I don't take up a story and follow it as if it were a road, taking me somewhere, with views and neat diversions along the way. I go into it, and move back and forth and settle here and there, stay in it for a while. It's more like a house. Everybody knows what a house does, how it encloses space and makes connections between one enclosed space and another and presents what is outside in a new way.

A story consists of episodes. Each episode consists of a set of events that take place sequentially and move rather evenly and steadily through time. Episodes are separated by a jump in time, a change in setting, or the appearance or departure of an important character (or a combination of these discontinuities). In fiction, these episodes are called *scenes*, and their arrangement is what we call *plot*.

Often our initial writing needs more attention to the development of individual scenes that will build into a larger plot. In "Crossing the Border," the excerpt from *The White Horse: A Colombian Journey*, the early drafts needed to be revised with more attention to building each small scene (this is discussed more fully in the revision narrative in the "Revision" section of this book). Details that were discussed as "afterthoughts" in an early draft, such as the passport official kissing my picture, were moved to "real time" to have more of an effect on the plot and buildup of tension in the book.

Even though plot almost always moves forward in time (in other words, the end of a story is at a point in time later than the beginning), it rarely does so continuously. Very often several scenes happen at the same time (they show events that happen in different places and involve different characters). These are *parallel* scenes and are a very useful way for the writer to describe the experiences of different characters either as a consequence of, or in preparation for, a significant event.

Another device that is used very frequently is the *flashback*—a scene that takes place at an earlier time than the main flow of the plot (the *base time* of the story). Flashbacks show the reader significant past events that help explain current actions and events; they help layer the motivation of characters.

Moving forward in time in a *flash-forward* is a technique used much less frequently. It invariably has the effect of distancing the reader from the characters and is therefore useful when the writer wants to inject objectivity and decrease the impact on the reader of situations that affect the characters strongly.

Suggestions for Writing

1. Write a short piece based on the following premise. You run into a person with whom you used to be friends. One of you begins to apologize to the other for the action or actions that caused the demise of the friendship. Use flashbacks to reveal the event that caused the end of the friendship and to layer the motivation of each person for the events taking place in the present (e.g., why has one decided to apologize? will the other accept the apology or not? why?).

2. Write a short piece about two people (e.g., you and a partner, your mother and father) who are involved in a romantic relationship. They are having a fight. They either break up or make up. Open the piece with a flash-forward that shows what happens to each of the characters and their relationship some years later.

Vignettes

Read/Revisit

Naomi Shihab Nye, "Three Pokes of a Thistle" (see page 215)

We all tell anecdotes of our lives, and jokes. The vignette is this type of form—short prose, complete on its own, but often woven together into a larger piece. Although it is short, it may actually be difficult to write because of this very compression.

Naomi Shihab Nye, in her "Three Pokes of a Thistle," groups together three vignettes, each of which seems to stand on its own as a moment captured in a life. Note the way the final sentence of each vignette also provides a fine example of the distance a single sentence can travel, through layers of meaning.

Eduardo Galeano (b. 1940), in his three-volume *Memory of Fire*, tells the history of the Americas in a series of short, poignant depictions, which reverberate because of their compression:

1908, San Andrés de Sotavento

The Government Decides That Indians Don't Exist

The governor, General Miguel Marino Torralvo, issues the order for the oil companies operating on the Colombia coast. The Indians do not exist, the governor certifies before a notary and witnesses. Three years ago, Law No. 1905/55, approved in Bogotá by the National Congress, established that Indians did not exist in San Andrés de Sotavento and other Indian communities where oil had suddenly spurted from the ground.

Suggestions for Writing

1. Write about an event in history. Imitate Galeano's compression of events.

2. Write a vignette about family life. Start, perhaps, with your favorite anecdote, which you have only shared aloud. Choose one that has a clear opening and closure. Let it find its way to paper. As you write others, you may find that together they build a continuous story: of a family, a job, a love.

Mapping Your Memory

Read/Revisit

Wendell Berry, "An Entrance to the Woods" (see page 139)
Edwidge Danticat, "Westbury Court" (see page 171)
Fred D'Aguiar, "A Son in Shadow" (see page 160)
Diane Thiel, "Crossing the Border" from *The White Horse: A Colombian Journey* (see page 245)

Drawing a map of a place can help access more specific physical memories and sensory images from the past. Edwidge Danticat opens her essay "Westbury Court" with a paragraph capturing very visual and aural images:

> When I was fourteen years old, we lived in a six-story building in a cul-de-sac off of Flatbush Avenue, in Brooklyn, called Westbury Court. Beneath the building ran a subway station through which rattled the D, M, and Q trains every fifteen minutes or so. Though there was graffiti on most of the walls of Westbury Court, and hills of trash piled up outside, and though the elevator wasn't always there when we opened the door to step inside and the heat and hot water weren't always on, I never dreamed of leaving Westbury Court until the year of the fire.

The final line is a powerful lead-in as well. The reader hears about the fire, but just enough to ensure that one will keep reading.

Fred D'Aguiar also seems to have an element of a map built into his essay. He describes how Georgetown, Guyana's "two-lane streets with trenches on either side mean a mostly single-file walk, she in front probably looking over her shoulder when he says something worthy of a glance . . ." One can almost see a drawing his memory would have made of the town.

You can use "mapping" to remember a place you spent many years, such as a room or a family home. You might also use it for a more expansive setting, such as a neighborhood or a village. I have found it useful to "map" on both the micro and macro scales. In travel writing, I have found it evocative to establish a sense of an actual map, to heighten the reader's sense of traveling along a coastal border, for instance. The map and general use of "sense of place" can even bring forth a number of political questions, as in this excerpt from *The White Horse: A Colombian Journey*, included in the anthology section of this book:

> As the officials looked at our papers and heard where we were headed, they began discussing whether the tiny village of Punta Ardita was Panama or Colombia. They were in disagreement as to whether we were actually leaving the country. Jaqué and Jurado were the two border towns, but Punta Ardita and Ricardo's place sat somewhere between them.
> "*Ardita es Colombia*," said the older official.
> "No, I think it's Panama." said the younger.
> "Are you going anywhere else?" they asked.
> "To visit an indigenous village up the river from Jurado," Ana Maria said.

"Now Jurado, that's Colombia," a third man piped in. "Terrible town. Dirty. Are you sure you want to go to Jurado?"

"Well, we're not really going to Jurado," Ana Maria answered. "Just around it."

One official pulled out a map, and the three men leaned into it, noting where *la frontera* actually was. The older one ran a thick finger down a dotted line to the ocean, hesitated, and then made his decision: "*Ardita es Colombia*," he proclaimed.

At first, I thought it strange that they didn't know where the country ended and the new one began. But then I thought about the imaginary lines which make such demarcations, and the fact that Panama was part of Colombia until the turn of the century, when the Canal made Panama such valuable territory to foreign interests. This tiny checkpoint suddenly felt like a huge border, a significant frontier rich with history, the edge of the other continent.

Making maps has also helped me re-create much smaller settings. In an early draft (included and discussed in the revision section of this book) of the chapter discussed above, I had not depicted the room in which the passport officials had their conversation. Mapping the room reminded me of the oscillating fan, as well as the bullet hole, which now feels like a crucial detail to depicting both the tension and the element of the unknown:

They sent our passports into the back room, and after a few moments we were called in. A middle-aged uniformed man with slicked-back hair sat behind a desk. An oscillating fan sat on a box in the corner, nearly blowing the one decoration, a calendar, off the wall. I noticed what looked like a bullet hole in the wall under the calendar. The hole reappeared each time the fan turned.

Suggestions for Writing

1. Choose a small place from your childhood, such as a room or a backyard. Take about 10 minutes to draw your memory of the place. Map the details carefully. For instance, where was the kitchen? How large was it in relation to the rest of the house? Was there a table around which many family discussions took place? After 10 minutes of drawing, take 15 minutes to "translate" your drawing into a few paragraphs. Set the scene for a piece about family memory.

2. Map a larger setting, a neighborhood or village, for instance. Was there a park? A "haunted" house that people avoided? A house with fierce dogs? You might put details such as these on your neighborhood map. Now translate some of the map into words, as D'Aguiar does with his imagining that "Georgetown's two-lane streets with trenches on either side mean a mostly single-file walk."

3. In "An Entrance to the Woods," Wendell Berry opens his essay with a maplike passage. We join Berry on his journey into the woods.

One feels a sense of leaving larger roads for smaller and smaller ones, and then beginning on foot:

> On a fine sunny afternoon at the end of September I leave my work in Lexington and drive east on I-64 and the Mountain Parkway. When I leave the Parkway at the little town of Pine Ridge I am in the watershed of the Red River in the Daniel Boone National Forest. From Pine Ridge I take Highway 715 out along the narrow ridgetops, a winding tunnel through the trees. And then I turn off on a Forest Service Road and follow it to the head of a foot trail that goes down the steep valley wall of one of the tributary creeks. I pull my car off the road and lock it, and lift on my pack.

Take a few minutes to draw the maplike quality of this paragraph. Now think of a journey you have taken. Take 10 minutes and sketch a map of a piece of the journey. You might try to remember significant elements of landscape or buildings on the way, as markers. Now try a paragraph or two that maps the leg of the journey with words.

Writing Inside the Story: Metawriting

Read/Revisit

> Fred D'Aguiar, "A Son in Shadow" (see page 160)
> Hilda Raz, "Looking at Aaron" (see page 218)
> Margaret Atwood, "Nine Beginnings" (see page 257)

Your journal holds many ideas for stories you did not develop because they seemed to go nowhere. Perhaps you had a good beginning, but nothing seemed to work in trying to develop a story from it. Perhaps a story seems flat; it may have an interesting premise, but you have been able to do little to render it in an interesting way. Is there anything you can do, you wonder, with these ideas and fragments?

It is possible that the process of rendering a piece could make for a more interesting story than the piece itself. Perhaps the different beginnings you tried tell an interesting story when put together. Perhaps you had an interesting conversation with a friend or relative when talking about a story you've been working on. This type of writing—called metawriting—can open up interesting possibilities for the story. Writing about the process of writing, of course, injects a direct and clear element of reality into the piece, blurring to some degree the genre distinction between fiction and nonfiction. In his "A Son in Shadow," D'Aguiar straddles genre boundaries. On the one hand, his story is about real people in real situations, but on the other, the author has to imagine events that he doesn't know much about, and he lets us know he is doing so.

In "Looking at Aaron," Hilda Raz's excerpt from *What Becomes You*, a memoir coauthored by Aaron Raz Link and Hilda Raz, the authors discuss the writing of the book: "So what's this book we're writing?" Aaron asks, and Hilda answers:

> I don't know, I say.
> He shifts impatiently. As far as I can tell, his part of the book is done. I hope to finish my part now, the mother's part, years after his surgery.
> Aaron says he hates everything he's written. His voice is speeding up. He articulates very clearly.
> "Who cares about this kind of book" he asks me. "You don't read books about breast cancer, right Mom?" He's talking fast now. He knows I've been well for twelve years.
> "Transformation happens in all lives. We'll tell about ours," I say in a soothing voice.
> "Okay," he says. His shoulders relax a little as he leans back in the driver's seat.
> I lean forward in the passenger seat. "Okay," I say. "But don't expect me to provide any analysis of our experience. Analysis is beyond me."

The rich element of metawriting in "Looking at Aaron" allows the reader to accompany the authors on the journey of both the experience and the process of finding the way to tell the story.

Suggestions for Writing

1. From your journal, pick an idea for a beginning of a story you have not been able to develop successfully. Write the beginning the story. Emulate both Atwood and D'Aguiar and write several different versions of this beginning (sketch five to ten). For each version, change a few details of the scene but keep the physical setting the same. For some of the versions try extending the story slightly beyond the original scene: what happened right before? right after? Write each version on a separate piece of paper (or two). When you are done try different arrangements. How do the versions work when put together as a single "story"?

2. Write a few paragraphs about the process of trying to find the way to render a particular story. This might involve a conversation with someone about the intended piece, perhaps even a coauthor, as in "Looking at Aaron."

3. Write a short story about the workshop experience. Center the story on a single very short piece of prose that you had workshopped. Include in your story two versions of the piece: the first draft presented to the workshop and a second draft that incorporates some of the critique offered in the workshop. What were the responses of the workshop participants to the first draft? What were their responses to the revised piece? What might these comments reveal about the workshop participants? What were your own thoughts about the process? What might these thoughts reveal about you? How much did the piece benefit from the workshop?

4. See the revision narrative in this book's section on revision. A revision narrative could be a kind of metawriting. Try incorporating a revision narrative as part of a longer piece, perhaps a piece about an event or an essay about the process of writing.

PART FOUR
A Collection of Creative Nonfiction

Diane Ackerman (B. 1948)

The Truth About Truffles

From *A Natural History of the Senses*

"The world's homeliest vegetable," it's been called, but also "divinely sensual" and possessing "the most decadent flavor in the world." As expensive as caviar, truffles sell for over $500 a pound in Manhattan these days, which makes it the most expensive vegetable on earth. Or, rather, under earth. Truffle barons must depend on luck and insight. A truffle may be either black (*melanosporum*) or white (*magnata*), and can be cooked whole, though people usually shave raw slivers of it over pasta, eggs, or other culinary canvases. For 2,000 years it's been offered as an aphrodisiac, prized by Balzac, Huysmans, Colette, and other voluptuous literary sorts for its presumed ability to make one's loins smolder like those of randy lions. When Brillat-Savarin describes the dining habits of the duke of Orleans, he gets so excited about the truffles that he uses three exclamation points:

> Truffled turkeys!!! Their reputation mounts almost as fast as their cost! They are lucky stars, whose very appearance makes gourmands of every category twinkle, gleam, and caper with pleasure.

One writer describes the smell of truffles as "the muskiness of a rumpled bed after an afternoon of love in the tropics." The Greeks believed truffles were the outcome of thunder, reversed somehow and turned to root in the ground. Périgord, in southwest France, produces black truffles that ooze a luscious perfume and are prized as the ne plus ultra of truffles, essential black sequins in the famous Périgord goose-liver pâté. The best white truffles come from the Piedmont region, near Alba in Italy. Napoleon is supposed to have conceived "his only legitimate son after devouring a truffled turkey," and women throughout history have fed their male companions truffles to rouse their desire. Some truffle dealers use trained dogs to locate the truffles, which tend to grow close to the roots of some lindens, scrub oaks, and hazelnut trees; but sows are still the preferred truffle hunters, as they have been for centuries. Turn a sow loose in a field where there are truffles, and she'll sniff like a bloodhound and then dig with manic passion. What is the sow's obsession with truffles? German researchers at the Technical University of Munich and the Lübeck School of Medicine have discovered that truffles contain twice as much androstenol, a male pig hormone, as would normally appear in a male pig. And boar pheromone is chemically very close to the human male hormone, which may be why we find truffles arousing, too. Experiments have shown that if a little bit of androstenol is sprayed into a room where women are looking at pictures of men, they'll report that the men are more attractive.

For the truffle farmer and his sow, walking above a subterranean orchard of truffles, it must be hysterically funny and sad. Here this beautiful, healthy sow smells the sexiest boar she's ever encountered in her life, only for some reason he seems to be underground. This drives her wild and she digs frantically, only to turn up a strange, lumpy, splotched mushroom. Then she smells another supermacho boar only a few feet away—also buried underground—and dives in, trying desperately to dig up that one. It must make her berserk with desire and frustration. Finally, the truffle farmer gathers the mushrooms, puts them in his sack, and drags his sow back home, though behind her the whole orchard vibrates with the rich aromatic lust of handsome boars, every one of them panting for her, but invisible!

1990

Sherman Alexie (B. 1966)

Superman and Me

I learned to read with a Superman comic book. Simple enough, I suppose. I cannot recall which particular Superman comic book I read, nor can I remember which villain he fought in that issue. I cannot remember the plot, nor the means by which I obtained the comic book. What I can remember is this: I was 3 years old, a Spokane Indian boy living with his family on the Spokane Indian Reservation in eastern Washington state. We were poor by most standards, but one of my parents usually managed to find some minimum-wage job or another, which made us middle-class by reservation standards. I had a brother and three sisters. We lived on a combination of irregular paychecks, hope, fear and government surplus food.

My father, who is one of the few Indians who went to Catholic school on purpose, was an avid reader of westerns, spy thrillers, murder mysteries, gangster epics, basketball player biographies and anything else he could find. He bought his books by the pound at Dutch's Pawn Shop, Goodwill, Salvation Army and Value Village. When he had extra money, he bought new novels at supermarkets, convenience stores and hospital gift shops. Our house was filled with books. They were stacked in crazy piles in the bathroom, bedrooms and living room. In a fit of unemployment-inspired creative energy, my father built a set of bookshelves and soon filled them with a random assortment of books about the Kennedy assassination, Watergate, the Vietnam War and the entire 23-book series of the Apache westerns.

My father loved books, and since I loved my father with an aching devotion, I decided to love books as well.

I can remember picking up my father's books before I could read. The words themselves were mostly foreign, but I still remember the exact moment when I first understood, with a sudden clarity, the purpose of a paragraph. I didn't have the vocabulary to say "paragraph," but I realized that a paragraph was a fence that held words. The words inside a paragraph worked together for a common purpose. They had some specific reason for being inside the same fence. This knowledge delighted me. I began to think of everything in terms of paragraphs. Our reservation was a small paragraph within the United States. My family's house was a paragraph, distinct from the other paragraphs of the LeBrets to the north, the Fords to our south and the Tribal School to the west. Inside our house, each family member existed as a separate paragraph but still had genetics and common experiences to link us. Now, using this logic, I can see my changed family as an essay of seven paragraphs: mother, father, older brother, the deceased sister, my younger twin sisters and our adopted little brother.

At the same time I was seeing the world in paragraphs, I also picked up that Superman comic book. Each panel, complete with picture, dialogue and narrative was a three-dimensional paragraph. In one panel, Superman breaks through a door. His suit is red, blue and yellow. The brown door shatters into many pieces. I look at the narrative above the picture. I cannot read the words, but I assume it tells me that "Superman is breaking down the door." Aloud, I pretend to read the words and say, "Superman is breaking down the door." Words, dialogue, also float out of Superman's mouth. Because he is breaking down the door, I assume he says, "I am breaking down the door." Once again, I pretend to read the words and say aloud, "I am breaking down the door" In this way, I learned to read.

This might be an interesting story all by itself. A little Indian boy teaches himself to read at an early age and advances quickly. He reads "Grapes of Wrath" in kindergarten when other children are struggling through "Dick and Jane." If he'd been anything but an Indian boy living on the reservation, he might have been called a prodigy. But he is an Indian boy living on the reservation and is simply an oddity. He grows into a man who often speaks of his childhood in the third-person, as if it will somehow dull the pain and make him sound more modest about his talents.

A smart Indian is a dangerous person, widely feared and ridiculed by Indians and non-Indians alike. I fought with my classmates on a daily basis. They wanted me to stay quiet when the non-Indian teacher asked for answers, for volunteers, for help. We were Indian children who were expected to be stupid. Most lived up to those expectations inside the classroom but subverted them on the outside. They struggled with basic reading in school but could remember how to sing a few dozen powwow songs. They were monosyllabic in front of their non-Indian teachers but could tell complicated stories and jokes at the dinner table. They submissively ducked their heads when confronted by a non-Indian adult but would slug it out with the Indian bully who was 10 years older. As Indian children, we were expected to fail in the non-Indian world. Those who failed were ceremonially accepted by other Indians and appropriately pitied by non-Indians.

I refused to fail. I was smart. I was arrogant. I was lucky. I read books late into the night, until I could barely keep my eyes open. I read books at recess, then during lunch, and in the few minutes left after I had finished my classroom assignments. I read books in the car when my family traveled to powwows or basketball games. In shopping malls, I ran to the bookstores and read bits and pieces of as many books as I could. I read the books my father brought home from the pawnshops and secondhand. I read the books I borrowed from the library. I read the backs of cereal boxes. I read the newspaper. I read the bulletins posted on the walls of the school, the clinic, the tribal offices, the post office. I read junk mail. I read auto-repair manuals. I read magazines. I read anything that had words and paragraphs. I read with equal parts joy and desperation. I loved those books, but I also knew that love had only one purpose. I was trying to save my life.

Despite all the books I read, I am still surprised I became a writer. I was going to be a pediatrician. These days, I write novels, short stories, and poems. I visit schools and teach creative writing to Indian kids. In all my years in the reservation school system, I was never taught how to write poetry, short stories or novels. I was certainly never taught that Indians wrote poetry, short stories and novels. Writing was something beyond Indians. I cannot recall a single time that a guest teacher visited the reservation. There must have been visiting teachers. Who were they? Where are they now? Do they exist? I visit the schools as often as possible. The Indian kids crowd the classroom. Many are writing their own poems, short stories and novels. They have read my books. They have read many other books. They look at me with bright eyes and arrogant wonder. They are trying to save their lives. Then there are the sullen and already defeated Indian kids who sit in the back rows and ignore me with theatrical precision. The pages of their notebooks are empty. They carry neither pencil nor pen. They stare out the window. They refuse and resist. "Books," I say to them. "Books," I say. I throw my weight against their locked doors. The door holds. I am smart. I am arrogant. I am lucky. I am trying to save our lives.

1998

Rudolfo Anaya (B. 1937)

Why I Love Tourists: Confessions of a Dharma Bum

I was born on the eastern llano of New Mexico—at just the right moment, so my mother said—a tourist from the great beyond. Just another guest on Earth looking for his dharma nature. I discovered the core of my nature in the people of my region. But we also discover elements of our essential nature by traveling to other places, by meeting other people. To tour is to move beyond one's circle. So we're all tourists on Earth, we go from here to there if only to just have a look.

But tourists and natives often clash, perhaps because the tourist cannot love the place as much as the native. We learn to love the land that nurtures us. We, the natives, become possessive about "our place." Westerners especially feel a great love toward this land that stretches north and south along the spine of the Rocky Mountains. I believe this sense of possessiveness about "our land" means we, the denizens of the West, are turning inward. We now truly understand that "there's no where else to go," so we had better take care of what's left.

The open spaces of the West once allowed for great mobility, and so the nature of those who came here was more ample, more extroverted. Today the real and the mythic frontier has disappeared, so we seem to be growing more introverted. Maybe we just want to be left alone.

Change and the progress of technology are bothering us. Next to Alburquerque where I live, a city has been built around the Intel Corporation; the subdivisions spread across sand hills where once only coyotes and jackrabbits roamed. Along the Rio Grande valley subdivisions cover farming land. We know what overdevelopment of the land can do. We know we're running out of water, out of space, out of clean air to breathe.

Westerners seem bound by one desire: to keep the land the way it was. Now the megacities are crowding us in. More and more people seem to be touring our turf. Are all those tourists looking for a place to settle? That's what bothers us. There are just too many tourists discovering and rediscovering the West. The tourist has become the "other" to the westerner. I hear my New Mexican paisanos say: "Take their money but let them go back where they came from. Please don't let them settle here."

Tourism is a very important segment of the western economy. Tourists bring bucks to grease Las Vegas, Disneyland, L.A., Seattle, and San Francisco, bucks to oceanside resorts and Rocky Mountain ski slopes, bucks for boating and hunting and fishing. Tourism has become the West's clean industry. But deep inside we, the natives, know it's got its inherent problems.

Tourism affects our lives, we believe, because it affects not only the topography; it also affects the sacred. We believe there is a spirit in the land; we know we cannot trample the flesh of the Earth and not affect its soul. Earth and spirit of the place go hand in hand. The transcendent has blessed this land and we don't want it ruined, we don't want it destroyed. We have a covenant with the land, we have become the keepers of the land. No wonder so many dharma bums—those looking for their essential relationship to the Earth—have crossed the West's rugged terrain, looking for a home, not just a home with a majestic view, but a home rooted to a landscape that allows the true nature of the person to develop.

We have all been tourists at one time or another. We have traveled to distant places to entertain and rest the body, and also to enlighten the spirit. The two are intertwined. We go looking for that revelation on the face of the Earth that speaks to the soul.

There are sensitive tourists, dharma bums who care about illuminating their nature and who appreciate the region and people they experience on their journey. There are some who respect the place and allow themselves to be changed by the people and region they visit. They return from the journey fulfilled, more aware of other cultures.

Then there are those who breeze through the place, accepting nothing of the local culture, learning little, complaining constantly, and leaving in their wake a kind of displacement. The natives take their money and are thankful when they're gone. Those travelers return home to complain about the food, the natives, and about the different lifestyles they encountered. They should never have left home. They did not travel to illuminate the spirit.

The land draws tourists to the West. They come to see the majestic mountains, arid deserts, the Pacific Ocean. Some come to experience our diverse cultural groups. Others come only to visit the cultural artifacts of the West: Las Vegas, Disneyland, L.A., Silicon Valley, Hoover Dam. Those who experience only the artifacts miss the spirit we natives find imbued in the landscape. Those who deal *only* in artifacts miss the history and culture of the West's traditional communities. And so tourists also symbolize the tension between tradition and change, a change that in some places carries the weight of impending doom.

Have the traditionalists grown tired of sharing the spirit of the West? Are we tired of those who come and trample our sacred land? And is the West really one unified region? When we speak of tourism are we only talking about people visiting here from outside the West, or do we also speak of internal tourism? From Montana to New Mexico, we hear complaints about tourists from outside the region. But in New Mexico, for example, we also complain about the Texans as tourists. Today I hear complaints about the nouveau riche Californians. Even Oregonians shrink from California tourists: "Please don't let them settle here," they whisper to each other.

The West was never one homogenous region; it is not only the land of the pioneers and the cowboy of the western movies. The West is a grouping of micro-regions and cultural groups. Even the grandeur of the Rocky

Mountains can't unify us, because there are too many different landscapes in the West, too many different indigenous histories. My home, the northern Rio Grande, is such a micro-region, with its unique history and people. It is—and here I show my indigenous bias—one of the most interesting multicultural areas of the West.

The Spanish/Mexicano side of my ancestors were tourists who journeyed to this region in the late sixteenth century. Imagine the Pueblo Indians seeing the Spanish colonists coming up the Rio Grande in 1598. I'm sure they shook their heads and said, "There goes the neighborhood." In many ways *it did go.* If anyone has suffered from tourists, it is the Native American communities.

But the tourists kept coming into the land of the pueblos. The first entradas were from south to north as Spanish-speakers expanded north. In the nineteenth century the east to west migrations began. In a scene from my novel *Shaman Winter,* I describe Kearny marching into New Mexico with the Army of the West in 1846. The Mexicanos in the crowd yell: "Why don't you go back where you came from!" "Go home gringos!" "Hope they keep going right on to California." "We ought to pass a Spanish Only law if they stay."

Of course those "tourists" didn't go home. And they changed the West forever. Each group introduced a new overlay of culture. Each brought a new set of stories, their own history and mythology to the West. Now the balance of what the land can hold has reached a critical point. Maybe we're uncertain about tourists because they represent the unknown. If the tourist decides to return to settle—and history teaches us that's the pattern— each one is a potential threat to the land, each one represents one more house to be built, more desert to be plowed up, more water consumed. They represent development in a fragile land already overdeveloped.

It's not just the growth in numbers we fear. We are convinced that outsiders know nothing of the nature of our relationship to the earth. This relationship defines our nature. I feel connected to la tierra de Nuevo México. This earth is all I know, it nourishes my soul, my humanity. The gods live in the Earth, the sky, the clouds.

Growing up in eastern New Mexico, I felt the llano speak to me. The llano as brother, father, mother. Constant breezes caressed me, sang to me, whispered legends, stirred my memory. The Pecos River engulfed me with its bosque of alamos, river willows, Russian olives, thick brush. It sang a song of memory as it flowed south to empty into the Rio Grande, from there into the Gulf of Mexico. Truly, time and the river sang in my heart.

This early attachment and sensibility to the land became love, love for the place and the people. The people molded me. The Hispano/Mexicanos of the llano were cattlemen and sheepmen who taught me a way of relating to the earth. The farmers from the Pecos River Valley initiated me into another relationship with nature; they planted my roots in that earth as they planted seeds. I saw the people struggle to make a living, I heard the stories they told. History and traditions were passed down, and everything related to the place and the people. Some of the teaching was unspoken; it was there in the silence of the llano, the faces of the people.

People told stories, joys and tragedies carried in the breezes, so I, too, became a storyteller. Listening to the people's story and then retelling the story relates one to the place. Will tourists who visit our land pause long enough to listen to our stories? The bones buried in the earth tell the story. Who will listen?

This spiritual connection to the land seems to describe the westerner. Even in the harshest weather and the longest drought, we stand in awe of the earth. Awe describes our relationship to the land. Perhaps tourists are simply people who don't stand still long enough to feel the immediacy of awe. They don't understand the intimacy of relationships woven into the people of the land.

As a child I felt this awe on the llano, along the river, on those hills which shaped my childhood. So the Earth for me has a particular feel, it is the New Mexican landscape, the llano and Pecos River of childhood, the Rio Grande and Sangre de Cristo Mountains of my later life, the desert which is always at the edge.

Still, we must be kind to tourists. It's part of our heritage to be kind to strangers. And we have all been tourists at one time or another. I, too, have been a tourist, a seeker who wanted to explore beyond the limits of my immediate environment.

One description of the Anglo-American culture has been its mobility. Anglo-Americans, we are told, are a restless lot. They couldn't just stay over there in the thirteen colonies, no, they had to go West. They love to quote the oft-repeated "Go west, young man, go west." So much a part of the history and mythology of this country is known from that western movement. Land, they smelled land, and gold and beaver pelts and gas and oil, all of which drew them west. So, Anglos are natural-born tourists. Now they've even been to the moon. Maybe some people just take to touring better than others. Or perhaps there are times when mass migrations take place; need and adventure move entire populations.

The Indohispanos of New Mexico have ancient roots in the land. Our European ancestors settled in the Hispano homeland along the northern Rio Grande in 1598. Remember those Espanioles coming up the Rio Grande? They took to the land, became as indigenous and settled as their vecinos in the pueblos. Wars, adventure, and extreme economic necessity have taken them beyond the homeland's frontier.

In this region Hispanics also claim tourist heroes. Cabeza de Vaca comes to mind. Shipwrecked on the coast of Texas, he set out on an odyssey that lasted seven or eight years. He is the Odysseus of the Southwest. Never mind that he was lost. Perhaps to be "lost" as a tourist is essential. Only thus can you enter fully into the place and the people. He was the first European tourist in Texas. Can you imagine the awe he experienced?

And he turned out to be a typical tourist. He went back to Mexico and spread the word. "Texas was great," Cabeza de Vaca told the viceroy in Mexico City. "The streets are paved with gold. There are pueblos four or five stories high. And a strange animal called a buffalo roams the plains by the millions."

Other Spanish explorers quickly followed Cabeza de Vaca. Coronado came north. A tourist looking for gold and the fabled cities of Cibola. He found only Indian pueblos, the original natives living in houses made of adobes. Accommodations in Native America weren't the best in the sixteenth century, so the Spanish tourists returned home, discouraged they hadn't found cities with streets paved with gold.

But the Spaniards were consumate note-takers. They mapped the land, described it and the natives, and they sent letters to their neighbors back in Mexico. "You've got to see this place. La Nueva México is virgin land. Very little traffic, and the native arts and crafts are out of this world. I bought a clay pot for dos reales. I can sell it in Spain for twice that. In a few years the place will be spoiled. Come see it before it's gone."

Gone? That's what we fear. What if the spirit that attracted us here in the first place leaves?

Tourists do spoil things. The minute tourists discover a new place, they also bring their garbage with them. Some set up businesses to ship the clay pots back home, organizing the natives in ways the natives never wanted to be organized. Tourism leads to strange kinds of enterprises, some good, some not very humanistic.

But I didn't learn about tourism in the West by reading the Spanish explorers' notes. In my childhood we weren't taught the history of our land as it occurred from the colonizations that came to el norte from the south. We were only taught the history of the pioneers, the western movement. How many times did little Chicanitos in school have to sing "Oh My Darling Clementine"?

The first tourists I encountered were in Santa Rosa, New Mexico, my home town. On highway 66, right after World War II. It was the best of times, it was the worst of times. People were moving west, tourists in search of California. I remember one particular afternoon at a gas station where we went to fill our bike tires after goathead punctures. A car stopped. Dad, mom, son, and daughter. Blonde, blue-eyed gringos from the east. They usually didn't pay attention to the brown Mexicanitos gathered at the gas station. But this Ozzie and Harriet Nelson family did. They talked briefly to me.

"Where you from?" Ozzie asked.
"Here," I said.
"Just here?" he said, looking around.
"Yes." I had never considered anyplace other than just here.
Here was home.
He wasn't too interested. "Oh," he said and went off to kick his
    car's tires.
"Where are *you* from?" I asked Harriet.

"Back east."

"Where are you going?" I asked.

"We're tourists," she answered. "We're going to California."

Heading west on highway 66, into the setting sun.

Imagine, I thought to myself. A family can travel to California as tourists. Just to go look. Look at what? The Pacific Ocean. I knew it from the maps at school. I knew then I wanted to be a tourist.

I ran home and told my mother. "Mama, I want to be a tourist."

Her mouth dropped. She stopped rolling tortillas and made the sign of the cross over me. "Where did you get that idea?" I told her about the family I had just met.

"No, mijito," she said. "Only the Americanos can be tourists. Now go help Ultima with her herbs and get those crazy ideas out of your mind."

I went away saddened. Why was it a crazy idea to be a tourist? Was my mother telling me to beware of tourists?

"Why is it only the Americanos get to be tourists?" I asked Ultima. She knew the answer to almost any question that had to do with healing and sickness of the soul, but I could see that tourists puzzled her.

"They have cameras, they take pictures," she finally answered.

"What's wrong with that?"

"The spirit of who we are cannot be captured in the picture," she said. "When you go to a different place you can know it by taking a picture, or you can let the place seep into your blood. A real turista is one who allows the spirit of that place to enter."

She looked across the hills of the llano, then turned her gaze to the river. "The river is like a turista. The water moves, but yet the river remains constant. So to travel also means to go within. This place, or any place, can change you. You discover pieces of yourself when you go beyond your boundaries. Or you can stay in one place and learn the true nature of your soul."

I knew Ultima had never been a tourist. She only knew the few villages around Santa Rosa. But she was far wiser than anyone I knew. She had traveled within, and so she knew herself. She knew the land and its people.

Still I questioned her. "My tio Benito and his family are tourists, aren't they? They're always going to Colorado or Texas."

Again she shook her head. "They go to work in the beet fields of Colorado and to pick cotton in Texas. Poor people who go to work aren't turistas."

So, tourists didn't go to work. They just went to look, and maybe take pictures. What a life. I knew I *really* wanted to be tourist.

"Who knows," Utima said, "maybe someday you will travel beyond this river valley. You may even go to China."

China, I thought. On the round world globe at school it was directly across from Santa Rosa. One day I dug a hole in the schoolyard. "You better watch out, Rudy," the girls warned me. "You could fall through to China." They ran away laughing.

For a class project I wrote away to cruise lines and did a report on cruise ships. They circled the globe. They went to Greece. Spain. Italy. They went to the Mediterranean world. Maybe someday I will take a ship on the Mediterranean, I thought.

For another project I made a sculpture of clay. The pyramids of Giza and the Sphinx. Set on a plaster board with sand for the desert and twigs for palm trees. It was real to me. I got an A.

"What do you want to be when you grow up?" the teacher asked.

"I want to be a tourist," I said.

"Esta loco," the kids whispered.

Yes, to dream of travel in that time and place was to be a little crazy. I settled for books to bring distant places to me.

But I did go to China. In 1984 my wife and I and a small group of colleagues traveled through China. I saw wonders my ancestors of the Pecos River could only imagine. Beijing, Xian, the Yangtze River, the Great Wall. I got so much into the place and the people at one point I felt transformed into a Chinese man. That's the kind of transformation the sensitive tourist looks for, becoming one with the place and people. If only for a short while. I have never written travel journals, but I did write one about China. *A Chicano in China.*

The memory of who I am stretches beyond the here and now. It resides in the archetypes, a biologic stream that is a strand into the past, to distant places and people. We sense the truth of images in stories and myths. And so we set out to test the memory. Was I related to China and its people? Was the Chinese dragon the Quetzalcoatl of the Aztecs? Was the god of nature, the golden carp which I described in *Bless Me, Ultima,* related to the golden carp that thrive in Chinese lakes? Was the bronze turtle resting at temple entrances related to the boy called Tortuga in my novel by that name?

We travel to seek connections. What are the tourists who come west seeking? Is our job to take their money and be done with them, or should we educate them? Should they read our books and history before applying for visas to our sacred land?

Later in life I did cruise on the Mediterranean, from the Greek Isles through the Bosporus into magical Constantinople. From Spain—where I practiced my New Mexican Spanish in many a tapas bar—to Italy down to Israel and into Egypt. Cruising the Nile, like a lowrider on Saturday night, I was transported into a past so deep and meaningful, I became Egyptian. I cut my hair like an Egyptian, wore the long robe, prayed at the temples, and entered into the worship. A tourist must also be a pilgrim.

I didn't participate in any revolutions like Lawrence of Arabia. I was a tourist. I knew my role and my parameters. But even as tourists we can enter the history of the place. I would go back to the Nile at the drop of a tortilla. Now I consider my Rio Grande a sister of the Nile. Long ago Mediterranean people, my ancestors, came to Rio Grande, bringing their dreams. I am part of that dream that infused the land. I am part of all the dreams that have settled here.

How do we teach these connections to tourists that visit our Rio Grande, or the Colorado River, or the Columbia? There are relationships of rivers. Those from the east bring knowledge of their Mississippi, their Ohio, their

Hudson. They bring a knowledge of their place and history. How we connect to each other may show us how we can save the West, and save the world.

Still we fear that tourism has become just one more consumer item on the supermarket shelf. Tourists who come only to consume and don't connect their history to ours leave us empty.

Is there an answer to this topic of tourism in the West? The issue is complex. My tio Benito and his family, who as I mentioned earlier went as workers to Texas and Colorado, weren't considered tourists, and yet they gave their work and sweat to the land. But they remained invisible. They worked the earth of the West, like prior groups have worked the western land, but they remained invisible.

The Mexicano workers who right now are constructing the history of the West through their work in the fields are not considered tourists. And yet they are lending their language, their music, and their food to enrich our region. The Pacific Rim has been connected to Asia for a long time, and that relationship continues to thrive in our time. The West now speaks, Japanese, Chinese, and Korean.

Maybe the West is going through a new era. We are a vast and exciting region where new migrations of people are creating an exciting multicultural world, one that has very little in common with the older, conservative myth of the West. Perhaps the idea of the West as the promised land isn't dead; a new infusion of cultures continues even as postmodern technology changes our landscape once again.

I am fascinated with the migrations of people. I have tried to emphasize this by saying some of those past migrations to the West were tourists. I don't mean to be flippant. We know most often it is necessity that moves groups of people. But migrations are a normal course of human events. Today, as in the past, it isn't only curiosity and available leisure time that creates the tourist. When people have to feed their families they will migrate.

Our challenge is to be sensitive to those who migrate across the land. A lot of mistakes were made in the past by those too arrogant to appreciate the native ways. Clashes between the cultural groups of the West exploded into atrocities. That, too, is part of our history. To not repeat that waste is the challenge. The answer lies in how we educate ourselves and those tourists exploring our region. In this effort major attention has to be paid to the migrant workers, those who put sweat and labor into the land but may not have the leisure time we normally associate with tourists. In many ways they know our region better than most of us, and many are settling into the land.

In Spanish we have a saying: Respeto al ajeno. Respect the other person's property, respect the foreigner. As we respect places and people in our travels, we expect to be respected by those who travel through our land. Respect can be taught. After all, we are on Earth "only for a while" as the Aztec poet said. We are all dharma bums learning our true nature from the many communities of the West. Let us respect each other in the process.

2001

Wendell Berry (B. 1934)

An Entrance to the Woods

On a fine sunny afternoon at the end of September I leave my work in Lexington and drive east on I-64 and the Mountain Parkway. When I leave the Parkway at the little town of Pine Ridge I am in the watershed of the Red River in the Daniel Boone National Forest. From Pine Ridge I take Highway 715 out along the narrow ridgetops, a winding tunnel through the trees. And then I turn off on a Forest Service Road and follow it to the head of a foot trail that goes down the steep valley wall of one of the tributary creeks. I pull my car off the road and lock it, and lift on my pack.

It is nearly five o'clock when I start walking. The afternoon is brilliant and warm, absolutely still, not enough air stirring to move a leaf. There is only the steady somnolent trilling of insects, and now and again in the woods below me the cry of a pileated woodpecker. Those, and my footsteps on the path, are the only sounds.

From the dry oak woods of the ridge I pass down into the rock. The foot trails of the Red River Gorge all seek these stony notches that little streams have cut back through the cliffs. I pass a ledge overhanging a sheer drop of the rock, where in a wetter time there would be a waterfall. The ledge is dry and mute now, but on the face of the rock below are the characteristic mosses, ferns, liverwort, meadow rue. And here where the ravine suddenly steepens and narrows, where the shadows are long-lived and the dampness stays, the trees are different. Here are beech and hemlock and poplar, straight and tall, reaching way up into the light. Under them are evergreen thickets of rhododendron. And wherever the dampness is there are mosses and ferns. The faces of the rock are intricately scalloped with veins of ironstone, scooped and carved by the wind.

Finally from the crease of the ravine I am following there begins to come the trickling and splashing of water. There is a great restfulness in the sounds these small streams make; they are going down as fast as they can, but their sounds seem leisurely and idle, as if produced like gemstones with the greatest patience and care.

A little later, stopping, I hear not far away the more voluble flowing of the creek. I go on down to where the trail crosses and begin to look for a camping place. The little bottoms along the creek here are thickety and weedy, probably having been kept clear and cropped or pastured not so long ago. In the more open places are little lavender asters, and the even smaller-flowered white ones that some people call beeweed or farewell-summer. And in low wet places are the richly flowered spikes of great lobelia, the blooms an intense startling blue, exquisitely shaped. I choose a place in an open thicket near the stream, and make camp.

It is a simple matter to make camp. I string up a shelter and put my air mattress and sleeping bag in it, and I am ready for the night. And supper is even simpler, for I have brought sandwiches for this first meal. In less than an hour all my chores are done. It will still be light for a good while, and I go over and sit down on a rock at the edge of the stream.

And then a heavy feeling of melancholy and lonesomeness comes over me. This does not surprise me, for I have felt it before when I have been alone at evening in wilderness places that I am not familiar with. But here it has a quality that I recognize as peculiar to the narrow hollows of the Red River Gorge. These are deeply shaded by the trees and by the valley walls, the sun rising on them late and setting early; they are more dark than light. And there will often be little rapids in the stream that will sound, at a certain distance, exactly like people talking. As I sit on my rock by the stream now, I could swear that there is a party of campers coming up the trail toward me, and for several minutes I stay alert, listening for them, their voices seeming to rise and fall, fade out and lift again, in happy conversation. When I finally realize that it is only a sound the creek is making, though I have not come here for company and do not want any, I am inexplicably sad.

These are haunted places, or at least it is easy to feel haunted in them, alone at nightfall. As the air darkens and the cool of the night rises, one feels the immanence of the wraiths of the ancient tribesmen who used to inhabit the rock houses of the cliffs; of the white hunters from east of the mountains; of the farmers who accepted the isolation of these nearly inaccessible valleys to crop the narrow bottoms and ridges and pasture their cattle and hogs in the woods; of the seekers of quick wealth in timber and ore. For though this is a wilderness place, it bears its part of the burden of human history. If one spends much time here and feels much liking for the place, it is hard to escape the sense of one's predecessors. If one has read of the prehistoric Indians whose flint arrowpoints and pottery and hominy holes and petroglyphs have been found here, then every rock shelter and clifty spring will suggest the presence of those dim people who have disappeared into the earth. Walking along the ridges and the stream bottoms, one will come upon the heaped stones of a chimney, or the slowly filling depression of an old cellar, or will find in the spring a japonica bush or periwinkles or a few jonquils blooming in a thicket that used to be a dooryard. Wherever the land is level enough there are abandoned fields and pastures. And nearly always there is the evidence that one follows in the steps of the loggers.

That sense of the past is probably one reason for the melancholy that I feel. But I know that there are other reasons.

One is that, though I am here in body, my mind and my nerves too are not yet altogether here. We seem to grant to our high-speed roads and our airlines the rather thoughtless assumption that people can change places as rapidly as their bodies can be transported. That, as my own experience keeps proving to me, is not true. In the middle of the afternoon I left off being busy at work, and drove through traffic to the freeway, and then for a solid hour or more I drove sixty or seventy miles an hour, hardly aware of the country I was passing through, because on the freeway one does not have to be. The landscape has been subdued so that one may drive over it at seventy miles per hour without any concession whatsoever to one's whereabouts. One might as well be flying. Though one is in Kentucky one is not experiencing Kentucky; one is experiencing the highway, which might be in nearly any hill country east of the Mississippi.

Once off the freeway, my pace gradually slowed, as the roads became progressively more primitive, from seventy miles an hour to a walk. And now, here at my camping place, I have stopped altogether. But my mind is still keyed to seventy miles an hour. And having come here so fast, it is still busy with the work I am usually doing. Having come here by the freeway, my mind is not so fully here as it would have been if I had come by the crookeder, slower state roads; it is incalculably farther away than it would have been if I had come all the way on foot, as my earliest predecessors came. When the Indians and the first white hunters entered this country they were altogether here as soon as they arrived, for they had seen and experienced fully everything between here and their starting place, and so the transition was gradual and articulate in their consciousness. Our senses, after all, were developed to function at foot speeds; and the transition from foot travel to motor travel, in terms of evolutionary time, has been abrupt. The faster one goes, the more strain there is on the senses, the more they fail to take in, the more confusion they must tolerate or gloss over—and the longer it takes to bring the mind to a stop in the presence of anything. Though the freeway passes through the very heart of this forest, the motorist remains several hours' journey by foot from what is living at the edge of the right-of-way.

But I have not only come to this strangely haunted place in a short time and too fast. I have in that move made an enormous change: I have departed from my life as I am used to living it, and have come into the wilderness. It is not fear that I feel; I have learned to fear the everyday events of human history much more than I fear the everyday occurrences of the woods; in general, I would rather trust myself to the woods than to any government that I know of. I feel, instead, an uneasy awareness of severed connections, of being cut off from all familiar places and of being a stranger where I am. What is happening at home? I wonder, and I know I can't find out very easily or very soon.

Even more discomforting is a pervasive sense of unfamiliarity. In the places I am most familiar with—my house, or my garden, or even the woods near home that I have walked in for years—I am surrounded by associations; everywhere I look I am reminded of my history and my hopes; even unconsciously I am comforted by any number of proofs that my life on the earth is an established and a going thing. But I am in this hollow for the first time in my life. I see nothing that I recognize. Everything looks as it did before I came, as it will when I am gone. When I look over at my little camp I see how tentative and insignificant it is. Lying there in my bed in the dark tonight, I will be absorbed in the being of this place, invisible as a squirrel in his nest.

Uneasy as this feeling is, I know it will pass. Its passing will produce a deep pleasure in being here. And I have felt it often enough before that I have begun to understand something of what it means:

Nobody knows where I am. I don't know what is happening to anybody else in the world. While I am here I will not speak, and will have no reason or need for speech. It is only beyond this lonesomeness for the places I have come from that I can reach the vital reality of a place such as this. Turning toward this place, I confront a presence that none of my schooling and none of my usual assumptions have prepared me for: the wilderness, mostly unknowable and mostly alien, that is the universe. Perhaps the most difficult labor for my species is to accept its limits, its weakness and ignorance. But here I am. This wild place where I have camped lies within an enormous cone widening from the center of the earth out across the universe, nearly all of it a mysterious wilderness in which the power and the knowledge of men count for nothing. As long as its instruments are correct and its engines run, the airplane now flying through this great cone is safely within the human freehold; its behavior is as familiar and predictable to those concerned as the inside of a man's living room. But let its instruments or its engines fail, and at once it enters the wilderness where nothing is foreseeable. And these steep narrow hollows, these cliffs and forested ridges that lie below, are the antithesis of flight.

Wilderness is the element in which we live encased in civilization, as a mollusk lives in his shell in the sea. It is a wilderness that is beautiful, dangerous, abundant, oblivious of us, mysterious, never to be conquered or controlled or second-guessed, or known more than a little. It is a wilderness that for most of us most of the time is kept out of sight, camouflaged, by the edifices and the busyness and the bothers of human society.

And so, coming here, what I have done is strip away the human facade that usually stands between me and the universe, and I see more clearly where I am. What I am able to ignore much of the time, but find undeniable here, is that all wildernesses are one: there is a profound joining between this wild stream deep in one of the folds of my native country and the tropical jungles, the tundras of the north, the oceans and the deserts. Alone here, among the rocks and the trees, I see that I am alone also among the stars. A stranger here, unfamiliar with my surroundings, I am aware also that I know only in the most relative terms my whereabouts within the black reaches of the universe. And because the natural processes are here so little qualified by anything human, this fragment of the wilderness is also joined to other times; there flows over it a nonhuman time to be told by the growth and death of the forest and the wearing of the stream. I feel drawing out beyond my comprehension perspectives from which the growth and the death of a large poplar would seem as continuous and sudden as the raising and the lowering of a man's hand, from which men's history in the world, their brief clearing of the ground, will seem no more than the opening and shutting of an eye.

And so I have come here to enact—not because I want to but because, once here, I cannot help it—the loneliness and the humbleness of my kind. I must see in my flimsy shelter, pitched here for two nights, the transience of capitols and cathedrals. In growing used to being in this place, I will have to accept a humbler and a truer view of myself than I usually have.

A man enters and leaves the world naked. And it is only naked—or nearly so—that he can enter and leave the wilderness. If he walks, that is; and if he doesn't walk it can hardly be said that he has entered. He can bring only what he can carry—the little that it takes to replace for a few hours or a few days an animal's fur and teeth and claws and functioning instincts. In comparison to the usual traveler with his dependence on machines and highways and restaurants and motels—on the economy and the government, in short—the man who walks into the wilderness is naked indeed. He leaves behind his work, his household, his duties, his comforts—even, if he comes alone, his words. He immerses himself in what he is not. It is a kind of death.

The dawn comes slow and cold. Only occasionally, somewhere along the creek or on the slopes above, a bird sings. I have not slept well, and I waken without much interest in the day. I set the camp to rights, and fix breakfast, and eat. The day is clear, and high up on the points and ridges to the west of my camp I can see the sun shining on the woods. And suddenly I am full of an ambition: I want to get up where the sun is; I want to sit still in the sun up there among the high rocks until I can feel its warmth in my bones.

I put some lunch into a little canvas bag, and start out, leaving my jacket so as not to have to carry it after the day gets warm. Without my jacket, even climbing, it is cold in the shadow of the hollow, and I have a long way to go to get to the sun. I climb the steep path up the valley wall, walking rapidly, thinking only of the sunlight above me. It is as though I have entered into a deep sympathy with those tulip poplars that grow so straight and tall out of the shady ravines, not growing a branch worth the name until their heads are in the sun. I am so concentrated on the sun that when some grouse flush from the undergrowth ahead of me, I am thunderstruck; they are already planing down into the underbrush again before I can get my wits together and realize what they are.

The path zigzags up the last steepness of the bluff and then slowly levels out. For some distance it follows the backbone of a ridge, and then where the ridge is narrowest there is a great slab of bare rock lying full in the sun. This is what I have been looking for. I walk out into the center of the rock and sit, the clear warm light falling unobstructed all around. As the sun warms me I begin to grow comfortable not only in my clothes, but in the place and the day. And like those light-seeking poplars of the ravines, my mind begins to branch out.

Southward, I can hear the traffic on the Mountain Parkway, a steady continuous roar—the corporate voice of twentieth-century humanity, sustained above the transient voices of its members. Last night, except for an occasional airplane passing over, I camped out of reach of the sounds of engines. For long stretches of time I heard no sounds but the sounds of the woods.

Near where I am sitting there is an inscription cut into the rock:

A • J • SARGENT
fEB • 2♮ •1903

Those letters were carved there more than sixty-six years ago. As I look around me I realize that I can see no evidence of the lapse of so much time. In every direction I can see only narrow ridges and narrow deep hollows, all covered with trees. For all that can be told from this height by looking, it might still be 1903—or, for that matter, 1803 or 1703, or 1003. Indians no doubt sat here and looked over the country as I am doing now; the visual impression is so pure and strong that I can almost imagine myself one of them. But the insistent, the overwhelming, evidence of the time of my own arrival is in what I can hear—that roar of the highway off there in the distance. In 1903 the continent was still covered by a great ocean of silence, in which the sounds of machinery were scattered at wide intervals of time and space. Here, in 1903, there were only the natural sounds of the place. On a day like this, at the end of September, there would have been only the sounds of a few faint crickets, a woodpecker now and then, now and then the wind. But today, two-thirds of a century later, the continent is covered by an ocean of engine noise, in which silences occur only sporadically and at wide intervals.

From where I am sitting in the midst of this island of wilderness, it is as though I am listening to the machine of human history—a huge flywheel building speed until finally the force of its whirling will break it in pieces, and the world with it. That is not an attractive thought, and yet I find it impossible to escape, for it has seemed to me for years now that the doings of men no longer occur within nature, but that the natural places which the human economy has so far spared now survive almost accidentally within the doings of men. This wilderness of the Red River now carries on its ancient processes *within* the human climate of war and waste and confusion. And I know that the distant roar of engines, though it may *seem* only to be passing through this wilderness, is really bearing down upon it. The machine is running now with a speed that produces blindness—as to the driver of a speeding automobile the only thing stable, the only thing not a mere blur on the edge of the retina, is the automobile itself—and the blindness of a thing with power promises the destruction of what cannot be seen. That roar of the highway is the voice of the American economy; it is sounding also wherever strip mines are being cut in the steep slopes of Appalachia, and wherever cropland is being destroyed to make roads and suburbs, and wherever rivers and marshes and bays and forests are being destroyed for the sake of industry or commerce.

No. Even here where the economy of life is really an economy— where the creation is yet fully alive and continuous and self-enriching, where whatever dies enters directly into the life of the living—even here one cannot fully escape the sense of an impending human catastrophe. One cannot come here without the awareness that this is an island surrounded by the machinery and the workings of an insane greed, hungering for the world's end—that ours is a "civilization" of which the work of no builder or artist is symbol, nor the life of any good man, but rather the bulldozer, the poison spray, the hugging fire of napalm, the cloud of Hiroshima.

Though from the high vantage point of this stony ridge I see little hope that I will ever live a day as an optimist, still I am not desperate. In fact, with the sun warming me now, and with the whole day before me to wander in this beautiful country, I am happy. A man cannot despair if he can imagine a better life, and if he can enact something of its possibility. It is only when I am ensnarled in the meaningless ordeals and the ordeals of meaninglessness, of which our public and political life is now so productive, that I lose the awareness of something better, and feel the despair of having come to the dead end of possibility.

Today, as always when I am afoot in the woods, I feel the possibility, the reasonableness, the practicability of living in the world in a way that would enlarge rather than diminish the hope of life. I feel the possibility of a frugal and protective love for the creation that would be unimaginably more meaningful and joyful than our present destructive and wasteful economy. The absence of human society, that made me so uneasy last night, now begins to be a comfort to me. I am afoot in the woods. I am alive in the world, this moment, without the help or the interference of any machine. I can move without reference to anything except the lay of the land and the capabilities of my own body. The necessities of foot travel in this steep country have stripped away all superfluities. I simply could not enter into this place and assume its quiet with all the belongings of a family man, property holder, etc. For the time, I am reduced to my irreducible self. I feel the lightness of body that a man must feel who has just lost fifty pounds of fat. As I leave the bare expanse of the rock and go in under the trees again, I am aware that I move in the landscape as one of its details.

Walking through the woods, you can never see far, either ahead or behind, so you move without much of a sense of getting anywhere or of moving at any certain speed. You burrow through the foliage in the air much as a mole burrows through the roots in the ground. The views that open out occasionally from the ridges afford a relief, a recovery of orientation, that they could never give as mere "scenery," looked at from a turnout at the edge of a highway.

The trail leaves the ridge and goes down a ravine into the valley of a creek where the night chill has stayed. I pause only long enough to drink the cold clean water. The trail climbs up onto the next ridge.

It is the ebb of the year. Though the slopes have not yet taken on the bright colors of the autumn maples and oaks, some of the duller trees are already shedding. The foliage has begun to flow down the cliff faces and the slopes like a tide pulling back. The woods is mostly quiet, subdued, as if the pressure of survival has grown heavy upon it, as if above the growing warmth of the day the cold of winter can be felt waiting to descend.

At my approach a big hawk flies off the low branch of an oak and out over the treetops. Now and again a nuthatch hoots, off somewhere in the woods. Twice I stop and watch an ovenbird. A few feet ahead of me there is a sudden movement in the leaves, and then quiet. When I slip up and examine the spot there is nothing to be found. Whatever passed there has disappeared, quicker than the hand that is quicker than the eye, a shadow fallen into a shadow.

In the afternoon I leave the trail. My walk so far has come perhaps three-quarters of the way around a long zigzagging loop that will eventually bring me back to my starting place. I turn down a small unnamed branch of the creek where I am camped, and I begin the loveliest part of the day. There is nothing here resembling a trail. The best way is nearly always to follow the edge of the stream, stepping from one stone to another. Crossing back and forth over the water, stepping on or over rocks and logs, the way ahead is never clear for more than a few feet. The stream accompanies me down, threading its way under boulders and logs and over little falls and rapids. The rhododendron overhangs it so closely in places that I can go only by stooping. Over the rhododendron are the great dark heads of the hemlocks. The streambanks are ferny and mossy. And through this green tunnel the voice of the stream changes from rock to rock; subdued like all the other autumn voices of the woods, it seems sunk in a deep contented meditation on the sounds of *l*.

The water in the pools is absolutely clear. If it weren't for the shadows and ripples you would hardly notice that it is water; the fish would seem to swim in the air. As it is, where there is no leaf floating, it is impossible to tell exactly where the plane of the surface lies. As I walk up on a pool the little fish dart every which way out of sight. And then after I sit still a while, watching, they come out again. Their shadows flow over the rocks and leaves on the bottom. Now I have come into the heart of the woods. I am far from the highway and can hear no sound of it. All around there is a grand deep autumn quiet, in which a few insects dream their summer songs. Suddenly a wren sings way off in the underbrush. A redbreasted nuthatch walks, hooting, headfirst down the trunk of a walnut. An ovenbird walks out along the limb of a hemlock and looks at me, curious. The little fish soar in the pool, turning their clean quick angles, their shadows seeming barely to keep up. As I lean and dip my cup in the water, they scatter. I drink, and go on.

When I get back to camp it is only the middle of the afternoon or a little after. Since I left in the morning I have walked something like eight miles. I haven't hurried—have mostly poked along, stopping often and looking around. But I am tired, and coming down the creek I have got both feet wet. I find a sunny place, and take off my shoes and socks and set them to dry. For a long time then, lying propped against the trunk of a tree, I read and rest and watch the evening come.

All day I have moved through the woods, making as little noise as possible. Slowly my mind and my nerves have slowed to a walk. The quiet of the woods has ceased to be something that I observe; now it is something that I am a part of. I have joined it with my own quiet. As the twilight draws on I no longer feel the strangeness and uneasiness of the evening before. The sounds of the creek move through my mind as they move through the valley, unimpeded and clear.

When the time comes I prepare supper and eat, and then wash kettle and cup and spoon and put them away. As far as possible I get things ready for an early start in the morning. Soon after dark I go to bed, and I sleep well.

I wake long before dawn. The air is warm and I feel rested and wide awake. By the light of a small candle lantern I break camp and pack. And then I begin the steep climb back to the car.

The moon is bright and high. The woods stands in deep shadow, the light falling soft through the openings of the foliage. The trees appear immensely tall, and black, gravely looming over the path. It is windless and still; the moonlight pouring over the country seems more potent than the air. All around me there is still that constant low singing of the insects. For days now it has continued without letup or inflection, like ripples on water under a steady breeze. While I slept it went on through the night, a shimmer on my mind. My shoulder brushes a low tree overhanging the path and a bird that was asleep on one of the branches startles awake and flies off into the shadows, and I go on with the sense that I am passing near to the sleep of things.

In a way this is the best part of the trip. Stopping now and again to rest, I linger over it, sorry to be going. It seems to me that if I were to stay on, today would be better than yesterday, and I realize it was to renew the life of that possibility that I came here. What I am leaving is something to look forward to.

1981

Philip Brady (B. 1955)

Myth & Uncertainty

From *To Prove My Blood: A Tale of Emigration and the Afterlife*

But what else
Can a mother give her daughter but such
Beautiful rifts in time?

—Eavan Boland

Although Aunt Mary moved back to Brooklyn after Brian's birth, she was never really gone; she merely faded to a voice humming in the phone, though it seldom occurred to me to listen. Now that she's the last sister alive, spirited to Ohio to live down the block, now that I want to hear all that she could teach, she's not really here.

It's a paradox that my students, studying Heisenberg in "Myth & Science," might appreciate. According to his Uncertainty Principle, no one knows where anything is at a given time, but every Monday-Wednesday-Friday at 8 a.m. on my way to class I drive the same three blocks and take the same elevator and tramp to the same room where the same ninety-five-year-old woman, my link to myth, snores. I bring cafeteria tea to her bedside and recall her to her fate. If she knows me, she takes the cup, and thanks me, calls me "son." But some mornings, she wakes to Heisenberg—white beard, skull gaunt as a key.

"Where's Flip?" she cries; "Where's my nephew?"

"It's alright, Aunt Mary, it's me."

"Oh, Gorgeous. What a face on you," she sniffs, then bursts into laughter.

Mary Martin knows all about uncertainty. In 1924, when Dick Martin, Belfast Presbyterian, died of stomach cancer at the age of twenty-nine, his Papist widow Mary made no trouble about returning obediently to childhood. There was no question of remaining in the gardener's cottage of the Long Island estate where her husband had worked; she simply left with her baby daughter for her parents' Brooklyn railroad flat. Even when Dick Martin's parents crossed the water like God's wrath, it was not Mary but my grandmother who barred the door and kept the Martins from taking Mary's infant back to Ulster. And if Mary couldn't hold on to the shirttail of a Protestant too feckless to stay alive, she wasn't about to seek another man.

"You never know what you might get," she told me on one rare occasion when I questioned her, as I decanted foam from a blender of whisky sours in the kitchen of 53-28. It was the Fourth of July, 1982, and Brian had ferried Mary in from Brooklyn, and I had just returned from Africa, where I had touched, near dawn, with undisguised wonder, a woman whose image no distance could dispel. When my left forefinger brushed her right breast, when the shirr of that touch speared my skull, one lobe knew instantly that I had met my bride; the other, that I would never marry.

"But Aunt Mary, it's been so long," I leered, tapping my glass.

Here in Ohio, at the end of Mary's century, all the intervening years having passed in an instant, Heisenberg taps a finger on her teacup.

"Aunt Mary, I've got to go teach."

"Of course, son," Mary says, squinting up at a face she knows or doesn't. "You're off now; I'll be grand. Do you get more money to teach college boys? Less? You're joking. Ah son, don't worry about me."

What theories could explain Aunt Mary's zigzagging? In the year Einstein first read *Faust,* she crossed the ocean. Her nuptials spirited her to Long Island just as the Grand Mufti's Fatwa endorsed consensual contraception, and her child was born the very month the Bronx-Whitestone Bridge linked two bleak cornices. She returned to her parents' Brooklyn flat on the second anniversary of Hart Crane's death, and her move to 53-28 with her widowed mother occurred the day Walter O'Malley told the *Daily News,* "If they have to be the Flushing Dodgers, they might as well be the Los Angeles Dodgers." Then back to Brooklyn on Kennedy's inauguration, and finally, after my mother's death, she was whisked off with all her kit stuffed into the trunk of her nephew's Taurus to some region beyond time and story.

But Deirdre, her fatherless daughter whose name means Sorrow, aspired to the absolute, craved certainty like salt. Catechized by a family that yo-yoed between skyscraper-awe and piety toward some Hibernian utopia, Deirdre could barely approximate who was above ground and who below. The only certainties were soup, and coins plumbed from purses on nightstands; and men—their shoulderly angles, bourbon and sedans, the hatchets buried in their throats. When she turned sixteen, the beaus who'd fox-trotted her cousins came for her. Deirdre was sure of their doorbell ring, the jangle of their pockets. How easy to churn them; she could draft lust the way a child dials Etch-A-Sketch. A glance, and their pulse quickened. Glare, and they veered off. The fact that men dodged, simpered, or scrammed didn't daunt her. They remained constant as soup, as purses. At seventeen, when the flash of Zeroes over Pearl Harbor blinded her guardians, she shimmied out of their grasp and fled across the river to New Jersey. It wasn't one of the dance-hall dandies who stole her, but a shy boy from Cathedral Prep, a character from the myth I tell my students, the story of Deirdre's name.

In Ulster, millennia before McCann and Martin sowed teeth into each other's flesh, a warrior's widow gave birth to a girl and named her "Sorrow," appealing to King Conchobor for protection. Presented with an infant, the king's eyes gleamed with a design that no woeful prophecy could deter: he'd raise the girl in secret, closeted in the usual fairy-tale minaret, where she'd see no face but his, hear only his voice. Season by season, Deirdre seemed to grow in devotion to the king, who taught her names of stars and essences, elk dances and spells, chariot-fighting and ogham mathematics. "Sorrow," he'd simper, locking her gaze and guiding her slim fingers to his wrist. Then one winter morning, Deirdre glimpsed from her window a young peasant, and that night she endured dreams of ravens diving toward bloodstained snow. How feeble the king seemed now, how banal his lessons compared to this blossoming of exotic faces and bodies, visions that filled her with an ineluctable power. When the next man passed by—a nobleman on horseback—Deirdre didn't just dream, she gave chase.

"What's your name, handsome?" Deirdre asked.

"Niall, first born son of Usnach," the nobleman said, keeping the horse's flanks to the young siren.

"Will you take me, Niall?" Deirdre asked.

"The king's Sorrow?" said Niall. "A made-to-order bride, adopted from scratch? Not a chance. Easier to filch his crown than his clone."

"Then I'll shame you," said Deirdre, stripping off her gown.

She wondered herself where she'd learned that, since stoking lust hadn't been on Conchobor's curriculum. But no education is soporific enough to keep certain kinds of knowledge from Sorrow.

All over Ireland the lovers wandered, even as far as Scotland, taking refuge at Usnach's castle, where Deirdre bore a girl, and was happy, though never able completely to forget her fear. As for the king, rage sharpened his cunning. Promising amnesty, his spies coaxed the fugitives back to Ulster, where the king murdered Niall and his brothers, fulfilling the dream of bloody snow. Conchobor had a baby girl again. As they approached her familiar prison, Deirdre screamed and split her own skull with a spear.

Was this the doppelgänger ensorcelling Deirdre Martin, the certainty she envisioned, tried to grasp? She had her own String Theory, webbing past and future; but the others above ground—grandfather, mother, cousins, lover—plied their roles from the ancient script.

On cue, Francis McCann marched across the bridge to retrieve his charge. Reinstalled in her grandparents' flat, Deirdre carried in her body a rune of certainty's helix: an infant. McCann raged; her cousins hemmed in, their ululations giving grief a skin. But Deirdre would not sway, would not turn back as Mary Martin had been turned. Nor would she split her own skull with a spear. Instead, she locked herself in the bathroom and wedged a chair against the pounding that grew frantic when her moans ceased with a thud and a crash of shattering glass. When they broke through, her cousins found her naked on the linoleum, awash in blood, the mirror sharded, a coat hanger lodged in her womb.

But she did not die, and when she fled again at the age of twenty-two, it was under a shield even her grandfather could not dent, marrying a man to double McCann's rage, a pock-faced Italian with a split-level in Bayside.

Soon, her husband unleashed the savagery that Mary Martin feared, flashing Deirdre's brain with blows until she went snow-blank. But still she would not die, raised three living daughters, found work in a flower shop, still bent on her own certainty, charting quarks with bifocals.

When I last saw Deirdre, one summer day on the patio of 53-28 two years before her death, she was already legend: her arms scaly, her hair a hag's nest. Her cousins called her *caution* and spooned the story under my night lamp.

Though I didn't speak to her then, I wonder what I'd say now that she's found certainty. "Only when all are dead is anyone certain," I might say; but that sounds like a Greek chorus. "Let the dead and the living join hands," I'd try; but Deirdre might roll her bloodshot eyes, hearing another crib of the motherly dogma that drove her to flee. Perhaps I wouldn't speak, would pass her unkempt shade, dreading the sisters' caution. Instead, I return to earth, to Ohio, where I stop in Mary's room, find her asleep.

"Is it safe now, Aunt Mary, can I tell?"

"Ah, son, you're back now." Not asleep at all. "Grand. I've been ringing this blessed bell for eons. Nobody comes. Not a soul. I'd like a bit of soup."

"You have to press the button. See, like this. Aunt Mary, listen. Do you remember Deirdre? What was Deirdre like? Tell me about your daughter."

"Ah Deirdre, son, Deirdre was a caution. I took her to Radio City, to the show, with your mother and Betty and Kay, to the Rockettes, do you remember the dancers, son? Gorgeous, they were, and Radio City all lit up and the men in fancy suits, and there she was, Deirdre, the scamp, she let go my hand and skipped down the aisle to join the dancing girls. Imagine. Long gone, she is, long gone. What's that fuzz on your face?"

Even in Ohio, Mary and I hum in the weft of the orbits Deirdre set in motion—doubling above, below: mothers, cousins, daughters, fathers, husbands; and at the gyre's vortex, an empty purse.

2003

Bruce Chatwin (1942–1989)

From *In Patagonia*

In my grandmother's dining-room there was a glass-fronted cabinet and in the cabinet a piece of skin. It was a small piece only, but thick and leathery, with strands of coarse, reddish hair. It was stuck to a card with a rusty pin. On the card was some writing in faded black ink, but I was too young then to read.

"What's that?"

"A piece of brontosaurus."

My mother knew the names of two prehistoric animals, the brontosaurus and the mammoth. She knew it was not a mammoth. Mammoths came from Siberia.

The brontosaurus, I learned, was an animal that had drowned in the Flood, being too big for Noah to ship aboard the Ark. I pictured a shaggy lumbering creature with claws and fangs and a malicious green light in its eyes. Sometimes the brontosaurus would crash through the bedroom wall and wake me from my sleep.

This particular brontosaurus had lived in Patagonia, a country in South America, at the far end of the world. Thousands of years before, it had fallen into a glacier, travelled down a mountain in a prison of blue ice, and arrived in perfect condition at the bottom. Here my grandmother's cousin, Charley Milward the Sailor, found it.

Charley Milward was captain of a merchant ship that sank at the entrance to the Strait of Magellan. He survived the wreck and settled nearby, at Punta Arenas, where he ran a ship-repairing yard. The Charley Milward of my imagination was a god among men—tall, silent and strong, with black mutton-chop whiskers and fierce blue eyes. He wore his sailor's cap at an angle and the tops of his sea-boots turned down.

Directly he saw the brontosaurus poking out of the ice, he knew what to do. He had it jointed, salted, packed in barrels, and shipped to the Natural History Museum in South Kensington. I pictured blood and ice, flesh and salt, gangs of Indian workmen and lines of barrels along a shore—a work of giants and all to no purpose; the brontosaurus went rotten on its voyage through the tropics and arrived in London a putrefied mess; which was why you saw brontosaurus bones in the museum, but no skin.

Fortunately cousin Charley had posted a scrap to my grandmother.

My grandmother lived in a red-brick house set behind a screen of yellow-spattered laurels. It had tall chimneys, pointed gables and a garden of blood-coloured roses. Inside it smelled of church.

I do not remember much about my grandmother except her size. I would clamber over her wide bosom or watch, slyly, to see if she'd be able to rise from her chair. Above her hung paintings of Dutch burghers, their fat buttery faces nesting in white ruffs. On the mantelpiece were two Japanese homunculi with red and white ivory eyes that popped out on stalks. I would play with these, or with a German articulated monkey, but always I pestered her: "Please can I have the piece of brontosaurus."

Never in my life have I wanted anything as I wanted that piece of skin. My grandmother said I should have it one day, perhaps. And when she died I said: "Now I *can* have the piece of brontosaurus," but my mother said: "Oh, that thing! I'm afraid we threw it away."

At school they laughed at the story of the brontosaurus. The science master said I'd mixed it up with the Siberian mammoth. He told the class how Russian scientists had dined off deep-frozen mammoth and told me not to tell lies. Besides, he said, brontosauruses were reptiles. They had no hair, but scaly armoured hide. And he showed us an artist's impression of the beast—so different from that of my imagination—grey-green, with a tiny head and gigantic switchback of vertebrae, placidly eating weed in a lake. I was ashamed of my hairy brontosaurus, but I knew it was not a mammoth.

It took some years to sort the story out. Charley Milward's animal was not a brontosaurus, but the mylodon or Giant Sloth. He never found a whole specimen, or even a whole skeleton, but some skin and bones, preserved by the cold, dryness and salt, in a cave on Last Hope Sound in Chilean Patagonia. He sent the collection to England and sold it to the British Museum. This version was less romantic but had the merit of being true.

My interest in Patagonia survived the loss of the skin; for the Cold War woke in me a passion for geography. In the late 1940s the Cannibal of the Kremlin shadowed our lives; you could mistake his moustaches for teeth. We listened to lectures about the war he was planning. We watched the civil defence lecturer ring the cities of Europe to show the zones of total and partial destruction. We saw the zones bump one against the other leaving no space in between. The instructor wore khaki shorts. His knees were white and knobbly, and we saw it was hopeless. The war was coming and there was nothing we could do.

Next, we read about the cobalt bomb, which was worse than the hydrogen bomb and could smother the planet in an endless chain reaction.

I knew the colour cobalt from my great-aunt's paintbox. She had lived on Capri at the time of Maxim Gorky and painted Capriot boys naked. Later her art became almost entirely religious. She did lots of St Sebastians, always against a cobalt-blue background, always the same beautiful young man, stuck through and through with arrows and still on his feet.

So I pictured the cobalt bomb as a dense blue cloudbank, spitting tongues of flame at the edges. And I saw myself, out alone on a green headland, scanning the horizon for the advance of the cloud.

And yet we hoped to survive the blast. We started an Emigration Committee and made plans to settle in some far corner of the earth. We pored over atlases. We learned the direction of prevailing winds and the likely patterns of fall-out. The war would come in the Northern Hemisphere, so we looked to the Southern. We ruled out Pacific Islands for islands are traps. We ruled out Australia and New Zealand, and we fixed on Patagonia as the safest place on earth.

I pictured a low timber house with a shingled roof, caulked against storms, with blazing log fires inside and the walls lined with the best books, somewhere to live when the rest of the world blew up.

Then Stalin died and we sang hymns of praise in chapel, but I continued to hold Patagonia in reserve.

1977

Judith Ortiz Cofer (B. 1952)

Silent Dancing

We have a home movie of this party. Several times my mother and I have watched it together, and I have asked questions about the silent revellers coming in and out of focus. It is grainy and of short duration but a great visual aid to my first memory of life in Paterson at that time. And it is in color—the only complete scene in color I can recall from those years.

We lived in Puerto Rico until my brother was born in 1954. Soon after, because of economic pressures on our growing family, my father joined the United States Navy. He was assigned to duty on a ship in Brooklyn Yard, New York City—a place of cement and steel that was to be his home base in the States until his retirement more than twenty years later.

He left the Island first, tracking down his uncle who lived with his family across the Hudson River, in Paterson, New Jersey. There he found a tiny apartment in a huge apartment building that had once housed Jewish families and was just being transformed into a tenement by Puerto Ricans overflowing from New York City. In 1955 he sent for us. My mother was only twenty years old, I was not quite three, and my brother was a toddler when we arrived at *El Building,* as the place had been christened by its new residents.

My memories of life in Paterson during those first few years are in shades of gray. Maybe I was too young to absorb vivid colors and details, or to discriminate between the slate blue of the winter sky and the darker hues of the snow-bearing clouds, but the single color washes over the whole period. The building we lived in was gray, the streets were gray with slush the first few months of my life there, the coat my father had bought for me was dark in color and too big. It sat heavily on my thin frame.

I do remember the way the heater pipes banged and rattled, startling all of us out of sleep until we got so used to the sound that we automatically either shut it out or raised our voices above the racket. The hiss from the valve punctuated my sleep, which has always been fitful, like a non-human presence in the room—the dragon sleeping at the entrance of my childhood. But the pipes were a connection to all the other lives being lived around us. Having come from a house made for a single family back in Puerto Rico—my mother's extended-family home—it was curious to know that strangers lived under our floor and above our heads, and that the heater pipe went through everyone's apartments. (My first spanking in Paterson came as a result of playing tunes on the pipes in my room to see if there would be an answer.) My mother was as new to this concept of beehive life as I was, but had been given strict orders by my father to keep the doors locked, the noise down, ourselves to ourselves.

It seems that Father had learned some painful lessons about prejudice while searching for an apartment in Paterson. Not until years later did I hear how much resistance he had encountered with landlords who were panicking at the influx of Latinos into a neighborhood that had been Jewish for a couple of generations. But it was the American phenomenon of ethnic turnover that was changing the urban core of Paterson, and the human flood could not be held back with an accusing finger.

"You Cuban?" the man had asked my father, pointing a finger at his name tag on the Navy uniform—even though my father had the fair skin and light brown hair of his northern Spanish family background and our name is as common in Puerto Rico as Johnson is in the U.S.

"No," my father had answered looking past the finger into his adversary's angry eyes "I'm Puerto Rican."

"Same shit." And the door closed. My father could have passed as European, but we couldn't. My brother and I both have our mother's black hair and olive skin, and so we lived in El Building and visited our great-uncle and his fair children on the next block. It was their private joke that they were the German branch of the family. Not many years later that area too would be mainly Puerto Rican. It was as if the heart of the city map were being gradually colored in brown—*café-con-leche* brown. Our color.

The movie opens with a sweep of the living room. It is "typical" immigrant Puerto Rican decor for the time: the sofa and chairs are square and hard-looking, upholstered in bright colors (blue and yellow in this instance, and covered in the transparent plastic) that furniture salesmen then were adept at making women buy. The linoleum on the floor is light blue, and if it was subjected to the spike heels as it was in most places, there were dime-sized identations all over it that cannot be seen in this movie. The room is full of people dressed in mainly two colors: dark suits for the men, red dresses for the women. I have asked my mother why most of the women are in red that night, and she shrugs, "I don't remember. Just a coincidence." She doesn't have my obsession for assigning symbolism to everything.

The three women in red sitting on the couch are my mother, my eighteen-year-old cousin, and her brother's girlfriend. The "novia" is just up from the Island, which is apparent in her body language. She sits up formally, and her dress is carefully pulled over her knees. She is a pretty girl but her posture makes her look insecure, lost in her full skirted red dress which she has carefully tucked around her to make room for my gorgeous cousin, her future sister-in-law. My cousin has grown up in Paterson and is in her last year of high school. She doesn't have a trace of what Puerto Ricans call "la mancha" (literally, the stain: the mark of the new immigrant—something about the posture, the voice, or the humble demeanor making it obvious to everyone that that person has just arrived on the mainland; has not yet acquired the polished look of the city dweller). My cousin is wearing a tight red-sequined cocktail dress. Her brown hair has been lightened with peroxide around the bangs, and she is holding a cigarette very expertly between her fingers, bringing it up to her mouth in a sensuous arc of her arm to her as she talks animatedly with my mother, who has come to sit between the two women, both only a few years younger than herself. My mother is somewhere halfway between the poles they represent in our culture.

It became my father's obsession to get out of the barrio, and thus we were never permitted to form bonds with the place or with the people who lived there. Yet the building was a comfort to my mother, who never got over yearning for *la isla*. She felt surrounded by her language: the walls were thin, and voices speaking and arguing in Spanish could be heard all day. *Salsas* blasted out of radios turned on early in the morning and left on for company. Women seemed to cook rice and beans perpetually—the strong aroma of red kidney beans boiling permeated the hallways.

Though Father preferred that we do our grocery shopping at the supermarket when he came home on weekend leaves, my mother insisted that she could cook only with products whose labels she could read, and so, during the week, I accompanied her and my little brother to *La Bodega*—a hole-in-the-wall grocery store across the street from *El Building*. There we squeezed down three narrow aisles jammed with various products. Goya and Libby's—those were the trademarks trusted by her Mamá and so my mother bought cans of Goya beans, soups and condiments. She bought little cans of Libby's fruit juices for us. And she bought Colgate toothpaste and Palmolive soap. (The final *e* is pronounced in both those products in Spanish, and for many years I believed that they were manufactured on the Island. I remember my surprise at first hearing a commercial on television for the toothpaste in which Colgate rhymed with "ate.")

We would linger at La Bodega, for it was there that mother breathed best, taking in the familiar aromas of the foods she knew from Mamá's, kitchen, and it was also there that she got to speak to the other women of El Building without violating outright Father's dictates against fraternizing with our neighbors.

But he did his best to make our "assimilation" painless. I can still see him carrying a Christmas tree up several flights of stairs to our apartment, leaving a trail of aromatic pine. He carried it formally, as if it were a flag in a parade. We were the only ones in El Building that I knew of who got presents on both Christmas Day and on *Día de Reyes*, the day when the Three Kings brought gifts to Christ and to Hispanic children.

Our greatest luxury in El Building was having our own television set. It must have been a result of Father's guilt feelings over the isolation he had imposed on us, but we were one of the first families in the barrio to have one. My brother quickly became an avid watcher of Captain Kangaroo and Jungle Jim. I loved all the family series, and by the time I started first grade in school, I could have drawn a map of Middle America as exemplified by the lives of characters in "Father Knows Best," "The Donna Reed Show," "Leave It to Beaver," "My Three Sons," and (my favorite) "Bachelor Father," where John Forsythe treated his adopted teenage daughter like a princess because he was rich and had a Chinese houseboy to do everything for him. Compared to our neighbors in El Building, we were rich. My father's Navy check provided us with financial security and a standard of life that the factory workers envied. The only thing his money could not buy us was a place to live away from the barrio—his greatest wish and Mother's greatest fear.

In the home movie the men are shown next, sitting around a card table set up in one corner of the living room, playing dominoes. The clack of the ivory pieces is a familiar sound. I heard it in many houses on the Island and in many apartments in Paterson. In "Leave It to Beaver," the Cleavers played bridge in every other episode; in my childhood, the men started every social occasion with a hotly debated round of dominoes: the women would sit around and watch, but they never participated in the games.

Here and there you can see a small child. Children were always brought to parties and, whenever they got sleepy, put to bed in the host's bedrooms. Babysitting was a concept unrecognized by the Puerto Rican women I knew: a responsible mother did not leave her children with any stranger. And in a culture where children are not considered intrusive, there is no need to leave the children at home. We went where our mother went.

Of my pre-school years I have only impressions: the sharp bite of the wind in December as we walked with our parents towards the brightly lit stores downtown, how I felt like a stuffed doll in my heavy coat, boots and mittens; how good it was to walk into the five-and-dime and sit at the counter drinking hot chocolate.

On Saturdays our whole family would walk downtown to shop at the big department stores on Broadway. Mother bought all our clothes at Penney's and Sears, and she liked to buy her dresses at the women's specialty shops like Lerner's and Diana's. At some point we would go into Woolworth's and sit at the soda fountain to eat.

We never ran into other Latinos at these stores or eating out, and it became clear to me only years later that the women from El Building shopped mainly at other places—stores owned either by other Puerto Ricans, or by Jewish merchants who had philosophically accepted our presence in the city and decided to make us their good customers, if not neighbors and friends. These establishments were located not downtown, but in the blocks around our street, and they were referred to generically as *La Tienda, El Bazar, La Bodega, La Botánica.* Everyone knew what was meant. These were the stores where your face did not turn a clerk to stone, where your money was as green as anyone else's.

On New Year's Eve we were dressed up like child models in the Sears catalogue—my brother in a miniature man's suit and bow tie, and I in a black patent leather shoes and a frilly dress with several layers of crinolines underneath. My mother wore a bright red dress that night, I remember, and spike heels; her long black hair hung to her waist. Father, who usually wore his Navy uniform during his short visits home, had put on a dark civilian suit for the occasion: we had been invited to his uncle's house for a big celebration. Everyone was excited because my mother's brother, Hernán—a bachelor who could indulge himself in such luxuries—had bought a movie camera which he would be trying out that night.

Even the home movie cannot fill in the sensory details such a gathering left imprinted in a child's brain. The thick sweetness of women's perfume mixing with the ever-present smells of food cooking in the kitchen: meat and plantain *pasteles,* the ubiquitous rice dish made special with pigeon peas—*gandules*—and seasoned with the precious *sofrito* sent up from the island by somebody's mother or smuggled in by a recent traveler. *Sofrito* was one of the items that women hoarded, since it was hardly ever in stock at La Bodega. It was the flavor of Puerto Rico.

The men drank Palo Viejo rum and some of the younger ones got weepy. The first time I saw a grown man cry was at a New Year's Eve party. He had been reminded of his mother by the smells in the kitchen. But what I remember most were the boiled *pasteles*—the plantain or yucca rectangles stuffed with corned beef or other meats, olives, and many other savory ingredients, all wrapped in banana leaves. Everyone had to fish one out with a fork. There was always a "trick" pastel—one without stuffing—and whoever got that one was the "New Year's Fool."

There was also the music. Long-playing albums were treated like precious china in these homes. Mexican recordings were popular, but the songs that brought tears to my mother's eyes were sung by the melancholic Daniel Santos, whose life as a drug addict was the stuff of legend. Felipe Rodríguez was a particular favorite of couples. He sang about faithless women and broken hearted men. There is a snatch of a lyric that has stuck in my mind like a needle on a worn groove: "De piedra ha de ser mi cama, de piedra la cabecera . . . la mujer que a mi me quiera . . . ha de quererme de veras. Ay, Ay, corazón ¿por qué no amas . . . ?" I must have heard it a thousand times since the idea of a bed made of stone, and its connection to love, first troubled me with its disturbing images.

The five-minute home movie ends with people dancing in a circle. The creative filmmaker must have asked them to do that so that they could file past him. It is both comical and sad to watch silent dancing. Since there is no justification for the absurd movements that music provides for some of us, people appear frantic, their faces embarrassingly intense. It's as if you were watching sex. Yet for years, I've had dreams in the form of this home movie. In a recurring scene, familiar faces push themselves forward into my mind's eye, plastering their features into distorted close-ups. And I'm asking them: "Who is she? Who is the woman I don't recognize? Is she an aunt? Somebody's wife? Tell me who she is. Tell me who these people are."

"No, see the beauty mark on her cheek as big as a hill on the lunar landscape of her face—well, that runs in the family. The women on your father's side of the family wrinkle early; it's the price they pay for that fair skin. The young girl with the green stain on her wedding dress is *La Novia*—just up from the island. See, she lowers her eyes as she approaches the camera like she's supposed to. Decent girls never look you directly in the face. *Humilde,* humble, a girl should express humility in all her actions. She will make a good wife for your cousin. He should consider himself lucky to have met her only weeks after she arrived here. If he marries her quickly, she will make him a good Puerto Rican-style wife; but if he waits too long, she will be corrupted by the city, just like your cousin there."

"She means me. I do what I want. This is not some primitive island I live on. Do they expect me to wear a black *mantilla* on my head and go to mass every day? Not me. I'm an American woman and I will do as I please. I can type faster than anyone in my senior class at Central High, and I'm going to be a secretary to a lawyer when I graduate. I can pass for an American girl anywhere—I've tried it—at least for Italian, anyway. I never speak Spanish in public. I hate these parties, but I wanted the dress. I look better than any of these *humildes* here. My life is going to be different. I have an American boyfriend. He is older and has a car. My parents don't know it, but I sneak out of the house late at night sometimes to be with him. If I marry him, even my name will be American. I hate rice and beans. It's what makes these women fat."

"Your *prima* is pregnant by that man she's been sneaking around with. Would I lie to you? I'm your great-uncle's common-law wife—the one he abandoned on the island to marry your cousin's mother. I was not invited to this party, but I came anyway. I came to tell you that story about your cousin that you've always wanted to hear. Remember that comment your mother made to a neighbor that has always haunted you? The only thing you heard was your cousin's name and then you saw your mother pick up your doll from the couch and say: 'It was as big as this doll when they flushed it down the toilet.' This image has bothered you for years, hasn't it? You had nightmares about babies being flushed down the toilet, and you wondered why anyone would do such a horrible thing. You didn't dare ask your mother about it. She would only tell you that you had not heard her right and yell at you for listening to adult conversations. But later, when you were old enough to know about abortions, you suspected. I am here to tell you that you were right. Your cousin was growing an *Americanito* in her belly when this movie was made. Soon after she put something long and pointy into her pretty self, thinking maybe she could get rid of the problem before breakfast and still make it to her first class at the high school. Well, *Niña*, her screams could be heard downtown. Your aunt, her Mamá, who had been a midwife on the Island, managed to pull the little thing out. Yes, they probably flushed it down the toilet, what else could they do with it—give it a Christian burial in a little white casket with blue bows and ribbons? Nobody wanted that baby—least of all the father, a teacher at her school with a house in West Paterson that he was filling with real children, and a wife who was a natural blond.

"Girl, the scandal sent your uncle back to the bottle. And guess where your cousin ended up? Irony of ironies. She was sent to a village in Puerto Rico to live with a relative on her mother's side: a place so far away from civilization that you have to ride a mule to reach it. A real change in scenery. She found a man there. Women like that cannot live without male company. But believe me, the men in Puerto Rico know how to put a saddle on a woman like her. *La Gringa*, they call her. Ha, ha. ha. *La Gringa* is what she always wanted to be . . . "

The old woman's mouth becomes a cavernous black hole I fall into. And as I fall, I can feel the reverberations of her laughter. I hear the echoes of her last mocking words: *La Gringa, La Gringa!* And the conga line keeps moving silently past me. There is no music in my dream for the dancers.

When Odysseus visits Hades asking to see the spirit of his mother, he makes an offering of sacrificial blood, but since all of the souls crave an audience with the living, he has to listen to many of them before he can ask questions. I, too, have to hear the dead and the forgotten speak in my dream. Those who are still part of my life remain silent, going around and around in their dance. The others keep pressing their faces forward to say things about the past.

My father's uncle is last in line. He is dying of alcoholism, shrunken and shriveled like a monkey, his face is a mass of wrinkles and broken arteries. As he comes closer I realize that in his features I can see my whole family. If you were to stretch that rubbery flesh, you could find my father's face, and deep within *that* face—mine. I don't want to look into those eyes ringed in purple. In a few years he will retreat into silence, and take a long, long time to die. *Move back, Tío,* I tell him. *I don't want to hear what you have to say. Give the dancers room to move, soon it will be midnight. Who is the New Year's Fool this time?*

1990

Fred D'Aguiar (B. 1960)

A Son in Shadow

I know nothing about how they meet. She is a schoolgirl. He is at work, probably a government clerk in a building near her school. At the hour when school and office are out for lunch their lives intersect at sandwich counters, soft-drink stands, traffic lights, market squares. Their eyes meet or their bodies collide at one of these food queues. He says something suggestive, complimentary. She suppresses a smile or traps one beneath her hands. He takes this as encouragement (as if any reaction of hers would have been read as anything else) and keeps on talking and following her and probably misses lunch that day. All the while she walks and eats and drinks and soaks up his praise, his sweet body-talk, his erotic chatter and sexy pitter-patter, his idle boasts and ample toasts to his life, his dreams about their future, the world their oyster together.

Am I going too fast on my father's behalf? Should there have been an immediate and cutting rebuttal from her and several days before another meeting? Does he leave work early to catch her at the end of the school day and follow her home just to see where she lives and to extend the

boundaries of their courtship? Throwing it from day to night, from school
to home, from childhood play to serious adult intent? Georgetown's two-
lane streets with trenches on either side mean a mostly single-file walk,
she in front probably looking over her shoulder when he says something
worthy of a glance, or a cut-eye look if his suggestions about her body or
what he will do with it if given half a chance exceed the decorum of the
day—which is what, in mid-Fifties Guyana? From my grandmother it's,
"Don't talk to a man unless you think you're a big woman. Man will bring
you trouble. Man want just one thing from you. Don't listen to he. Don't
get ruined for he. A young lady must cork her ears and keep her eye straight
in front of she when these men start to flock around. The gentleman among
them will find his way to her front door. The gentleman will make contact with the parents first. Woo them first before muttering one thing to
the young lady. Man who go directly to young ladies only want to ruin
them. Don't want to make them into respectable young women—just
whores. Mark my words." My grandfather simply thinks that his little girl
is not ready for the attentions of any man, that none of them is good enough
for his little girl, and so the man who comes to his front door had better
have a good pretext for disturbing his reverie. He had better know something about merchant seamen and the character of the sea, and about
silence—how to keep it so that it signifies authority and dignity, so when
you speak you are heard and your words, every one of them, are rivets. That
man would have to be a genius to get past my grandfather, a genius or a
gentleman. And since my father is neither, it's out of the question that
he'll even use the front door of worship. His route will have to be the yard
and the street of ruination.

So he stands in full view of her house at dusk. It takes a few nights
before her parents realize he is there for their daughter. Then one day her
father comes out and tells him to take his dog behavior to someone else's
front door, and the young man quickly turns on his heel and walks away.
Another time her mother opens the upstairs window and curses him, and
he laughs and saunters off as if her words were a broom gently ushering him
out of her yard. But he returns the next night and the next, and the daughter can't believe his determination. She is embarrassed that her body has
been a magnet for trouble, that she is the cause of the uproar, then angry
with him for his keen regard of her at the expense of her dignity, not to mention his. Neighbors tease her about him. They take pity on the boy, offer
him drinks, some ice-cold mauby, a bite to eat, a dhalpouri, all of which
he declines at first, then dutifully accepts. One neighbor even offers him
a chair, and on one night of pestilential showers an umbrella, since he
does not budge from his spot while all around him people dash for shelter, abandoning a night of liming (loitering) and gaffing (talking) to the per-
sistence and chatter of the rain. Not my father. He stands his ground with
only the back of his right hand up to his brow to shelter his eyes zeroed
in on her house. She steals a glance at him after days of seeming to ignore
the idea of him, though his presence burns brightly inside her heart. She

can't believe his vigilance is for her. She stops to stare in the mirror and for the first time sees her full lips, long straight nose, shoulder-length brunette hair, and dark green eyes with their slight oval shape. Her high cheekbones. Her ears close to her skull. She runs her fingers lightly over these places as if to touch is to believe. Her lips tingle. Her hair shines. Her eyes smile. And she knows from this young man's perseverance that she is beautiful, desirable. She abandons herself to chores, and suppresses a smile and a song. She walks past windows as much as possible to feed the young man's hungry eyes with a morsel of that which he has venerated to the point of indignity. She rewards his eyes by doing unnecessary half-turns at the upstairs window. A flash of clavicle, a hand slowly putting her hair off her face and setting it down behind her ears, and then a smile, a demure glance, her head inclined a little, her eyes raised, her eyelids batted a few times—she performs for him though she feels silly and self-conscious. What else is there for a girl to do? Things befitting a lady that she picked up from the cinema. Not the sauciness of a tramp.

Her mother pulls her by one of those beautiful close-skulled ears from the window and curses her as if she were a ten-cent whore, then throws open the window and hurtles a long list of insults at this tall, silent, rude, good-for-nothing streak of impertinence darkening her street. The father folds his paper and gets up, but by the time he gets to the window the young man is gone.

My mother cries into the basin of dishes. She rubs a saucer so hard that it comes apart in her hands. She is lucky not to cut herself. She will have to answer to her mother for that breakage. In the past it meant at least a few slaps and many minutes of curses for bringing only trouble into her mother's house. Tonight her mother is even angrier. Her father has turned his fury against her for rearing a daughter who is a fool for men. Her mother finds her in the kitchen holding the two pieces of the saucer together and then apart—as if her dread and sheer desire for reparation would magically weld them whole. Her tears fall like drops of solder on that divided saucer. Her mother grabs her hands and strikes her and curses her into her face so that my mother may as well have been standing over a steaming, spluttering pot on the stove. She drops the two pieces of saucer and they become six pieces. Her mother looks down and strides over the mess with threats about what will happen if her feet find a splinter. She cries but finds every piece, and to be sure to get the splinters too she runs her palms along the floor, this way and that, and with her nails she prizes out whatever her hand picks up. She cries herself to sleep.

The next night he is back at his station, and her mother and father, their voices, their words, their blows sound a little farther off, fall a little lighter. His presence, the bare-faced courage of it, becomes a suit of armor for her to don against her mother's and father's attacks. She flies through her chores. She manages under her mother's watchful eye to show both sides of her clavicle, even a little of the definition down the middle of her chest— that small trench her inflated chest digs, which catches the light and takes the breath away, that line drawn from the throat to the uppermost rib exuding warmth and tension, drawing the eyes twenty-five yards away with its radiance in the half-light of dusk, promising more than it can possibly contain, than the eye can hold, and triggering a normal heart into palpitations, a normal breath into shallowness and rapidity.

"Miss Isiah, howdy! How come you house so clean on the west side and not so clean on the east? It lopsided! Dirt have a preference in your house? Or is that saga boy hanging around the west side of your house a dirt repellent?" The gossip must have been rampant in the surrounding yards, yards seemingly designed deliberately so people could see into one another's homes and catch anything spilling out of them—quarrels, courtships, cooking pots, music—and sometimes a clash of houses, a reaction against the claustrophobia of the yard, but not enough yards, not enough room to procure a necessary privacy in order to maintain a badly sought-after dignity—clean, well dressed, head high in the air on Sundays—impossible if the night before there is a fight and everyone hears you beg not to be hit anymore, or else such a stream of obscenities gushes from your mouth that the sealed red lips of Sunday morning just don't cut it.

My father maintains his vigil. Granny threatens to save the contents of her chamber pot from the night before and empty it on his head. Could she have thrown it from her living room window to his shaded spot by the street? Luckily she never tries. She may well be telling him that he doesn't deserve even that amount of attention. If there is any creature lower than a gutter rat—one too low to merit even her worst display of disdain—then he is it. How does my father take that? As a qualification he can do without? How much of that kind of water is he able to let run off his back? Poor man. He has to be in love. He has to be wearing his own suit of armor. Lashed to his mast like Odysseus, he hears the most taunting, terrible things, but what saves him, what restores him, are the ropes, the armor of his love for my mother. Others without this charm would have withered away, but my father smiles and shrugs at the barrage of looks, insults, gestures, silence, loneliness.

Watch his body there under that breadfruit or sapodilla tree; the shine of his status as sentry and his conviction are twin headlights that blind her parents. They redouble their efforts to get rid of his particular glare, then are divided by the sense of his inevitability in their daughter's life. My grandmother stops shouting at him while my grandfather still raises his cane and causes the young man to walk away briskly. My grandmother then opens the windows on the west side, ostensibly to let in the sea breeze but really to exhibit in all those window frames a new and friendly demeanor. My grandfather shouts at her that he can smell the rank intent of that black boy, rotten as a fish market, blowing into his living room and spoiling his thoughts.

But the windows stay open. And my mother at them. With the love Morse of her clavicles and her cleavage as she grows bolder. Smiling, then waving. And no hand in sight to box her or grip her by the ear and draw her away from there. Until one night she boldly leaves the house and goes to him and they talk for five minutes rapidly as if words are about to run out in the Southern Hemisphere.

My father's parents wonder what has become of their Gordon.
"The boy only intend to visit town."
"Town swallow him up."
"No, one woman turn he head, stick it in a butter churn and swill it."
"He lost to us now."
"True."
They say this to each other but hardly speak to him except to make pronouncements on the size of foreign lands.
"Guyana small?"
"What's the boy talking about?"
"Why, England and Scotland combined are the size of Guyana."
"How much room does a man need?"
"That woman take he common sense in a mortar and pound it with a pestle."
The two voices are one voice.
Opportunity is here now. The English are letting go of the reins, a whole new land is about to be fashioned. And he is planning to leave! What kind of woman has done this to our boy? The boy is lost. Talking to him is like harnessing a stubborn donkey. This isn't love but voodoo, obeah, juju, some concoction in a drink, some spell thrown in his locus. A little salt over the shoulder, an iodine shower, a rabbit foot on a string, a duck's bill or snake head dried and deposited into the left trouser pocket, a precious stone, lapis lazuli, amethyst, or anything on the middle finger, a good old reliable crucifix around the neck, made of silver, not gold, and at least one ounce in weight and two inches in diameter. A psalm in papyrus folded in a shirt pocket next to the heart. A blessing from a priest, a breathing of nothing but incense with a towel over the head. A bout of fasting, one night without sleep, a dreamless night, and a dreamless, sleepless, youngest son restored to them. He wants to stay around the house, he shows them why he loves his mummy and poppy and the bounteous land. There is no plan to flee. There is no city woman with his heart in her hand. And his brain is not ablaze in his pants. His head is not an empty, airless room.

They have one cardboard suitcase each, apart from her purse and his envelope tied with a string that contains their passports and tickets, birth certificates, and, for him, a document that he is indeed a clerk with X amount of experience at such-and-such a government office, signed "supervisor"—a worthless piece of shit, of course, in the eyes of any British employer. But for the time being, these little things are emblematic of the towering, staggering optimism that propels them out of Georgetown, Guyana, over the sea to London, England.

So what do they do? My mother is a shy woman. My father, in the two photos I've seen of him, is equally reserved. Not liable to experimentation. The big risk has been taken—that of leaving everything they know for all that is alien to them. My mother knows next to nothing about sex, except perhaps a bit about kissing. My father may have experimented a little, as boys tend to do, but he, too, when faced with the female body, confronts unfamiliar territory. Each burns for the other, enough to pull up roots and take off into the unknown. Yet I want to believe that they improvise around the idea of her purity and respect it until their marriage night. That they keep intact some of the moral system they come from even as they dismantle and ignore every other stricture placed on them by Guyanese society: honor your father and mother; fear a just and loving God; pledge allegiance to the flag; lust is the devil's oxygen. All that circles in their veins.

Over the twelve days at sea they examine what they have left and what they are heading toward. At sea they are in between lives: one life is over but the other has not yet begun. The talking they do on that ship without any duties to perform at all! My mother tells how her father, despite his routine as a merchant seaman, finds time to memorize whole poems by the Victorians: Tennyson, Longfellow, Browning, Jean Ingelow, Arnold, and Hopkins. The sea is his workplace, yet he makes time to do this marvelous thing. She tells how when he comes back to land he gathers them all in the living room and performs "The Charge of the Light Brigade" or "Maud" or "My Last Duchess" or "Fra Lippo Lippi" or "The High Tide on the Coast of Lincolnshire" or "Dover Beach" or "The Kingfisher" or "The Wreck of the Deutschland." He recites these poems to his creole-thinking children, who sit there and marvel at the English they are hearing, not that of the policeman or the teacher or the priest, but even more difficult to decipher, full of twists and impossible turns that throw you off the bicycle of your creole reasoning into the sand. If any of them interrupts my grandfather he stops in midflow, tells them off in creole, and resumes his poem where he left off. When particularly miffed by the disturbance he starts the poem from the beginning again. Does my grandfather recite these verses before or after he gets drunk, swears at the top of his voice, and chases my grandmother around the house with his broad leather belt?

But when my parents are out at sea, they have only the King James Bible in their possession. What they plan and rehearse is every aspect of their new life.

"Children. I want children."

"Me too. Plenty of them."

"I can work between births."

"Yes, both of us. Until we have enough money for a house. Then you can stay home with the kids."

"A nanny. Someone to watch the kids while we work. What kind of house?"

"Three bedrooms. A garden at the front, small, and back, large. A car—a Morris Minor. With all that room in the back for the children and real indicators and a wood finish." Neither has a notebook or dreamed of keeping one. They do not write their thoughts, they utter them. If something is committed to memory, there has to be a quotidian reason for it, apart from bits of the Bible and a few calypsos. My grandfather's labor of love, his settling down with a copy of Palgrave's *Golden Treasury* and memorizing lines that bear no practical relationship to his life, must seem bizarre to his children. Yet by doing so he demonstrates his love of words, their music, the sense of their sound, their approximation to the heartbeat and breath, their holding out of an alternative world to the one surrounding him, their confirmation of a past and another's life and thoughts, their luxury of composition, deliberation, their balancing and rebalancing of a skewered life. I imagine my mother benefits from this exposure in some oblique way—that the Victorians stick to her mental makeup whether she cares for them or not, that a little of them comes off on me in the wash of my gestation in her.

There is an old black-and-white photo (isn't there always?) and fragments of stories about his comings and goings, his carryings-on, as the West Indian speak goes, his mischief. "Look pan that smooth face, them two big, dark eye them, don't they win trust quick-time? Is hard to tie the man with them eye in him head to any woman and she pickney them. He face clean-shaven like he never shave. He curly black hair, dougla-look, but trim neat-neat. The man got topside." His hair, thick and wavy because of the "dougla" mix of East Indian and black, exaggerates an already high forehead. Automatically we credit such an appearance, in the Caribbean and elsewhere, with intelligence—"topside." And a European nose, not broad, with a high bridge (good breeding, though the nostrils flare a bit—sign of a quick temper!). And lips that invite kisses. "They full-full and pout like a kiss with the sound of a kiss way behind, long after that kiss come and gone." He is six feet tall and thin but not skinny, that brand of thin that women refer to as elegant, since the result is long fingers and economic gestures. Notice I say economic and not cheap. A man of few words. A watcher. "But when he relax in company he know and trust, then he the center of wit and idle philosophizing. He shoot back a few rums, neat no chaser, with anyone, and hold his own with men more inclined to gin and tonic. He know when to mind he Ps and Qs and when to gaff in the most lewd Georgetown, rumshop talk with the boys. What chance a sixteen-year-old closeted lady got against such a man, I ask you?"

But most of the puzzle is missing. So I start to draw links from one fragment to the next. He begins to belong—fleetingly, at first—in my life. As a man in poor light seen crossing a road mercifully free of traffic, its tarmacadam steamy with a recent downpour. As a tall, lank body glimpsed ducking under the awning of a shop front and disappearing inside and never emerging no matter how long I wait across the street, watching the door with its reflecting plate glass and listening for the little jingle of the bell that announces the arrival and departure of customers.

Or I cross Blackheath Hill entranced by the urgent belief that my father is in one of the cars speeding up and down it. Blackheath Hill curves a little with a steep gradient—less than one in six in places. It's more of a ski slope than a hill. Cars and trucks, motorbikes and cyclists all come down the road as if in a race for a finish line. Going up it is no different. Vehicles race to the top as if with the fear that their engines might cut off and they will slide back down. I want to be seen by my father. I have to be close to his car so that he does not miss me. I measure the traffic and watch myself get halfway, then, after a pause to allow a couple of cars to pass on their way up, a brisk walk, if I time it right, to allow the rest of the traffic to catch up with me, to see the kid who seems to be in no particular hurry to get out of their way looking at them. I step onto the sidewalk and cherish the breeze of the nearest vehicle at my back—Father, this is your son you have just missed. Isn't he big? Pull over and call his name. Take him in your arms. Admonish him. Remind him that cars can kill and his little body would not survive a hit at these high speeds. Tell him to look for his father under less dangerous circumstances.

I am searching the only way I know how, by rumination, contemplation, conjecture, supposition. I try to fill the gaps, try to piece together the father I never knew. I imagine everything where there is little or nothing to go on. And yet, in going back, in raking up bits and pieces of a shattered and erased existence, I know that I am courting rejection from a source hitherto silent and beyond me. I am conjuring up a father safely out of reach and taking the risk that the lips I help to move, the lungs I force to breathe, will simply say "No." No to everything I ask of them, even the merest crumb of recognition.

"Father." The noun rings hollowly when I say it, my head is empty of any meaning the word might have. I shout it in a dark cave but none of the expected bats come flapping out. Just weaker and weaker divisions of my call. "Father." It is my incantation to bring him back from the grave to the responsibility of his name. But how, when I only know his wife, my mother, and her sudden, moody silence whenever he crops up in conversation?

You ever have anyone sweet-talk you? Fill your ears with their kind of wax, rub that wax with their tongue all over your body with more promises than the promised land itself contains, fill your head with their sweet drone, their buzz that shuts out your parents, friends, your own mind from its own house? That's your father, the bumblebee, paying attention to me.

My sixteenth birthday was a month behind. He was nearly twenty. A big man in my eyes. What did he want with me? A smooth tongue in my ears. Mostly, though, he watched me, my house, my backside when he followed me home from school. His eyes gleamed in the early evening, the whites of his eyes. He stood so still by the side of the road outside my house that he might have been a lamppost, planted there, shining just for me.

My father cursed him, my mother joined in, my sisters laughed at his silence, his stillness. They all said he had to be the most stupid man in

Georgetown, a dunce, a bat in need of a perch, out in the sun too long, sun fry his brain, cat take his tongue, his head empty like a calabash, his tongue cut out, he look like a beggar. They felt sorry for him standing there like a paling, his face a yard long, his tongue a slab of useless plywood in his mouth. "Look what Ingrid gone and bring to the house, shame, dumbness, blackness follow she here to we house to paint shame all over it and us. Go away, black boy, take your dumb misery somewhere else, crawl back to your pen in the country, leave we sister alone, she got more beauty than sense to listen to a fool like you, to let you follow her, to encourage you by not cursing the day you was born and the two people who got together to born you and your people and the whole sorry village you crawl out of to come and plant yourself here in front of we house on William Street, a decent street, in Kitty, in we capital."

I should have thanked my sisters; instead I begged them to leave him alone. Ignore him and he'll go away. My father left the house to get hold of the boy by the scruff of his neck and boot his backside out of Kitty, but he ran off when my father appeared in the door frame. With the light of the house behind him and casting a long, dark shadow, he must have looked twice his size and in no mood to bargain. Your father sprinted away, melting into the darkness. I watched for his return by checking that the windows I'd bolted earlier really were bolted, convincing myself that I had overlooked one of them, using my hands to feel the latch as I searched the street for him. But he was gone for the night. My knight. Shining eyes for armor.

My mother cursed him from the living room window, flung it open and pointed at him and with her tongue reduced him to a pile of rubble and scattered that rubble over a wide area then picked her way through the strewn wreckage to make sure her destruction was complete: "Country boy, what you want with my daughter? What make you think you man enough for her? What you got between your legs that give you the right to plant yourself in front of my house? What kind of blight you is? You fungus!"

As she cursed him and he retreated from the house sheepishly, she watched her husband for approval. These were mild curses for her, dutiful curses, a warm-up. When she really got going her face reddened and her left arm carved up the air in front of her as if it were the meat of her opponent being dissected into bite-size bits. That's how I knew she was searching for a way to help me but hadn't yet found it. Not as long as my father was at home. Soon he would be at sea, away for weeks, and things would be different.

That is, if my onlooker, my remote watcher, my far-off admirer wasn't scared off forever. And what if he was? Then he didn't deserve me in the first place. If he couldn't take a few curses he wasn't good for anything. If I wasn't worth taking a few curses for . . . well, I didn't want a man who didn't think I was worth taking a few curses for . . . well, I loved him for coming back night after night when all he got from me was a glance at the window. Sometimes less than a glance. Just me passing across the window frame as I dashed from chore to chore under four baleful eyes.

It seemed like he was saving all his breath and words for when he could be alone with me. Then he turned on the bumblebee of himself and I was the hapless flower of his attentions. He told me about my skin that it was silk, that all the colors of the rainbow put together still didn't come close to my beautiful skin. That my face, my eyes, my mouth, my nose, the tip of my nose, my ears, my fingertips, each was a precious jewel, precious stone. He likened the rest of me to things I had read about but had never seen, had dreamed about but had never dreamed I would see: dandelions, apples, snow, spring in England's shires, the white cliffs of Dover. In his eyes my body, me, was everything I dreamed of becoming.

That was your father before any of you were a twinkle in his eye. More accurately, that was my lover and then my husband. Your father was a different man altogether. Suddenly a stranger occupied my bed. His tongue now turned to wood. All the laughter of my sisters, the half-hearted curses of my mother, my father's promise of blue misery, all came true in this strange man, this father, this latter-day husband and lover.

I saw the change in him. My hands were full with you children. He went out of reach. He cradled you as if he didn't know which side was up, which down. He held you at arm's length to avoid the tar and feathers of you babies. Soon I earned the same treatment, but if you children were tar and feathers I was refuse. His face creased when he came near me. What had become of my silk skin? My precious features disappeared into my face, earning neither praise nor blame—just his silence, his wooden tongue, and that bad-smell look of his. I kept quiet for as long as I could. I watched him retreat from all of us, hoping he'd reel himself back in since the line between us was strong and I thought unbreakable; but no. I had to shout to get him to hear me. I shouted like my mother standing at the upstairs window to some rude stranger in the street twenty-five yards away. I sounded like my father filling the door frame. My jeering sisters insinuated their way into my voice. And your father simply kept walking away.

Believe me, I pulled my hair and beat the ground with my hands and feet to get at him in my head and in the ground he walked on that I worshiped. Hadn't he delivered England to me and all the seasons of England, all England's shires and the fog he'd left out of his serenades, no doubt just to keep some surprise in store for me? The first morning I opened the door that autumn and shouted, "Fire!" when I saw all that smoke, thinking the whole street on fire, all the streets, London burning, and slammed the door and ran into his arms and his laughter, and he took me out into it in my nightdress, he in his pajamas, and all the time I followed him, not ashamed to be seen outside in my thin, flimsy nylon (if anyone could see through that blanket) because he was in his pajamas, the blue, striped ones, and his voice, his sweet drone, told me it was fine, this smoke without fire was fine, "This is fog."

He walked away and everything started to be erased by that fog. That smoke without fire crossed the ocean into my past and obliterated Kitty,

Georgetown, the house on William Street, everything he had touched, every place I had known him in. I swallowed that fog. It poured into my ears, nose, eyes, mouth. He was gone. I got a chest pain and breathlessness that made me panic. There wasn't just me. There were you children. I had to breathe for you children. The pain in my chest that was your father had to be plucked out, otherwise I too would be lost to you all, and to myself.

The first time I see him is the last time I see him. I can't wait to get to the front of the queue to have him all to myself. When I get there my eyes travel up and down his body. From those few gray hairs that decorate his temples and his forehead and his nose to the cuffs at his ankles and sparkling black shoes. He wears a black suit, a double-breasted number with three brass buttons on the cuff of each sleeve. He lies on his back with his hands clasped over his flat stomach. There is too much powder on his face. Let's get out of this mournful place, Dad. We have a lot of catching up to do. He has the rare look—of holding his breath, of not breathing, in between inhaling and exhaling—that exquisitely beautiful corpses capture. For a moment after I invite him to leave with me, I expect his chest to inflate, his lids to open, and those clasped hands to unfold and pull him upright into a sitting position as if he really were just napping because he has dressed way too early for the ball.

There are myths about this sort of thing. Father enslaves son. Son hates father, bides his time, waits for the strong father to weaken. Son pounces one day, pounces hard and definite, and the father is overwhelmed, broken, destroyed with hardly any resistance, except that of surprise and then resignation. Son washes his hands but finds he is washing hands that are not bloodstained, not marked or blemished in any way. He is simply scrubbing hands that no longer belong to him—they are his father's hands, attached to his arms, his shoulders, his body. He has removed a shadow all the more to see unencumbered the father in himself. There is the widow he has made of his mother. He cannot love her as his father might. While his father lived he thought he could. The moment his father expired he knew his mother would remain unloved.

I alight too soon from a number 53 bus on Blackheath Hill, disembark while the bus is moving, and stumble, trip from two legs onto all fours, hands like feet, transforming, sprouting more limbs, becoming a spider and breaking my fall. That same fall is now a tumble, a dozen somersaults that end with me standing upright and quite still on two legs with the other limbs dangling. Onlookers, who fully expected disaster, applaud. I walk back up the hill to the block of council flats as a man might, upright, on two legs. My other limbs dangle, swing as if they are two hands. Some days I will be out of breath, I will gasp and exhale, and the cloud before me will not be my winter's breath but the silken strands of a web, or worse, fire. Other days I might look at a bed of geraniums planted on the council estate and turn all their numberless petals into stone. A diamond held between my thumb and index finger crumbles in this mood, in this light, like the powdery wings of a butterfly.

I stare out of an apartment on the twenty-fourth floor of a tower block overlooking the nut-brown Thames. That wasp on the window-pane nibbling up and down the glass for a pore to exit through, back into the air and heat, tries to sting what it can feel but cannot see. My father is the window. I am the wasp. Sometimes a helping hand comes along and lifts the window, and the wasp slides out. Other times a shadow descends, there is a displacement of air, and it is the last thing the wasp knows. Which of those times is this? I want to know. I don't want to know. I am not nibbling nor trying to sting. I am kissing, repeatedly, rapidly, the featureless face of my father. It feels like summer light. It reflects a garden. Whose is that interfering hand? Why that interrupting shadow? My child's hand. My child's shadow. My son or my father? My son and my father. Two sons, two fathers. Yet three people. We walk behind a father's name, shoulder a father's memory. Wear another's walk, another's gait. Wait for what has happened to their bodies, the same scars, maladies, aches, to surface in ours.

I want to shed my skin. Walk away from my shadow. Leave my name in a place I cannot return to. To be nameless, bodiless. To swim to Wallace Stevens's Key West, which is shoreless, horizonless. Blackheath Hill becomes Auden's Bristol Street, an occasion for wonder and lament. Blackheath at 5:45 A.M. on a foggy winter morning becomes Peckham Rye. There are no trees on Blackheath, but angels hang in the air if only Blake were there to see them. On the twenty-fourth floor towering above the Thames, water, not land, surrounds me. Everything seems to rise out of that water. Look up at ambling clouds and the tower betrays its drift out to sea.

1999

Edwidge Danticat (B. 1969)

Westbury Court

When I was fourteen years old, we lived in a six-story brick building in a cul-de-sac off of Flatbush Avenue, in Brooklyn, called Westbury Court. Beneath the building ran a subway station through which rattled the D, M, and Q trains every fifteen minutes or so. Though there was graffiti on most of the walls of Westbury Court, and hills of trash piled up outside, and though the elevator wasn't always there when we opened the door to step inside and the heat and hot water weren't always on, I never dreamed of leaving Westbury Court until the year of the fire.

I was watching television one afternoon when the fire began. I loved television then, especially the afternoon soap operas, my favorite of which was *General Hospital.* I would bolt out of my last high school class every day, pick up my youngest brother, Karl, from day care, and watch *General Hospital* with him on my lap while doing my homework during the commercials. My other two brothers, André and Kelly, would later join us in the apartment, but they preferred to watch cartoons in the back bedroom.

One afternoon while *General Hospital* and afternoon cartoons were on, a fire started in apartment 6E, across the hall. There in that apartment lived our new neighbors, an African-American mother and her two boys. We didn't know the name of the mother, or the names and ages of her boys, but I venture to guess that they were around five and ten years old.

I didn't know a fire had started until two masked, burly firemen came knocking on our door. My brothers and I rushed out into the hallway filled with smoke and were quickly escorted down to the first floor by some other firemen already on our floor. While we ran by, the door to apartment 6E had already been knocked over by the fire squad and inside was filled with bright flames and murky smoke.

All of the tenants of the building who were home at that time were crowded on the sidewalk outside. My brothers and I, it seemed, were the last to be evacuated. Clutching my brothers' hands, I wondered if I had remembered to lock our apartment door. Was there anything valuable we could have taken?

An ambulance screeched to a stop in front of the building, and the two firemen who had knocked on our door came out carrying the pliant and lifeless bodies of the two children from across the hall. Their mother jumped out of the crowd and ran toward them, screaming, "My babies—not my babies," as the children were lowered into the back of the ambulance and transferred into the arms of the emergency medical personnel. The fire was started by the two boys, after their mother had stepped out to pick up some groceries at the supermarket down the street. They had been playing with matches.

(Later my mother would tell us, "See, this is what happens to children who play with matches. Sometimes it is too late to say, 'I shouldn't have.'" My brother Kelly, who was fascinated with fire and liked to hold up a match to the middle of his palm until the light fizzled out, gave up this party trick after the fire.)

We were quiet that afternoon when both our parents came home. We were the closest to the fire in the building, and the most religious of our parents' friends saw it as a miracle that we had escaped safe and sound. When my mother asked how come I, the oldest one, hadn't heard the children scream or hadn't smelled the smoke coming from across the hall, I confessed that I had been watching *General Hospital* and was too consumed in the intricate plot.

(After the fire, my mother had us stay with a family on the second floor for a few months, after school. I felt better not having to be wholly responsible for myself and my brothers, in case something like that fire should ever happen again.)

The apartment across the hall stayed empty for a long time, and whenever I walked past it, a piece of its inner skeleton would squeak, and occasionally burnt wood that might have been hanging by a fragile singed thread would crash down and cause a domino effect of further ruptures, unleashed like those children's last cries, which I had not heard because I had been so wrapped up in the made-up drama of a world where, even though the adults' lives were often in turmoil, the children came home to the welcoming arms of waiting mommies and nannies who served them freshly baked cookies on porcelain plates and helped them to remove their mud-soaked boots, if it was raining, lest they soil the lily-white carpets. But should their boots accidentally sully the carpet, or should their bright yellow raincoats inadvertently drip on the sparkling linoleum, there would be a remedy for that as well. And if their house should ever catch fire, a smart dog or a good neighbor would rescue them just in time, and the fire trucks would come right quick because some attentive neighbor would call them.

Through the trail of voices that came up to comfort us, I heard that the children's mother would be prosecuted for negligence and child abandonment. I couldn't help but wonder, would our parents have suffered the same fate had it been my brothers and me who were killed in the fire?

When they began to repair the apartment across the hall, I would occasionally sneak out to watch the workmen. They were shelling the inside of the apartment and replacing everything from the bedroom closets to the kitchen floors. I never saw the mother of the dead boys again and never heard anything of her fate.

A year later, after the apartment was well polished and painted, two blind Haitian brothers and their sister moved in. They were all musicians and were part of a group called les Frères Parent, the Parent Brothers. Once my parents allowed my brothers and me to come home from school to our apartment, I would always listen carefully for our new tenants, so I'd be the first to know if anything went awry.

What I heard coming from the apartment soon after they moved in was music, "engagé" music, which the brothers were composing to protest against the dictatorship in Haiti, from which they had fled. The Parent Brothers and their sister, Lydie, did nothing but rehearse a cappella most days when they were not receiving religious and political leaders from Haiti and from the Haitian community in New York.

The same year after the fire, a cabdriver who lived down the hall in 6J was killed on a night shift in Manhattan; a good friend of my father's, a man who gave great Sunday afternoon parties in 6F, died of cirrhosis of the liver. One day while my brothers and I were at school and my parents were at work, someone came into our apartment through our fire escape and stole my father's expensive camera. That same year a Nigerian immigrant was shot and killed in front of the building across the street. To appease us, my mother said, "Nothing like that ever happens out of the blue. He was in a fight with someone." It was too troublesome for her to acknowledge that people could die randomly, senselessly, at Westbury Court or anywhere else.

Every day on my way back from school, I hurried past the flowers and candles piled in front of the spot where the Nigerian, whose name I didn't know, had been murdered. Still I never thought I was living in a violent place. It was an elevated castle above a clattering train tunnel, a blind alley where children from our building and the building across the street had erected a common basketball court for hot summer afternoon games, an urban yellow brick road where hopscotch squares dotted the sidewalk next to burned-out, abandoned cars. It was home.

My family and I moved out of Westbury Court three years after the fire. Every once in a while, though, the place came up in conversation, linked to either a joyous or a painful memory. One of the girls who had scalded her legs while boiling a pot of water for her bath during one of those no-heat days got married last year. After the burglar had broken into the house and taken my father's camera, my father—an amateur photography buff—never took another picture.

My family and I often reminisce about the Parent Brothers when we see them in Haitian newspapers or on television; we brag that we knew them when, before one of the brothers became a senator in Haiti and the sister, Lydie, became mayor of one of the better-off Haitian suburbs, Pétion-Ville. We never talk about the lost children.

Even now, I question what I remember about the children. Did they really die? Or did their mother simply move away with them after the fire? Maybe they were not even boys at all. Maybe they were two girls. Or one boy and one girl. Or maybe I am struggling to phase them out of my memory altogether. Not just them, but the fear that their destiny could have so easily been mine and my brothers'.

A few months ago, I asked my mother, "Do you remember the children and the fire at Westbury Court?"

Without missing a flutter of my breath, my mother replied, "Oh those children, those poor children, their poor mother. Sometimes it is too late to say, 'I shouldn't have.'"

1999

Rhina P. Espaillat (B. 1932)

Bilingual/Bilingüe

Recent interest in the phenomenon known as "Spanglish" has led me to reexamine my own experience as a writer who works chiefly in her second language, and especially to recall my father's inflexible rule against the mixing of languages. In fact, no English was allowed in that midtown Manhattan apartment that became home after my arrival in New York in 1939. My father read the daily paper in English, taught himself to follow disturbing events in Europe through the medium of English-language radio, and even taught me to read the daily comic strips, in an effort to speed my learning of the language he knew I would need. But that necessary language was banished from family conversation: it was the medium of the outer world, beyond the door; inside, among ourselves, only Spanish was permitted, and it had to be pure, grammatical, unadulterated Spanish.

At the age of seven, however, nothing seems more important than communicating with classmates and neighborhood children. For my mother, too, the new language was a way out of isolation, a means to deal with the larger world and with those American women for whom she sewed. But my father, a political exile waiting for changes in our native country, had different priorities: he lived in the hope of return, and believed that the new home, the new speech, were temporary. His theory was simple: if it could be said at all, it could be said best in the language of those authors whose words were the core of his education. But his insistence on pure Spanish made it difficult, sometimes impossible, to bring home and share the jokes of friends, puns, pop lyrics, and other staples of seven-year-old conversation. Table talk sometimes ended with tears or sullen silence.

And yet, despite the friction it caused from time to time, my native language was also a source of comfort—the reading that I loved, intimacy within the family, and a peculiar auditory delight best described as echoes in the mind. I learned early to relish words as counters in a game that could turn suddenly serious without losing the quality of play, and to value their sound as a meaning behind their meaning.

Nostalgia, a confusion of identity, the fear that if the native language is lost the self will somehow be altered forever: all are part of the subtle flavor of immigrant life, as well as the awareness that one owes gratitude to strangers for acts of communication that used to be simple and once imposed no such debt.

Memory, folklore, and food all become part of the receding landscape that language sets out to preserve. Guilt, too, adds to the mix, the suspicion that to love the second language too much is to betray those ancestors who spoke the first and could not communicate with us in the vocabulary of our education, our new thoughts. And finally, a sense of grievance and loss may spur hostility toward the new language and those who speak it, as if the common speech of the perceived majority could weld together a disparate population into a huge, monolithic, and threatening Other. That Other is then assigned traits and habits that preclude sympathy and mold "Us" into a unity whose cohesiveness gives comfort.

Luckily, there is another side to bilingualism: curiosity about the Other may be as natural and pervasive as group loyalty. If it weren't, travel, foreign residence, and intermarriage would be less common than they are. For some bilingual writers, the Other—and the language he speaks—are appealing. Some acknowledge and celebrate the tendency of languages to borrow from each other and produce something different in the process. That is, in part, the tendency that has given rise to "Spanglish."

It's dangerous, however, to accept the inevitable melding of languages over time as a justification for speaking, in the short run, a mix that impoverishes both languages by allowing words in one to drive out perfectly good equivalent words in the other. The habitual speaker of such a mix ends by speaking not two, or even one complete language, but fragments of two that are no longer capable of standing alone or serving the speaker well with any larger audience. As a literary device with limited appeal and durability, "Spanglish," like other such blends, is expressive and fresh. But as a substitute for genuine bilinguality—the cultivation and preservation of two languages—I suspect it represents a danger to the advancement of foreign speakers, and a loss to both cultures. My father sensed as much in 1939, and stubbornly preserved my native language for me, through his insistence that I be truly bilingual rather than a traveler across boundaries that "Spanglish" has made all too permeable.

My father, who never learned to think in English, was persuaded that the words of his own language were the "true" names for things in the world. But for me that link between fact and word was broken, as it is for many who grow up bilingual. Having been taught to love words and take them seriously as reflections of reality, I felt it a loss to learn that, in fact, words are arbitrary, man-made, no more permanent than clothing: somewhere under all of them reality is naked.

Disconcerting as it is, however, to lose the security of words that are perceived as single keys to what they unlock, it is also exhilarating to see oneself as the maker of those words, even if they are now impermanent, provisional artifacts that have value for us only because they're ours. Anybody who has ever gone hunting for that one right and elusive word knows what bilingualism feels like, even if he's never left his native country or learned a word in any language but his own. There is a sense in which every poet is bilingual, and those of us who are more overtly so are only living metaphors for the condition that applies to us all. We use a language that seems deceptively like the language of the people around us, but isn't quite. The words are the same, but the weight we give them, the connections we find among them, the criteria we use to choose this one rather than that one, are our own.

At a recent poetry reading I closed with a poem in Spanish, and a member of the English-speaking audience approached me afterward to remark how moved she had been by that poem, and how she wished I had read others.

"Where did you learn Spanish?" I asked.

"I don't speak any Spanish," she replied. "What I understood was the music of what you read."

It occurred to me, during our subsequent conversation, that poetry may be precisely what is almost lost, not in translation, but in the wording, the transit from experience to paper. If we succeed in salvaging anything, maybe it is most often in the music, the formal elements of poetry that do travel from language to language, as the formal music of classic Spanish poetry my father loved followed me into English and draws me, to this day, to poems that are patterned and rich and playful.

It's occurred to me since that conversation that a poem in Spanish may have more in common with a poem in English—or any other language— than with a grocery list, say, or a piece of technical writing that happens to use Spanish words. There is something in poetry that transcends specific language, that makes it possible for transplanted people like me to recognize the songs of the Other as his own even before he understands them fully. Poetry may be used to draw very small circles around itself, identifying its speaker as a member of a narrowly delineated group and looking at "outsiders" with eyes that discern less and less detail as distance increases. But it may also be used to draw very large circles, circles that will draw in rather than exclude, as in Edwin Markham's apt four-line metaphor titled "Outwitted":

> He drew a circle that shut me out—
> Heretic, rebel, a thing to flout.
> But Love and I had the wit to win:
> We drew a circle that shut him in.

1998

Shirley Geok-Lin Lim (b. 1944)

Splendor and Squalor

From *Among the White Moon Faces: An Asian-American Memoir of Homelands*

Years later, I lie awake
In the deep enclosing heart of a household.
Years later than in a crib
Floating among the white moon faces that beam and grasp.

Years later, flecking the eyes,
Faces like spheres wheeling, savoring myself.
Years later, I awake to see
Dust falling in the dark, in the house.

I know no other childhood than mine, and that I had left secret as something both treasured, the one talent that my parents unwittingly have provided me, and shameful, how these same parents have as unwittingly mutilated me. Moving myself from Malacca, a small town two degrees north of the equator, to New England, then to Brooklyn and to the rich New York suburb of Westchester County, and now to Southern California, I have attempted to move myself as far away from destitution as an ordinary human creature can. In the move from hunger to plenty, poverty to comfort, I have become transformed, and yet have remained a renegade. The unmovable self situated in the quicksand of memory, like those primeval creatures fixed in tar pits, that childhood twelve thousand miles and four decades away, is a fugitive presence which has not yet fossilized. Buried in the details of an American career, my life as a non-American persists, a parallel universe played out in dreams, in journeys home to Malaysia and Singapore, and in a continuous undercurrent of feelings directed to people I have known, feared, loved, and deserted for this American success.

The irony about a certain kind of immigrant is how little she can enjoy of the very things she chases. Even as she runs away from her first life, this other life that begins to accrue around her remains oddly secondary, unrooted in the sensuality of infancy and the intensities of first memory. Before I could learn to love America, I had to learn to love the land of unconditional choice. The searing light of necessity includes my mother and father, characters whom I never would have chosen had I choice over my history.

Before there is memory of speech, there is memory of the senses. Cold water from a giant tap running down an open drain that is greenish slime under my naked feet. My mother's hands are soaping my straight brown body. I am three. My trunk is neither skinny nor chubby. It runs in a smooth curve to disappear in a small cleft between my two legs. I am laughing as her large palms slide over my soapy skin which offers her no resistance, which slips out of her hands even as she tries to grasp me. I do not see her face, only her square body seated on a short stool and a flowered *samfoo* that is soaked in patches.

The same open area, the same large green-brass tap above my head, only this time I am crying. My anus hurts me. My mother is whittling a sliver of soap. I watch the white piece of Lifebuoy grow sharper and sharper, like a splinter, a thorn, a needle. She makes me squat down, bare-assed, pushes my body forward, and inserts the sliver up my anus. The soap is soft, it squishes, but it goes up and hurts. This is my mother's cure for constipation. I cry but I do not resist her. I do not slide away but tense and take in the thorn. I have learned to obey my mother.

Both scenes occur in my grandfather's house. The house is full of the children who belong to his sons. It is already overflowing with my brothers and cousins. But all I remember of this early childhood are my aunts. They bulk like shadows to the pre-verbal child, very real and scary. One aunt is tall and stringy; her face, all planes and bolted bones, stares and scowls, her voice a loud screech. Another aunt is round; everything about her curves and presses out; her chest is a cushion, her stomach a ball, her face a full moon, and her smile grows larger and larger like a mouth that will eat you. I am afraid of them both. They wear black trousers and dull sateen *samfoo* tops, gray embossed with silver or light blue filigree. Their hair is very black, oiled to a high sheen, pulled tight off their faces into round buns, secured by long elaborate gold pins.

I do not remember my mother's figure in this infant's memory of my grandfather's house. She is an outsider, and silent in their presence. This is not her house as it is their house, although my father is a son here. In my infant memory my mother is never a Chinese woman the way my aunts, speaking in Hokkien, will always be Chinese.

Hokkien, a version of Southern Xiamen, the Min dialect from the Fujien Province, is the harsh voluble dialect of the Nanyang, the South Seas Chinese, directive, scolding, a public communication of internal states that by being spoken must be taken in by all. I heard Hokkien as an infant and resisted it, because my mother did not speak it to me. This language of the South Chinese people will always be an ambivalent language for me, calling into question the notion of a mother tongue tied to a racial origin. As a child of a Hokkien community, I should have felt that propulsive abrasive dialect in my genes. Instead, when I speak Hokkien, it is at the level of a five-year-old, the age at which I moved out of my grandfather's house on Heeren Street into my father's shoe store on Kampong Pantai. Hokkien remains for me an imperfectly learned system of grammar comprised of the reduced nouns and verbs of a child's necessary society—*chia puai* (eat rice); *ai koon* (want to sleep); *kwah* (cold); *ai kehi* (want to go); *pai* (bad); *bai-bai* (pray); *baba* (father); *mahmah* (mother). It remains at a more powerful level a language of exclusion, the speech act which disowns me in my very place of birth.

Chinese-speaking Malayans called me a "Kelangkia-kwei,"—or a Malay devil—because I could not or would not speak Hokkien. Instead I spoke Malay, my mother's language. My peranakan mother had nursed me in Malay, the language of assimilated Chinese who had lived in the peninsula, jutting southeast of Asia, since the first Chinese contact with the Malacca Sultanate in the fifteenth century. And once I was six and in a British school, I would speak chiefly English, in which I became "fluent," like a drop of rain returning to a river, or a fish thrown back into a sea.

Hokkien had never been a language of familiarity, affection, and home for me. Like the South Seas Chinese paternal house I was born in, Hokkien laid out a foreign territory, for I was of the South Seas Chinese but not one of them. Hokkien was the sounds of strong shadowy women, women who circled but did not welcome me, while in my grandfather's house my enclosing mother dimmed into two hands washing, holding, penetrating me, neither a face nor a shadow.

Then, when Baba opened his shoe shop, we had our own house. Here, in my memory, my mother becomes a woman. She chattered to us, her two sons, her daughter, her baby boy, in Malay. I do not remember moving to the shophouse on Kampong Pantai. It was as if I woke up from a dark and discordant infancy into a world of pleasure in which my mother was the major agent.

In my mother's presence there is memory of talk, not labor. Mother ordered my brothers around. She scolded us for getting ourselves wet or dirty or tired. She joked with her sisters on the manners, the bodies, and crude lusts of their acquaintances. Her *baba* Malay—the Malay spoken by assimilated Chinese—the idiomatic turns of her ethnic identity, was a waterfall whose drops showered me with sensuous music. She was funny, knowing, elegantly obscene. I remember the rhythms of her phrasings, gentle drumbeats that ended with a mocking laugh, short scolds that faded away, assuming assent.

In my mother's house, she was a *nonya,* a Malayan-native Chinese woman, whose voice ran soft-accented, filled with exclamations. Scatological phrases, wickedly funny and nasty comments on neighbors and relatives, numerous commands, an infinite list of do's and don'ts, her Malay speech was all social, all appearance and lively, never solo, always interweaving among familiar partners. How could she have talked alone to herself in *baba* speech? It would have been impossible. Even when alone, it would be speech addressed to kin, a form of *sembahyang,* prayers before the ancestral altar, to dead yet watchful fathers and mothers.

I listened and must have chattered in response. From a very early age, I was called teasingly by family and strangers a *manek manek,* a gossipy grandmother or an elderly woman who loves talk, her own and others'. I must have chattered in Malay, for just as the Hokkien-speaking elders named me as a Malay, so the Malay-speakers placed me as an ancestral talker. But I have little memory of what I said or of this precocious childhood tongue I associate with my mother's house. In memory it is my mother's speech but not mine; it was of my childhood but I do not speak it now.

My mother wore *nonya* clothing, the *sarong kebaya.* Her stiffly starched sarongs wrapped elegantly around her waist fell with two pleats in the front. Her sarongs were gold and brown, purple and brown, emerald and brown, crimson and brown, sky blue and brown. Ironed till they gleamed, they were stacked in the armoire like a queen's treasure. She wore white lace chemises under her *kebaya* tops. The breast-hugging, waist-nipping *kebayas* were of transparent material, the most expensive georgette. They were pale blue, mauve, lavender, white, yellow-green, pricked and patterned with little flowers or tiny geometric designs. They were closed in the front by triple pins or brooches, and these borders were always elaborately worked with a needle into delicate lacy designs, like scallops and shell shapes, or leaf and vine patterns. Women with time on their hands, needing food and money, meticulously picked the fragile threads apart and reworked them into an imitation of the free natural world around them. Each *kebaya* was a woman's work of art, and my mother changed her *sarong kebaya* daily as a curator changes an exhibition.

She was good-humored in this act, surrounded by many strange containers. One was filled with sweet-smelling talc and a pink powder puff like a rose that she dipped into white powder and lavishly daubed over her half-dressed body, under her armpits, around her neck and chest, and quickly dabbed between her legs like a furtive signal. Another was a blue-colored jar filled with a sugary white cream. She took a two-fingertip scoop of the shiny cream and rubbed it over her face, a face that I can still see, pale, smooth, and unmarred. She polished her clear fair face with this cream, over her forehead, her gently rounded cheeks, and the sloping chin. Her face shone like an angel's streaked with silver, and when she wiped the silvery streaks off, the skin glowed faintly like a sweet fruit. Later, I would discover that the blue jar was Pond's Cold Cream, the tub of powder, Yardley Talc. She was immersed in Western beauty, a Jean Harlow on the banks of a slowly silting Malacca River, born into a world history she did not understand.

More than store-bought magic, she was also my mother of peranakan female power. Like a native goddess she presided over an extended family— younger sisters Amy and Lei came to live with her, and younger brothers Ling, Charlie, and Mun passed through her home on their way to adult separation. She was surrounded by rituals that worshipped her being. The ritual of the peranakan female face began with white refined rice ground to a fine powder. This *badak* was dampened with rainwater to form a smooth paste that my mother smeared over her face. The rice paste caked and dried like a crackled crepe. It filled in the fine pores on her nose and cheeks, the tiny lines around her eyes and forehead; it turned gritty like bleached beach sand. Washed away, it left her face glimmering like a piece of new silk.

My mother was the goddess of smells. She perfumed herself with eau de cologne from cut-glass bottles that were imported from the Rhine Valley in Germany. She knotted one end of a sheer cambric handkerchief and sprinkled the cologne on the knot. I kept the handkerchief in my plaid smock pocket and took it out throughout the day to sniff the knotted end. The scent was intoxicatingly fresh. It was my mother's Hollywood smell.

Some days she dressed us both elaborately, herself in a golden brown sarong and gleaming puce *kebaya,* and I in a three-tiered, ruffled, and sashed organdy dress with a gold-threaded scarlet ribbon in my hair. We rode in a trishaw to a plain structure, its doorway flanked by banana palms. The walled courtyard led to an interior room; through the door there was darkness and a flickering oil lamp. Gradually my eyes adjusted to the darkness. The small room was empty except for an altar facing the door, and on the altar was a *lingam,* a black stone stump garlanded with wreaths of orange marigolds and white jasmines. A man as dark as the room, bare-chested and with a white cotton *dhoti* wrapped around his hips, his face marked with lines of ash, a thumbprint of red in the center of his forehead, took my mother's money. He gave her a small comb of *pisang emas*—perhaps ten to fifteen finger-sized bananas—and a clump of incense like a pebble of gray rock candy.

Later that evening she burned the incense on a brass saucer. As the smoke rose with a pleasantly acrid scent she walked from room to room, waving the saucer till the entire house was impregnated with smoke, the smell of frankincense, and the spirits that banish fear, pain, and illness. The gray smoke wavered across the rooms and shrouded me. My mother worked with deities to cast out the envious eye, the ill-wisher, and the intruding hungry ghosts attracted by the plenty in her home. This burning incense was the smell of my mother's faith.

My mother lived through her senses. I do not believe she was capable of thinking abstractly. Her actions even late in her life were driven by needs—for food, shelter, security, affection. When needy mothers love, there is a shameful nakedness about their emotions, a return to flagrant self-love, that embarrasses. Their heat is distancing: we are driven to reject them before they can eat us up. Because my mother abandoned us when I was eight, I was never certain that she loved her children till later in life, when she needed us. Living through her senses, she could not lie about her needs. In this way, my mother's actions were always honest.

When she lived with us, my mother did not read except for magazines on Hollywood stars. Father was enthralled by the movies that frequently came into our town, and he bought expensive copies of *Silver Screen* and *Motion Picture,* fan magazines imported from wildly distant cities like

Chicago and Burbank. I grew up in the company of glossy photographs of Leslie Caron, Doris Day, Fred Astaire, Ginger Rogers, Douglas Fairbanks, even Roy Rogers and Dale Evans, and those magnificent creatures Trigger, Lassie, and Francis the Talking Mule.

Other than these Hollywood familiars, we had few photographs and no pictures hanging on our walls. Framed certificates testifying to Father's success in passing the Senior Cambridge Examinations and in achieving the status of a Queen's Scout hung along the upper floor's corridors. So Father's identity was literally imprinted on the walls of our home. But Emak's presence wavered in our senses, entangled among our synapses, roused involuntarily by a scent from a perfume counter, a passing sadness at the sight of white-colored blossoms, an undercurrent of loneliness in a church or temple where old incense still lingers in the empty pews.

My mother's aesthetic sense was insensible to anything as abstract as a picture or a photograph. It must have been Father who cherished the photographs of actors and actresses, which came all the way from California, to be gazed upon by my five-year-old self. These portraits were as remote from me as the statues of Ganesha, the elephant-headed god, whose temple my mother visited, as remote as the gold-leafed, soot-covered seated figures of Kuan Yin, Goddess of Mercy, and Kwan Ti, God of Literature, War, and Justice, that rested on the tall altars where we placed joss-sticks twice a year in the Cheng Hoon Teng Temple—the Temple of The Green Merciful Clouds. Hollywood, Hindu, and Chinese spirits circled the maternal air, fit denizens whose presence in our lives gave comfort, interest, and security when we chose to remember them. But except for ancestral worship days and forays to temples, Mother lived chiefly from day to day without spirits.

In the background another woman ruled, a doughy-complexioned, large-boned woman in a cotton *samfoo*. Ah Chan washed our clothes, cooked our meals, and cleaned the bedrooms upstairs. Ah Chan came in the mornings and left every evening. She was and was not one of us.

Ah Chan made it possible for Mother always to be carefully dressed. She ironed our clothes to a high starched gloss. Often she sat on the little stool by the open-air bathroom area next to the kitchen, where she had a large zinc-plated tub full of water and dirty clothes. Or she stood in front of the baked clay charcoal braziers, raising a shower of ash with each blast of her breath, stirring the blackened wok with a huge cast-iron ladle. Ah Chan swept the rooms upstairs with a soft straw-plaited broom, pushing the skirt of straw from one corner of a room to the other. Stocky, broad, silent, she was always doing something. I never heard her speak.

Ah Chan's daughter, Peng, older than I was yet also a young girl, came to our house in the afternoons to help her mother with the laundry, ironing, cooking, and washing up. I did not play with Peng, for she was the servant's daughter and, like her mother, she remained busy and silent.

My earliest remembered dreams are of Ah Chan. Behind my shut eyelids white spots move and dance. Gradually, then faster and faster, the spots rotate and magnify till they each resolve into a round shining face with two bright black eyes and a beaming smile. They are all faces of the same woman. Her smile brightens till the myriad rows of white teeth shine and blind me, although my eyes are tightly shut. I am terrified of this female vision, these expanding faces with their pasted elongating grins spinning bodiless everywhere. Why should Ah Chan terrify me when she continues to remain in the background, seemingly screened and unheard?

Memory fixes two versions of Ah Chan, the maternal servant. In one she is stoically silent. Constantly moving, she works at small domestic chores, a necessary machine in the household. In the other version, a nightmare of beatific power, her face multiplies and expands to claim the entire ground of my vision. I wake up with my five-year-old heart racing. Awake I am careful to stay with my mother or to play in a room away from Ah Chan's presence.

Before there was trouble there were years I remember as happy, when we ventured out as a family to visit Grandma, Grand Auntie, and Mother's and Father's friends. In the evenings or on Sundays after Father had taken out the plank panels, fitted them into the metal tracks, and closed up his store which sold Bata shoes, we squeezed into his dark green Morris Minor and drove slowly up the coast with its old colonial houses, or to Bandar Pasir where friends lived in new housing estates.

It was a ritual my mother called *makan angin:* to eat the wind, to move as leisure. Not as a challenge or as a means to an end, which are Western notions of travel, but as easy pleasure. It held nothing of the association of speed that "wind" arouses in the West, but rather of slowness, a way of drawing life out so that time is used maximally. *Makan angin* makes sense only in a society in which time is valueless, a burden to be released with least financial loss and most pleasure. It speaks for lives that have not understood necessity or luxury, and that drift in dailiness, seeking escape from boredom of the senses through the senses.

The Tan family lived in a grand rambling house in Klebang. The circular driveway enclosed a flowered plot that was circled with yellow and blue tiles. Bachelor buttons, cockscombs, and zinnias glowed orange, blood red, and plum purple in the evenings when we visited. I wandered by the garden dazed by growing things. Pink clusters of sweet william flourished above me, and a thickly-branched *jambu-ayer* offered green-pink watery guavas. Inside the polished planked living room, the adults sat on rattan armchairs. Who knew what they said to each other, why the Tans felt it necessary to welcome us, what my parents intended by these visits?

I do not remember these relatives or friends visiting us except for Chinese New Year. There was something different about my parents: their restlessness to be out of the shophouse, shuttling their children, first three, made up of Beng, Chien, and myself, and gradually including Jen and Wun, all of us putt-putting into an unpaved driveway, stopping by to visit for an hour or two. Was there a pathos to this unreciprocated ritual? Even as a five-year-old child I understood social place. We were a piece of Malacca society but not secured in it.

Or less secured than the Malacca families we visited. My envy of intact families begins with those Sunday afternoons when, like a gypsy troupe or a circus mob, we stopped before a private home. Not a shophouse like ours, nor an ancestral house with five or six families in it like Grandfather's, but a house with a garden, a living room, a dining room, and bedrooms, possessing the banal regularity of the Western home.

So we made our way to another Lim home, no relative of ours but another businessman like my father, who sold books, magazines, stationery, and school supplies. The family had once lived above their shop the way we were living above the shoe store, but, newly prosperous, they were able to move into a bungalow in Bandar Hilir. The parents bustled each time we dropped by, and we never stayed long.

Their house seemed to have been constructed completely of cement. The rooms led one to another with no logic of space, no markers for inner and outer lives. They had two girls and only one son, their most valuable possession, whom they called Kau Sai, or Dogshit, for fear of the envious spirits. We thought Kau Sai was as obnoxious as his name, given to deceive the gods. The children, usually kept busy with tuition classes, piano lessons, and homework, played with their toys when we visited, disregarding our envious looks.

Perhaps we felt temporary and unimportant because we no longer lived in Grandfather's house, like the families of First Uncle, Second Uncle, Third Uncle, and Sixth Uncle. This ancestral home was a long, many-roomed, merchant's house Grandfather had built for his children. Grandfather had come to Malaya as a young man from a village near Amoy, in the Fujien province. He came as a coolie immigrant with no education or social rank, one of thousands of poor males from southern maritime China who poured into the British-controlled Straits Settlements at the beginning of the twentieth century. A common laborer, he carried sacks of charcoal wood, rice, dried foodstuffs, and agricultural imports from the cargo ships anchored off the narrow mouth of the Malacca River, onto the light boats that navigated the mud flats to unload on the quays. Through industriousness and foresight, he managed to save sufficient money to set up a chandler's shop beside the river mouth.

As a young child, I visited Grandfather's shop, a large room that opened immediately onto the street. Untidy and crowded, it was a child's fantasy of strange things, boxes and barrels that overflowed with nails, bolts, screws, brass fittings, washers, various thicknesses of ropes, steel wires, and other clunky metal fixtures. He must have done well, for he went on to buy farmland which he rented out. Grandfather weathered the world depression of 1929–32, and his store and farms prospered with the establishment of Malacca as a careening station, in the wake of British colonial and naval expansion in the Malayan peninsula.

With seven sons, the coolie transformed now into a merchant, a *towkay*, Grandfather built a handsome house on one end of Heeren Street, named after the Dutch burghers who had first settled along the coast by the mouth of the Malacca River. In the early twentieth century Heeren Street was where Malacca society lived. There, merchants like Grandfather built solid deep houses, ornately tiled, floored with quarried marble and fired red clay. I was born in such a house.

All my life I have dreamed about Grandfather's house, sometimes that I had bought the old house and was repairing it. These dreams are rarer now; more often I dream that I am exploring its rooms again. The rooms open up one into another, and old fragments of carved screens, an etched glass pane, antique spaces of yellowing marble and worn teak flooring flow in a visual stream. I am almost always delighted to rediscover its grandeur. A pride not of possession but of identity pushes the exploration. The images trigger a strong visceral sensation of identity. I know this material world, and know myself through it. The spaces are dream spaces, distorted, like the looming image of a cavernous hall for the altar room, or seeing an enormous room from under the altar table, as a child might have done, crouching in play, a long time ago. The dreams are usually pleasant, yet I am sad when I wake up.

I do not remember speech between my grandfather and myself, as if my early childhood were spent in a dumbshow, a silence of mutually uncomprehending animals. I see Grandfather in our home on Kampong Pantai. He is burnt brown, not so much scrawny as stringy, like dried toughened meat. His head is shaved and short gray bristles cover his scalp like pinpricks. His face is narrow, his cheeks drawn. He sits on the chair, an exhausted man, neither smiling nor talking. I know he is *Ah Kong,* but what does *Ah Kong* mean? With so many sons and grandsons already in the world, I must have struck him as insignificant. He is mute in my memory, giving nothing of himself except his utter weariness. He sits like a man who is only a dried burned body.

My other memory is of Grandfather's portrait which I first saw during his funeral, and then for a number of years on the altar table facing the front door, where anyone entering the house on Heeren Street would have to see it. Tinted in shades of gray, it shows the unsmiling face of a man in his early sixties, somber yet not grim, as if a history of hardship and sorrow were masked in the stoical mien and deliberately erased. It is not a face of suffering but of suffering blanked out.

This is how I envision the history of the Chinese pioneers to Malaya, the men who lived for three bowls of rice a day, and then for their sons, so that their sons would be able to feast on pork fat and white chicken meat. My grandfather's life repeats the myth of immigrant Chinese heroes, but his sons, my uncles, to whom he refused to show his sufferings, were beginning to fall away, even before he died, from the lives he had struggled to achieve for them. This truth may explain the exhaustion I saw in the man on the chair. It explains the hysteria that came over the extended family when he died.

My mother took us to a tailor's shop in the back streets of Malacca and had us measured for mourning clothes. We needed sufficient black clothes for six months, and because we had to wear black immediately, some of our other clothes were sent to be dyed. For a week until the tailor was able to complete the newly fashioned mourning clothes for us, we wore these stiff dyed cloths. They were more of an indigo than inky black. The dye penetrated the fibers and made them hard, as in a form of rigor mortis, and the seams of my blouse sat on my body like rulers. Through the day I walked in an ambience of indigo stink. It circled my head as the dye diffused with my body's heat, and its odor rose, wafted from my armpits and pores. I smelled like a corpse being prepared for burial, so that, although I was not permitted to see my grandfather's enormous teak coffin as it rested for five days on trestles in the front hall of his house, I was reminded every moment that a death had occurred.

On the day of the funeral, we joined our uncles, aunts, cousins, and numerous related people in accompanying the coffin as it moved out of the house to Bukit China, or Chinese Hill, the oldest and largest cemetery for Chinese in Malaya. We began the funeral procession at Grandfather's house. The coffin, carved with upturned ends like a pagoda roof, was hoisted with ropes and pulleys onto a lorry, and blanketed with wreaths and embroidered banners. Then, his portrait, set in an oval frame, was tied to the hood of the lorry. The scent of the cream and pink-centered frangipani wreaths masked our sweat and indigo heat, as we followed the lorry on foot, crying and lamenting. Hoods of sack cloth covered our heads, and we shuffled in straw sandals to show how his death had stripped us to destitution. First Aunt, half-carried by the other women through the hot streets, screamed the loudest.

The procession filled an entire street, the flower-bedecked lorry trailed by dozens of weeping adults and children, and they in turn followed by a solemn brass band, with drums, trumpets, and Chinese flutes blowing dirges. Behind the band fluttered banners carried streaming from a single pole or spanning the breadth of the street between two men. The banners of bright crimson, purple, midnight blue, and garish green satiny stuff were emblazoned with the names of associations and shops that had done business with Grandfather. Men in blue shirts and trousers ran up and down offering yellow "charm" papers, blessed by the Buddhist temple, to the passers-by. Grandfather's funeral was a civic occasion as much as it was a private grief, and as we dragged our fraying sandals behind the slow jerking lorry, the streets rang with the shouts of the banner carriers, and with the cries of the water carriers as they hurried from group to group dispensing bamboo joints of cool water from their covered buckets.

A photograph captures this single moment, when I felt Malacca not as a town but as a familiar spirit, a space extending from the family, and familiarity encompassing territory intimately inside my memory. In the photograph, the coffin-loaded lorry occupies center stage. The sons, faces visible under their sack-cloth hoods, kneel in front of the lorry and stare into the camera. Grandchildren stand on the sides, fanning outwards with mothers and related womenfolk behind us. There are so many grandchildren that the photograph, forming a broad, flattened rectangle, appears to have netted me within the psychic space of the extended family, that veining trajectory of multiple cousins, blooming for a shortened history in our lives.

This moment imprinted on me the sense of Malacca as my home, a sense I have never been able to recover anywhere else in the world. To have felt the familiar once is always to feel its absence after. The town through whose streets I mourned publicly, dressed in black, sack, and straw, weeping with kinfolk, united under one common portrait, is what my nerves understand as home. It doesn't matter that the family is lost, and that the town has been changed long ago by politics and economics. Every other place is foreign after this moment.

Father came from a family of six boys and one girl. He was the only son to have taken a peranakan woman as his wife. He broke away from being Chinese, and as soon as his children started school, he began to speak to them in English. As the fifth son, he had been left to his own devices, and, finding his pleasures in films and Western music, he constructed a life out of Western products. These included books. Before poverty stripped him down to essential pleasures, he read widely if with little depth. Newspapers, magazines, and omnibuses of *Reader's Digest* novels filled our home. He must have spent recklessly on subscriptions. We received *National Geographic* and two film magazines; later, as his tastes grew cruder, we received the *British Tatler* and *Tid-Bit*. He ordered copies of British funnies for my brothers, so that we were raised on popular British humor, with Desperate Dan, Billy Bunter, Dennis the Menace, and Gnasher.

When I study the few photographs I have of him as a young man, it becomes clear how differently he saw himself from his older Chinese-educated brothers. My father is almost always smiling in his photographs, as if there were an injunction against solemnity or misery in his world. In this way his image is already un-Chinese. The convention of individual portraits, a seriously considered expenditure when it wasn't an extravagance, taken perhaps only once in a lifetime, was that of the gaze across the centuries. One was looking at masses of one's great-grandchildren and expecting their worship. It was as human deities that Chinese parents looked into the camera, lofty, and as always under the eye of eternity, with a tragic cast. But my father's image for the future-capturing camera defies this Chinese deification. He sees before him the bent, tilted, shoulder-slanted pose of the Hollywood stars, the Howard Keels and Douglas Fairbanks of the non-Chinese world. His boyish head is always askew in the frame. He tilts it back as if to invite admiration. He has a smile that can charm any woman, even a five-year-old child. Sometimes he is posed with other men, but he is always in the center and at front. His pants are broad linen slacks, and he wears a cardigan whose sleeves are casually draped over his shoulders and tied loosely around his neck. In one photograph he wears a Panama hat and cradles a mandolin. He could have been a Chino in Cuba.

Where did my handsome father get his Western ways?

Father's imagination was possessed by Western images. He had a Gramophone that needed to be cranked up, and after he placed the needle in the groove of the heavy dinner-plate-sized records, music poured out of a mouthpiece curved elegantly like a horn of plenty. A little puppy with a brown-splashed ear guarded the instrument, and a man sang, "Oh Rosemarie, I love you, I'm always dreaming of you." A bright female voice promised, "Mangoes, papayas, chestnuts in the fire, the food is so good that you'll wanna stay!" My favorite was "The Mockingbird's Song," a tune which veered in my memory as the sound of happiness in the melancholic years that soon followed.

There was a time when Father and Mother enjoyed taking us to the Great World Amusement Park, a fenced-in area adjacent to the Rex Cinema. We bought entrance tickets for admission and filed through a narrow gate. Once inside, an entire brightly lit world surrounded us. Shops full of records, magazines, dolls, and knickknacks beckoned. A carousel of metal horses with large painted eyes and flying manes swirled giddily. A screen kept us from seeing into the darkened dance hall where sailors and playboys paid taxi-girls a dollar a dance. We could hear the brassy music of the Malay *joggett* or the slow thump of fox trots through the open yet hidden door. Food stands offered exotic cut apples, pears, and red plums from Australia. We sat around the rickety wooden tables of an open-air coffee shop, drinking colored syrups and listening to an ancient Chinese musician as he sawed on his two-stringed *erhu*. With an artist's pride, he placed a dried plum on our table, and in exchange we gave him some coins. He did not play for money, and we acknowledged this in accepting his plum for our coins.

Passing by the record shop we stopped to let Father browse. A large doll with bright yellow hair and blue irises stood propped by its box. "Look," the salesman said, "if you lay the doll down, it closes its eyes." Perhaps Father saw the way I held it, with incredulity and delight. A white and pink doll with the plumpest arms, and legs that moved the way the German soldiers marched in the movies! I went home that evening with my first doll, an alien almost half as big as I, so wonderful that it was placed in its box high on the highest cupboard, to be brought down only on special afternoons for me to play with gingerly.

Father was an inveterate movie fan. Although films from Hong Kong and Bombay also showed daily in Malacca, he seldom saw a movie that was not in English and imported from Britain or the United States.

There were at least three movie houses in Malacca in the 1940s and '50s: the Rex, the Lido, and Capitol. The names of these pleasure houses, owned by the Shaw Brothers who lived in Singapore and Hong Kong, blazed above two-storied buildings. These imperial Latin names hardly signified the cheap shambling structures in which light poured out through a peephole and filled a screen with new images of the West: white cavalry chasing after wild Indians; Errol Flynn with a kerchief round his forehead hoisting himself up a mast, pirate's shirt blowing in the wind and pressing against his giant pectorals, waving a cutlass and challenging a dozen sailors to a fight.

The cinema facades were festooned with giant posters advertising the latest Hollywood extravaganzas. A mustachioed Clark Gable, hair slicked back and head lowered, eyes half-closed, gazed into the green irises of a flaming red-haired beauty, her skin tinted pink, who tilted her giant head and lips to greet him. This fantastic American idealized passion, posed with broad male-clothed shoulders and bare woman's flesh, covered the Rex Cinema's facade for months. It dominated the entire open square where singlet-clad peddlers sold slices of pineapple, Chinese pears, apples, and *chiku,* packages of melon seeds, dried salted olives, sugared plums, and barbecued squid. We would stand over the dazzling array of snacks for long minutes, agonizing over what we should buy with our five-cent treat. We could already taste the tropical treasures in our eager mouths, together with the American imaginary—the luxurious orchestra sweep, panoramic scenes, close-ups of white male and female beauty—to be ingested in cool darkness and silence. We emerged from the cinema hall gorged with Western images, our ears ringing with the accumulated noise of the finale, our children's eyes blinking in the afternoon glare in which suddenly everything appeared dull, flat, and small.

Since Father's shop, which sold only fashionable, brand-name Bata shoes, was carried in the Rex Cinema's opening advertisements, we were given free admission to every show. Even after Father went bankrupt and lost the shop, the regular ushers knew us so well that they continued to allow us in without tickets. Some weeks we saw three or four movies at the Rex. On weekends Beng, Chien, Jen, little Wun, and I set off in a trishaw, the smaller boys balanced on the older, and myself, a small six-year-old, squatting, scrunched by the floor. We caught the 11 A.M. matinee, then the 2 A.M. main feature, and reeled home at five in the evening, drugged and speechless after so much spectacle.

A vivid memory at ages five and six is of being wakened by my mother who wraps me in a blanket. She carries me to the Morris Minor and my father drives us to the Rex Cinema. We climb up the stairs to the more expensive balcony seats where I doze in the midst of flashing pictures and glitzy amplified music. This ritual of the midnight show is repeated frequently. My brothers must have been left alone in the shophouse while my parents silently smuggled me out. But why me? Do they provide this midnight treat on alternative nights to my brothers? Or am I special, the only girl and my father's favorite child, the one he double-dates with my mother?

The pictures I absorbed in those late night moments now form part of my involuntary imagination. A Busby Berkeley musical with Esther Williams diving and backstroking, her strong muscular body pushing through the water. Then she stands perched on a carousel composed of long-legged sleek women, smiling and waving, a surprisingly asexual figure of womanhood. A clunky metal figure ominously emerges out of a metal hulk, the light dims, the music threatens. This image frightens me and I keep recalling it for years. Decades later, in New York, I learn that this is a shot from *The Day the Earth Stood Still*, a science-fiction fantasy that I believed a part of my Malacca world. I remember a musical with prancing men and pert women dressed in long flouncy gowns. That, I find in Boston, was *Seven Brides for Seven Brothers*. Each midnight show, I wake up in time to watch the finale and see the screen filled with loudily singing, gesturing, good-looking people.

I didn't ask in the morning about the dazed fantasies. I was too busy filling in the blanks of the day with sensory motions and with explorations of my body. The second story of bedrooms and a corridor play-area had a smooth polished wood floor, planked and deeply grained. Bored and delighted at the same time, I lay on the floor, feeling its cool surface on my cheek, and traced the wood grains with my fingers. I sat by the glassless window in my parents' bedroom that faced the street, a wooden balustrade like a fence marking the division between bedroom and open air. I held onto the round bars of the balustrade, pushed my head as far as it could go between two of the bars, and studied the street below. It was dazzling hot and sunny outside. A car drove slowly past, a trishaw moved languorously in search of a passenger. Across the street was a row of other shop fronts: the goldsmith's shop showed only a dark interior, although the steel accordion gates were pushed back all the way. A lorry was parked before the sundry shop, but no one was unloading anything. The street lay silent like a somnambulist's vision.

My father's shop had a prominent place on the street, but the street always appeared quiet and empty. Sometimes I went through the curtain that separated the family rooms from the sales area and found him sitting on a stool, slipping a customer's foot into a shoe with a shoehorn. He wore dark-rimmed glasses and appeared serious, a different person in his workplace, a person who frowned impatiently. After the customer left he wrapped the shoes back in their paper tissues, placed them in their boxes, and put away the boxes precisely in their places on the shelves, like a stack of catalogued books. He swept the floor and neatly rearranged the cushioned chairs. With a feather duster, a huge cluster of black and brown rooster feathers, he dusted the counters and chairs.

He was compact, efficient, and angry. When his anger erupted, he would seize the feather duster, chase after my brothers, and thrash them with the rattan handle, gripping the feathers so tightly that they shredded and fell like pieces of my brothers' bodies. The rattan whipped through the air with a singing tone, and red welts appeared on my brothers' bare legs and arms. They raised their arms to shield their heads. When they rolled themselves into balls, the rattan cut them on their backs and shoulders. I watched terrified, guilty: was it because of me that they were being caned? Had I cried, complained, or pointed a finger at them? I was aware that my father's arm, striking again and again at my brothers, could as well be aimed at me. I stayed in the corner of the room, unable to move away from his fury. Sometimes he yelled at me, "'You stay here and watch this. Don't think I won't cane you either!" I knew he would also beat me some day.

We were not allowed in the shop except on Sundays when I could stand on a cushioned chair and jump off, imitating my brothers. Once, I fell clumsily, my elbow wrenched out of its socket. I screamed with pain; the elbow bone stuck out of the skin like a sharp stick. Nevertheless, I was determined to follow my brothers, to act as they did. To be one of them, I had to keep up with them. And they were a bunch of demons. They shrieked and ran like crazed animals all over the neighborhood.

Indoors they had to be quieter, and they delighted in games that excluded me. I stood by the closed door of their bedroom; they were whispering, conspiring about a game that I was not permitted to play. I pushed at the door, but they had blocked it with the full weight of their four male bodies. I begged them to let me in, I wanted to play with them, but they refused with gleeful laughs. I cried, exhausted. Why was I outside the magic of their play? I knew it was because I was a girl. What did it mean, that I was a girl? It meant that I was slower than all of them, although my youngest brother, four years younger, was barely a toddler. I was unwanted and unloved by my brothers.

My oldest brother, Beng, the prized first-born, was the one who disliked me most. In my earliest memory, he was gruff and distant. He was comfortable in Malay, and over and over again I heard him. say of me, *"Benchi!"* signifying antipathy, even hatred. I understood he disapproved of me because I was a girl. The house was full of brothers, except for me, third-born. I was a despised female, but I was also the only girl whose tears, whines, requests, whims, and fancies my father responded to unashamedly. The only daughter overtook the first-born son in a family with too many boys. This childish anger that Beng showed me never shook my sense of being special, but it made me timid of the feelings of rivals.

Yet I held an unequal position over my brothers. All my brothers spoke of my father's favoritism toward me as a fact of life, and I assumed that I deserved my father's favors. Because my father treated me as a gift, a treasured child, I felt myself to be a gift, and that I held treasures within me.

Being a girl also made me precocious and edgy, asking not "Who am I?" but "How can I prove that I am not who I am?" From the moment my father dealt with me more gently than with my brothers, and I understood my oldest brother when he muttered *"Benchi,"* from the moment I stood outside a door and felt my sex make me unwelcome, I decided my brothers' acceptance was preferable to my father's favoritism. I rejected the identity of girl. Since I could not have both, I chose equality as a boy over privilege as a girl.

My parents explained to their friends with exasperation that I was a tomboy, born in the year of the monkey. But I was not born one. It did not come naturally to me to run fast, to jump from high walls, to speed on a bicycle, or to stay out late alone at night. I would not have wandered from place to place, except for the promise, barely sensed, that something was to be picked up, learned, found, discovered, given, taken, ingested, desired, something that I couldn't find in my home, that I would be stronger, better, improved, changed, transformed in a stranger's house.

I was given the trappings of a girl–child: like an antiquated pleasure machine, my memory churns out images of tea-sets, blond dolls, doll wicker furniture, frilly dresses, red tartan ribbons, and my power as the only girl. Lying on a rattan chaise lounge, with a high fever, I was a very small and sick four-year-old. But Baba hovered over me; he had bought grapes, rare delicious globes. Emak stripped the green skins from them. The flesh was translucent, pale jade, veined, and firm. Delirious with happiness, I held each cool fat fruit in my fevered mouth.

In a later image, I sat on the floor gravely arranging the plastic teacups and saucers, holding each teacup in turn by its little handle. Today, this child playing house is a mystery to me. What was she thinking of as she sipped the air and set the emptied cup on its daisied saucer? What company did she enjoy this solitary hot afternoon while her brothers were away in school? There was a stillness in this child, attentively at work with imaginary companions, that absorbs me now. Was she imitating her mother and the many aunts she had met? But Malacca society ran on glasses of Sarsi and Greenspot, frizzy, sugared pop, colored violent blood-brown and orange, rather than on cups of tea and cream. Tea in Malacca was Chinese tea, poured into small handleless cups that you clasped in one hand. Where had this girl–child learned to drink tea in the British way, grasping the handle gingerly between thumb and middle finger and sticking her pinkie out like a society woman? The illustration on the box that held the tea set showed a blond child, also on the floor, drinking tea with her equally blond dollies. The girl had studied the picture. She was more like this blond girl than like her aunts or even her mother. Her doll with the straw-textured blond curls sat upright across from her, the hard blue eyes wide open. The girl played not so much with the tea set as with the picture on the box. It was quite satisfactory.

But finally it was not as good as the real thing, which was my brothers' play. The boys played at fighting with each other, noisily and excessively. All kinds of sounds came from them—bangs, rattles, yells, screams, shouts, yipes, hollers, short murderous silences, stampings, thumps, pings, singing.

It seemed to me that none of the boys were ever alone. They were always whispering together, laughing, planning something, sharing a joke, exchanging a look, chasing each other, pushing, shoving, howling, pinching, punching, kicking, blaming each other. I whined because they would not tell me what they were doing, but that was their favorite game, conspiring to keep me out. And when I had begged enough, they let me run with them in their chases, but they ignored me. It was too easy to catch up with me. I cried and whimpered when I was hit, which was after all the aim of their games, to see how often they could hit each other.

And I? My chest hurt as I flew down the narrow sidewalks, trying not to stumble against the dustcans and baskets of garbage left by the sundry shops next to our home. My breath hammering against my ribs, I scrunched down inside a dry drain, fearing to be discovered, fearing my brothers' physical play, listening to their hoots as they galloped up and down above me. I wanted desperately to be up there, out in the open, whacking them as hard with an open palm as they were dealing each other. But I was grateful to be hiding, to be silent, secret, left alone, and safe. The minutes passed, and I leaped from the drain, scrambled in front of the three boys, raced panic-stricken, and touched the pillar that spelled home.

It was my brothers' enmity that made me refuse to be a girl. To be a girl, as I saw through their mocking distance, was to be weak, useless, and worse, bored. It was to stay in one place and gossip for hours the way my mother sat gossiping with my aunts and grandaunts.

My mother's parents had lived in Malacca State all their lives. Their parents were descendants of Chinese traders who had migrated to Malaya as early as the fifteenth century and who had married local Malay women. My mother's father had been a station master at Tampin, a civil servant for the British administration. He had moved his family, four boys and five girls, to a house in Klebang outside the town of Malacca, survived the Japanese Occupation, then died suddenly of a bad heart, leaving behind five children still at home. His wife died soon after, and Mother found herself hosting one teenage sibling after another as they passed from her older brother's hands to hers and then to Singapore where two married sisters were able to set them up with opportunities and jobs.

A series of aunts came through our home. First, Aunt Amy, sweet-faced, gentle, always with a smile that meant nothing except how good she felt to be simply wherever she was. If my mother was wickedly funny and driven by the needs of her senses, Aunt Amy was amusing and grateful to receive whatever was given to her. Her strange contentment made happiness inevitable for her, while my mother's uncontainable needs marked her for misery. Aunt Amy was a bowl of brown-sugared oatmeal, delicious yet surprisingly good for you. Her warm and easy temperament gave her the halo of good looks. When Aunt Amy left for Singapore, Auntie Lei, Mother's youngest sister, came to live with us.

Auntie Lei was a short woman, darker-complexioned than the rest of her siblings, and fiercely passionate, almost as I imagine I might have appeared at sixteen. She had a willful vivid face, not pretty at all but catching because the eyes were so restless, the compact shape of the skull and cheeks seemingly too small for the furrowed countenance, the concentrated inward focus of a furious self. Her slight body was dense with resistance; she was like an animal that would not be housebroken. She quarreled continuously with my mother, kept her distance from the rest of us, and finally ran away with a fair-skinned young man whose languid manners promised a life of poverty.

I watched these aunts, intimate, fleeting, subordinate in my mother's household, the only women of my blood I would know from the inside. They offered two different selves, but each inescapable from *kismat,* or fate, as Emak loved to say. Aunt Amy was tamed for pleasure; whatever entered her mouth turned sweet if insipid. The youngest sister, however, was ruled by passions. Intense, brooding, her eyes tugged inwards, she was blind to self-interest and to safety. They were both of marriageable age, but, orphaned and dowryless, with no parents to negotiate their value, they were social waste, excess, unhoused women to be taken in by their married sisters as unpaid domestic help. Aunt Amy willingly waited in another sister's home in Singapore in hopes of a meager marriage; Lei, sexuality brooding in her sullen body, defied social approval and gradually disappeared into the Malacca underclass. Appearing more and more worn through the years, her face never lost its countenance of discontented sexuality, as if in the narrow squalor she had chosen she had kept unscattered that appetite of the sixteen-year-old.

Uncle Ling came through, then Uncle Charlie, to be followed by Amy, Lei, and Mun. Ling and Charlie stayed only briefly, but long enough for me to remember Ling's good nature mixed with a cruelty that had him throwing me into the waves. I screamed with panic as he seized and tossed me casually like a sack of charcoal into the deep water into which I gurgled and could not find my footing. I was perhaps four, a child who could drape her entire body over a blown-up plastic tube and imagine it to be a ship, but who also had a mind that could understand cruelty and be afraid of it. My grandparents' orphans introduced me to tragedy, and I learned in self-defense to stand apart, not to be like Mother and her sisters, who wept helplessly and who ran away and gave themselves to helpless men, nor like her brothers who were forced to depend on reluctant relatives.

So much family! Uncles, brothers, cousins! But all were only one step from strangers. Baba and Emak were the bedrock, that which could not be lost, although they might lose each other and themselves. But by the time I was six, even they were changing into strangers moving away from me.

Baba's temper grew more uncertain and unchecked, and Emak became pregnant again. The house was permeated with the scents of chicken and pork liver in Chinese wine boiled with ginger and ginseng root. One night I saw her using the flowered porcelain-covered metal chamber pot placed in the corridor connecting the three bedrooms. No one went to the bathroom downstairs after we went to bed; life was lived upstairs after 8 P.M. She was huge, her belly floating in the dark like a boat. The night sarong barely needed to be folded over.

Weeks later we were told that we had another brother named Wilson, but that our *Tua Ee,* our maternal First Grandaunt, would be taking care of him. Lei told us that a fortuneteller had predicted that Wilson would be a difficult child who would bring disaster to his parents, and that he would have to be given away. *Tua Ee* took him in although she already had three sons of her own and an adopted daughter. Our baby brother came and left without our ever seeing him.

1996

Dana Gioia (B. 1950)

Lonely Impulse of Delight: One Reader's Childhood

Every reader has two lives—one public, the other secret. The public life is the one visible to our teachers, friends, and families, though none of them ever sees it fully. It consists of our homes and houses, schools and schoolmates, friends and enemies, lovers, colleagues, and competitors. This is the realm of experience universally known as real life. But every true reader has a secret life, which is equally intense, complex, and important. The books we read are no different from the people we meet or the cities we visit. Some books, people, or places hardly matter, others change our lives, and still others plant some idea or sentiment that influences our futures. No one else will ever read, reread, or misread the same books in the same way or in the same order. Our inner lives are as rich and real as our outer lives, even if they remain mostly unknowable to others. Perhaps that is why books matter so much. They serve as our intimate companions. Some books guide us. Others lead us astray. A few rescue or redeem us. All of them confide something of the wonder, joy, terror, and mystery of being alive.

I had a happy, lonely childhood characterized by many odd circumstances—two of which turned me into a passionate lifelong reader. First, both of my parents had full-times jobs, sometimes even two jobs. Among working-class Latin families fifty years ago, this situation was not only unusual but also slightly embarrassing, suggesting a certain financial desperation—not altogether mistaken in our case. Consequently, I spent a great deal of time alone in our apartment or sat awake with one of my parents asleep while the other was at work. (They worked entirely different hours.) The second odd circumstance was our apartment, which was full of books—not popular paperbacks or book-club selections, but serious hardbound volumes of fiction, poetry, drama, philosophy, art, and music. These books did not reflect my parent's tastes or interests. They read very little except newspapers and magazines. The large, eclectic, and intellectually distinguished library was the legacy of my mother's brother, Ted Ortiz, who had died in an airplane crash when I was six. An old-style proletarian intellectual, my uncle had served in the Merchant Marine and lived with my parents when he was not at sea.

Special shelves housed the heavier volumes—including more than a hundred bound folio scores, printed in Germany, of the complete works of Mozart, Beethoven, Brahms, Bach, and Haydn. (Tall plywood cabinets likewise lined one wall of our tiny garage holding hundreds of classical record albums.) Many books were in foreign languages—Dante in Italian, Goethe in German, Cervantes in Spanish. These were family books, not the possessions of a stranger or a school. They belonged to us, even if we didn't know exactly what to do with them.

I grew up in a tight enclave of Sicilian relations. My family lived in the large back apartment of a stucco triplex next door to a nearly identical triplex. Five of these six apartments were inhabited by relations, including my grandparents, my aunt and uncle, and various cousins. Other relations lived nearby. The older people had been born in Sicily and had made their arduous and often painful way to Los Angeles via New York City and Detroit. An Italian dialect was spoken when the older generation was in the room. Conversation shifted to English when they left. Although born in Detroit, my father had spoken no English until he started school. Most of my schoolmates in Hawthorne, California, came from similar backgrounds, though their families spoke Spanish. In my parish all grandparents spoke English with a foreign accent—if they spoke English at all.

None of my practical, hard-working relations read much, but neither did they disdain the activity. There were a few books in their homes, but they were mostly inexpensive encyclopedias and young adult classics—books bought, that is, for someone else to read. I never saw anyone open one of these decorative volumes except myself jealously examining them on a visit. In fact, during my entire childhood I don't recall ever seeing any adult relation, except my mother, read a book. Everyone was busy cooking, cleaning, building, or repairing something. Leisure time was spent together—eating, talking, or playing cards—not going off alone with a book. Kitchen table arguments were especially popular. Everyone argued about politics, religion, money, sports, and people. No one minded these often fiery debates. The only thing that disturbed people was being ignored.

My family had no idea what to make of my bookish habits, but they never mocked or discouraged them. Never before having encountered a bookworm, these stoical Sicilians hoped for the best. One reason Latin families stay tight is that they allow their members latitude for personal taste. Italians also admire any highly developed special skill—carpentry, cooking, gardening, singing, even reading. The best skills helped one make a living. The others helped one enjoy living.

My parents rarely brought home children's books, so my earliest memories of reading include taking down the uniformly black-bound novels of Thomas Mann or the green-bound plays of George Bernard Shaw looking vainly for something a kid might enjoy. Childhood was slower before cable television, videogames, DVDs, and the Internet. Kids had time on their hands. We had to entertain ourselves, which meant exploring every possible means of amusement our circumscribed lives afforded. I paged through every book on every shelf, however unlikely its appeal. I loved my uncle's Victor Book of Opera with its photographs and engravings of old singers and set designs, and I constructed my own plots for the operas based on these illustrations. I also grew up seeing reproductions of Botticelli, Michelangelo, Titian, Velazquez, and El Greco, mostly in black and white, before I ever saw the drawings of Dr. Seuss or his peers.

There were few religious books in our deeply Roman Catholic home. My parents owned only the Bible, *The Lives of the Saints,* several pocket-sized missals, and a single, inspirational paperback by Bishop Fulton Sheen. Although my Mexican uncle, a former Communist, had converted to Catholicism shortly before his sudden death, he had left no devotional texts, only books on comparative religion. I suspect that no other Sicilian or Mexican home in Hawthorne possessed a copy of the Koran. The family Bible proved a keen disappointment. This situation was no fault of God's word, only its inept illustrator. Our large, cheap edition contained two dozen color prints that were so awful that even a ten-year-old felt cheated. I found spiritual sustenance only in *The Lives of the Saints,* especially in its vivid accounts of legendary hermits and martyrs. This early imaginative nourishment explains far more about my inner life than I care to disclose.

Although I perused the title pages of *Heartbreak House* and *The Magic Mountain,* I never read them until college. I loved the books that boys love—stories of wonder, danger, and adventure. Among the earliest books I remember reading were young adult biographies of Julius Caesar, Alexander the Great, Joan of Arc, Marco Polo, Napoleon, and John Paul Jones, which were sold at the local toy store. (I had been alerted to Caesar's existence by a Classics Illustrated comic book.) Exhausting those volumes, I moved into the adult history section of the local library. It may seem odd that in fourth grade my favorite book was *Caesar's Gallic Wars,* but I was an odd child, and I can still remember the number of soldiers who fought on each side of the Roman general's major battles.

I delighted in books on mythology, especially Norse mythology, and devoured prose versions of *Beowulf, The Iliad, The Odyssey,* and *The Song of Roland.* (I had no idea then that these stories had originally been written in verse.) I also read and reread the elegant retellings of myths by Edith Hamilton, Charles Bulfinch, and Padric Colum. How few children's authors today write prose half as well as Hamilton or Colum did? In fourth grade I discovered unabridged editions of *Gulliver's Travels* and *Robinson Crusoe* in St. Joseph's tiny parochial school library, which was about the size of a large walk-in closet. No one told me the novels were too hard for a ten-year-old, so I adored them, and then passed them on to my best friend.

Toward the end of fourth grade I had one of my decisive experiences as a reader—my first great literary love affair. I came across a copy of Edgar Rice Burroughs's *At the Earth's Core* on the paperback rack of the corner drugstore. I liked the colorfully exciting cover so I plunked down forty cents and took the book home. It was, I joyfully discovered, the perfect novel—brilliantly plotted and full of action. Over the next few years I read everything I could find by Burroughs—except the perfunctory later Tarzan novels. I also got two of my parochial school friends hooked, Paul Lucero and Ernie Rael. We practiced literary criticism in its purest form—talking about and comparing the books we read in common. We held a general consensus that Burroughs's first three Mars novels were his masterpieces, with the first two Tarzan novels only slightly less thrilling. I still find it exciting to remember the titles and garishly exuberant covers of those Ace and Ballantine paperbacks—*Pellucidar, The Land that Time Forgot, Pirates of Venus, A Princess of Mars,* and *The Mad King.* I read at least forty of Burroughs's novels, and I have had the pleasure of rereading of the Mars, Venus, and early Tarzan novels aloud to my sons—now marveling less at the author's breathless plotting than at the huge vocabulary popular writers once took for granted among young readers.

I developed a passion for science fiction, adventure, and fantasy literature. A few of my favorite boyhood writers have now, I am sorry to say, entered the fringe of the academic canon. In my heart, however, they remain forever beyond the reach of pedagogic good taste—H.P. Lovecraft, H.G. Wells, Ray Bradbury, Olaf Stapledon, Arthur C. Clarke, and Isaac Asimov—as well as the now mostly forgotten Richard Matheson, Charles Beaumont, Charles G. Finney, and William Hope Hodgson. It was, in fact, dystopian sci-fi that gradually got me interested in literary fiction. I read Aldous Huxley, Kurt Vonnegut, and George Orwell initially as sci-fi writers, and only then discovered their literary novels. To a working-class, teenage Angeleno, who knew nothing first-hand of the larger world, I must confess that Huxley's futuristic fantasies, *Brave New World* and *Ape and Essence,* were novels I understood entirely, but his realistic social comedies, *Crome Yellow* and *Antic Hay,* were deeply obscure and mysterious. Mars I comprehended but an English country house was an utterly alien world.

In fifth grade, I became passionately interested in art after seeing television specials on Leonardo da Vinci and Michelangelo. I haunted the enormous Hawthorne public library and over the next four years voraciously read through hundreds of art books. I studied European painting the way other boys immersed themselves in sports statistics. I daydreamed about visiting the Alte Pinakothek, Hermitage, Uffizi, and Prado. At twelve, I could tell you the location of every Vermeer, Massacio, Giotto, or Bosch in the world—and weirder still—could identify the provenance of each painting in Washington's National Gallery, which I had never visited. I read S.N. Behrman's biography of the art dealer Joseph Duveen three times and kept track of Old Master auction prices in a little notebook. I spent the money I earned doing odd jobs by ordering museum catalogues and subscribing to *Art News* and *Connoisseur.* (One continuing pleasure of adulthood has been to visit the museums whose catalogues I studied as a child.) My parents approved of my odd behavior because they associated my interest in art with academic achievement—just as they associated my science fiction and fantasy reading with laziness and impracticality.

I must stress two crucial facts. First, no one—neither a relative nor a teacher—ever encouraged my reading or intellectual pursuits. Second, my bookish hobbies (except for science fiction) needed to be hidden from my friends. I never confided my passion for art to anyone at school. Luckily, none of my classmates ever seemed to visit the library, so my double life remained safe from their discovery. I was grateful for my anonymity. While I didn't need encouragement, I also felt no urge to court certain disapproval. Discretion was the better part of valor. My childhood secrecy proved good training. This pattern of a double life—one public, the other one imaginative—was repeated in adulthood when I worked in the business world while secretly writing poetry at night.

I have always been an insomniac. Even as a young boy, I had trouble falling asleep. My parents, both night owls, let their children keep late hours. Once we were in bed, they never forced us to turn off the lights—one of their countless kindnesses. Consequently, every night I read in bed, often for hours. When I remember my childhood reading, I see myself in Sears and Roebuck pajamas propped up under the covers devouring *The Circus of Dr. Lao, The Time Machine* or *The Lost World* while my younger brother Ted sleeps in the twin bed beside me. I usually kept the next book I planned to read on my nightstand—not so much as an incentive to finish my current selection but simply to provide anticipatory pleasure. "My library was dukedom large enough," Prospero says in *The Tempest,* and so seemed the kingdom of my childhood. The clock would tick toward midnight and beyond while I wandered through Rome and London, Lilliput and Mars. Today I am a world traveler, but life never seemed larger than in that tiny lamplit room.

In my childhood milieu, reading was associated with self-improvement. I suppose this uplifting motive played some role in my intellectual pursuits, but my insatiable appetite for books came mostly from curiosity and pleasure. I liked to read. I liked to study and investigate subjects that interested me—European painting, silent films, dinosaurs, great battles, and mythology. My interests changed and developed year by year. Some of the books I read were quite respectable, like *Gulliver's Travels* or Vasari's *Lives of the Artists,* but respectability never guided my choices.

By the standards of Hawthorne, a rough and ugly industrial town, my love of books was clearly excessive, indeed almost shameful. Not able to control this passion, I needed to hide it, if only to keep it pure. A private passion is free from public pressures. Then I could follow this "lonely impulse of delight," to borrow a phrase from William Butler Yeats, wherever it led. I read good books for enjoyment just as I did each issue of *Spiderman, The Incredible Hulk,* or *The Fantastic Four.* I can't think of better ways to learn than through pleasure and curiosity. I guess the reason these two qualities play so small a role in formal education is that they are so subjective and individual. Curiosity and delight can't be institutionalized.

Childhood and adolescence form our sensibilities. By the time I arrived in college, I had already developed a deep suspicion of all theories of art that did not originate in pleasure. Surely, this conviction developed from my own self-education in books, and in particular from exploring them with little tutorial assistance—except from an uncle who could not speak to me, except though the mute juxtaposition of subjects in his book collection.

My uncle must have been a remarkable man. Although raised in brutal poverty, he had supported himself at sea from the age of fifteen while also learning five languages and schooling himself in music, literature, and art. I don't honestly remember him—only stories about him and a few photographs. If I claimed to love him, I would really be saying that I loved the books and records he left behind. I'm not sure that distinction matters much. I think I know him pretty well. After all, he did help raise me.

2005

Guillermo Gómez-Peña (B. 1955)

Documented/ Undocumented

I live smack in the fissure between two worlds, in the infected wound: half a block from the end of Western Civilization and four miles from the start of the Mexican-American border, the northernmost point of Latin America. In my fractured reality, but a reality nonetheless, there cohabit two histories, languages, cosmologies, artistic traditions, and political systems which are drastically counterposed. Many "deterritorialized" Latin American artists in Europe and the U. S. have opted for "internationalism" (a cultural identity based upon the "most advanced" of the ideas originating out of New York or Paris). I, on the other hand, opt for "borderness" and assume my role: My generation, the *chilangos* [slang term for a Mexico City native], who came to "el norte" fleeing the imminent ecological and social catastrophe of Mexico City, gradually integrated itself into otherness, in search of that other Mexico grafted onto the entrails of the et cetera . . . became Chicanoized. We deMexicanized ourselves to

Mexi-understand ourselves, some without wanting to, others on purpose. And one day, the border became our house, laboratory, and ministry of culture (or counterculture).

Today, eight years after my departure (from Mexico), when they ask me for my nationality or ethnic identity, I can't respond with one word, since my "identity" now possesses multiple repertories: I am Mexican but I am also Chicano and Latin American. At the border they call me *chilango* or *mexiquillo;* in Mexico City it's *pocho* or *norteño;* and in Europe it's *sudaca.* The Anglos call me "Hispanic" or "Latino," and the Germans have, on more than one occasion, confused me with Turks or Italians. My wife Emilia is Anglo-Italian, but speaks Spanish with an Argentine accent, and together we walk amid the rubble of the Tower of Babel of our American post-modernity.

The recapitulation of my personal and collective topography has become my cultural obsession since I arrived in the United States. I look for the traces of my generation, whose distance stretches not only from Mexico City to California, but also from the past to the future, from pre-Columbian America to high technology and from Spanish to English, passing through "Spanglish."

As a result of this process I have become a cultural topographer, border-crosser, and hunter of myths. And it doesn't matter where I find myself, in Califas or Mexico City, in Barcelona or West Berlin; I always have the sensation that I belong to the same species; the migrant tribe of the fiery pupils.

1988

Joy Harjo (B. 1951)

The Flying Man

For Ratonia & Phil

As I was being born I fought my mother to escape, all the way out to the breathing world, until I was pulled abruptly by the doctor who was later credited with saving both my mother and me. I dangled there from his hands, a reluctant acrobat caught in flight. I took note there was a rush with the release, with flying free, and like an addict I flew whenever I could, from crib bars to jungle gyms and once the roof of the garage. Later, it was anything dangerous, like smoking cigarettes in the bathroom of the church, or jumping off a cliff into the lake after drinking illegal beer. And then the plain stupid: I leaped from the house of the proverbial cruel stepfather to the arms of a young dancer I met at Indian school who could not love me. And now we were stuffed into an apartment over a pizza restaurant, living from paycheck to paycheck. At 17, I was a mother with a nursing child and a hyperactive three-year-old stepdaughter.

When I looked out the window to where the sun, moon, and stars flew by, the only view was a rundown street bypassed by the freeway and progress. Anything that took root had to break through asphalt and concrete and climb the walls of decay. Anything that flew over this city of stolen land and oil had to have wings.

I could see the roof of my mother-in-law's apartment. She blamed me for the fix her son was in, as if it hadn't happened before. He was supposed to return from Indian school with a postgraduate degree and support her, his half-sister, and the daughter he kidnapped from her teenage mother in Oregon. Instead, he returned with yet another pregnant teenage wife who would once again shift the fortunes of her son. I was the other woman, the reason for his lack of success, for her suffering. I had the one man bound to her by blood and guilt, a most volatile bond. Every man she had been with had given her a child then abandoned her, including her son who had left her with his daughter while he went to school in the Southwest. I was in the way and she took every opportunity to remind me.

She was now without a man, but she made sure she wouldn't be without everything she and the children had ever owned. Every item of clothing that her children had ever worn, every toy they had ever played with, every piece of paper with their names on it, she packed into boxes she piled high into a maze that filled up her apartment to the ceiling. She threw nothing away. She would not throw away her son to a strange, foolish girl.

Of course I wasn't ecstatic about the situation, either. None of this had figured into my map for a life, though I must admit the map was never clearly drawn. My path meandered according to the whim of failed adults and chance. It headed wanly to the life of a painter, like my Aunt Lois, who traveled from the Creek Nation all over the country without the encumbrance of children or husband and had the money to buy paint, canvas, and a car. Living as an artist was as close to my now limited universe as the planet Mars. Despite all my attempts at flight I couldn't afford art supplies, not even a junked car.

Each day was predictable. We got up, ate cold pizza for breakfast leftover from my husband's shift at the restaurant the night before. I washed the children and cleaned, and he went to work, and I worried about money and what we would do when he lost his job. And he would lose it, as he had lose all the others. The only question was, when? The last time he walked out on a job we had only an industrial-sized box of pancake mix, a gift from my mother, for meals to supplement beans, commodity cheese, and a squirrel once in a while. My mother was disgusted with the mess I had found myself in and did everything she could to keep from coming to the side of town I was now living in. She had grown up in worse and had cleaned and cooked her way to decency. My life was now a mockery of her struggle.

Every night he came in from work in a furious cloud. He had yet another story of how someone had cried to pull one over on him. Most recently he had barely managed to keep from punching out the skinny white boss who was riding him even though the new waitress was the one screwing up the orders and apparently the boss, too. We had nearly starved until he got this job, and 1 hadn't been able to work yet because I was still recovering from birth. The baby was nearing eight weeks old, and, as I watched my husband open another beer and pace the room, I decided I had better start looking for work. I would wash dishes, dance on tables, or fly to the moon if I had to, rather than starve the children or myself again.

Some days his mother would come over and we would pool our resources for food. We were bound together for raw survival and her mood shifted according to the nature of our predicament. On the nice days we would hit the yard sales together. Then I was her ally as we searched through junk for dishes and clothes. If she were feeling especially hospitable she would buy me something to wear for under a dollar.

She felt sorry for me and even that was difficult for me to swallow, but understandable considering I had first shown up in that small town of the tribal capitol, where they were all living then, my blooming stomach leading the way. My then-to-be husband attempted to hide me from his mother at his grandmother's house, but it is impossible to hide a pregnant woman or anybody in a close Indian community in which everyone knows everyone else's business, or thinks they do. Word got out, especially after I was seen sitting in the town square with the old lady who spent the crisp mornings with her friends under the eaves of the old bandstand. They were the heart of the nation and made note of the current state of affairs as they watched people enter and leave the bank and the various establishments and agencies around the square. They were also still checking each other out for romantic liaisons. At least they didn't have to worry about getting pregnant at that age. They didn't say much and I didn't understand much of their Cherokee. To be included in this daily meeting under the oak trees gave me a fresh peace that was rare everywhere else.

Once, when the grandmother got her monthly check, we ate lunch at the diner across the street. I watched her unclasp her black patent bag and empty the basket of crackers into it to take home. I was horrified and tried to duck down, but my growing belly made it impossible. I bumped and spilled my glass of water, which called even more attention to us. She, however, had grace as she carefully left change for a tip, and we walked back to her house.

Soon thereafter I was summoned to my soon-to-be mother-in-law's house. I was nervous. I had been warned by anyone who could take me aside that she was jealous, overprotective, and mean. They were right. What they didn't say was how attractive she was, how she was still in perfect form despite the rough years, her dark hair thick and lightly curled with energy. It was her dark eyes that told the other story, took in the edges of things, the tatters, and left the good behind. My lively new daughter ran up to us as soon as she saw her father. My new sister-in-law quietly drew pictures of horses at the table.

We moved in with them to her tiny one-bedroom house that afternoon, because, as she told her son, "You can't stay there and live off your grand-mother." Which was true. But she also wanted to think she had some con-trol of the gossip. Of course, there's no controlling gossip, but if I were in her house she would know my whereabouts, could be the authority. She was also pragmatic. I could watch the children. And so it went day after day. I adjusted. I had no choice. My center of gravity plopped there, weighted with frustration and a baby who was growing pound by pound. There was no way I could fly.

I hated the days she was moody and critical. I could smell them coming from afar off, like the ozone in a storm front. She might start with: "Why aren't you with your mother?" meaning, why doesn't your mother take care of you? She would reproach me as I washed dishes after eating food bought with her hard-earned money. Or she would say, "Your mother is rich. Why can't she send us money?" I would be humiliated and swallow hard. I didn't like being at the mercy of someone else's kindness. I did everything I could to make myself useful around the house. "My mother isn't rich," I would answer, and knew that she assumed my mother was rich, because she was a lighter-skinned Cherokee who passed for white and lived in Tulsa. I promised myself that as soon as the baby was born we would find our own place.

I never knew what to expect. Strange things would happen around the house at dark. One night, one of her enemies came to her in the shape of a bird. It sat in a tree outside the living room window, I'll always remem-ber the sound, like the peculiar howl of the dog in my family that always foretold a death. It sent shivers through all of us. I picked up my newly born son and took my girl into my arms, while she sent out her son with a gun. She told him to get rid of it, that she knew who it was. I hummed to the children louder and louder so we wouldn't know anything, so we would-n't think about evil in the world. We heard the shot into the tree and the haunting singing abruptly stopped. It was shortly after that that we moved out of the house into Tulsa. My mother-in-law followed with her daugh-ter and moved in next door.

One morning as I was toweling off the children from their baths, she pushed her way roughly into the house, puffing, then blowing smoke from a cigarette into my face. This was a new one. She didn't smoke cigarettes and she had been nice lately, in fact, we had just taken a drive. She had a car. We didn't. My husband surprised me with the swiftness of his leap between us. He had never taken up for me before when she slid into her enemy mode. "Mom, get out of here, now!" he warned her. She stepped back, surprised at the vehemence of his reaction as he slapped the ciga-rette from her hand and determinedly pushed her out the door, slamming it behind her. The smoke followed her like a puppy. "That cigarette was doc-tored with curses," he told me. "She's witching you."

Then it began to make sense. One morning as we struggled to put a bag of stuff from a yard sale into the trunk of her car, she showed me the book of spells written in Cherokee that she had acquired during her last trip home. The book was so old the pages were turning to powder. I didn't touch it. I wanted no part of it. She had stolen it from the witch she saw regularly to combat the many enemies she had in the world: the terrible men, the minimum wage jobs, the unwanted daughters-in-law.

I didn't get sick or die that day or the weeks that followed, but neither did our fortunes change to happiness and luck. I began to believe that I dreamed the smoking curse, that it happened far away from my babies, my house. What I didn't dream was that each day after she blew the smoke in my face she began to stoop. Just a little at first, imperceptibly even. Then it became noticeable, how the weight of the smoke bore down on her as it sat on her back, kicking its legs as it rode.

We all have a story. They are a means to an introduction, shining markers on the map to destiny. The night my husband-to-be and I met it was an accident. We ran into each other as I flew down the sidewalk to a dance. He was on his way to party with the over-21s. There were a few of them at the school in the post-graduate program. Later, we sat out on the porch of the girls' dorm and talked about our plans to be artists, about our families. "My father is Creek," I told him, and built him up as a descendent of warriors, when he was running around somewhere south of Okmulgee with a woman or two on his arm. My husband-to-be's parents were both Cherokee, his father mixed with German. His mother was full-blood and had been adopted by another full-blood family in Tahlequah. This wasn't unusual in that many of our peoples had died of tuberculosis and other diseases that took root from loss. When her son was small, she had left him with her adoptive parents when she left for the city to find work. We discovered that our mothers were probably distantly related.

His first memory, he told me that night as we talked under a night sky rich with flying stars, was of a boy with burned skin being brought to his grandfather for a healing. The skin was flayed over the boy's face in waves. He watched as his grandfather sang and prayed, then took water in his mouth, spitting on the burn. He did this many times. The boy and the boy's father returned two weeks later with some bags of groceries and a wood carving in gratitude for the healing. There was no sign of the burn on the boy's body, no mark at all.

This was the truth of the world. "My story is like a falling star," I said as we watched a small universe blaze and fall from the sky. It was there and then it wasn't there. This state of affairs could go on nearly forever, until the law of stasis won out and the next world replaced this one. I knew that night I was headed in a new direction, stopped literally in flight. Everything turned.

I measured the falling world by the baby's small accomplishments. He could hold his head up, he smiled, he laughed. Each increment was a promise of change. Not long after the witching incident, his mother and I were allies again as we were short on food and resources. It was spring. My mother-in-law, the children and I went walking at dusk toward the rich neighborhood that bordered on our part of town. Most of the flowers lived there and were blooming. My stepdaughter was also blooming, outgrowing clothes and shoes that were difficult to afford. We stepped into an alley, attracted by a pile of used furniture and barely worn clothes thrown in a bin for trash pickup. We. sifted through, holding things up, chattering with our good fortune, until a child from the huge house spotted us from his immaculate yard and yelled to his parents that Indians were going through their trash. We ran, holding onto our new stuff and the children, until we reached our neighborhood. We laughed after we had made it, and felt rich enough with our new treasures to buy ice cream. I still harbored a vague sense of shame at being discovered digging through someone's trash, but was angry, too, that the residents would rather it be thrown away, than given to someone who could use it.

Another sign of spring were the posters announcing the circus coming to town. We got discount passes from the grocery store, and I took the kids and my sister-in-law to the Sunday matinée. It was my first venture out in over a year. I felt expansive, as if my orbit had changed to accommodate the light of a new path. The arena was packed with families that afternoon, the city's kids swirling with snacks, circus toys, and excitement. We sat next to a concrete aisle for easier access to the bathrooms. The girls asked about everything as we waited for the show. They, wanted to know what-time-the-show-started-exactly-how-long-would-it-be-before-the-show-started-where-were-the-tigers-could-they-have-balloons-if-they-couldn't-have-a-balloon-could-they-ride-the-elephant-and-why-couldn't-we-sit-closer-so-we-could-see-better-and-could-they-go-to-the-bathroom-even-though-they-had-just-been-a-few-minutes-ago? As I answered them, I watched people intensely, imagined their lives and how I would paint them, rejuvenated by the smell of popcorn, the change in scenery.

Out of the churning crowds came a slim man in tights and a cape. As he headed up from the ring, he grew larger and larger as people parted to let him by, an incongruous figure in the middle of the flatly ordinary. He stopped next to me and surprised me by speaking to me. At first I thought he needed directions or had mistaken me for someone else, but he casually introduced himself as one of the brothers of the featured trapeze act, the Flying-Something-or-Other Brothers. I felt suddenly awkward and mumbled a response. I didn't know what I had done to garner such attention. And I had forgotten how to speak to anyone but small children and a husband who was so desperate for youth and fun he had taken to riding around and drinking beer with his high school friends. This strange man from Italy was the first person who had talked to me in months, the only one who had asked me a direct question about my own life. I responded by talking about my husband. I told this caped performer who had suddenly befriended me that my husband had been a dancer who was compared by critics to Rudolf Nureyev when we performed together a little more than a year before. He had many offers to join dance companies in the East, but had turned them down. I nervously talked up his attributes, but didn't really know where I was going with any of it. Then I agreed to meet after the performance.

When I look back, I can imagine how I must have appeared that afternoon—a vulnerable young woman dressed neatly but poorly, fixed at point zero under the big top, accompanied by an infant, by children waving their cotton candy clouds, urgently asking for the bathroom after they had just returned from the bathroom. I was in terrible need of flight.

That afternoon the children and I watched the Flying Brothers swing gracefully from one small platform to another, suspended by muscle and nerve, as if by magic. I began to consider what it might be like to fly, like this man from Italy who traveled the world flying into the space beyond fear, risking his life while the crowd watched in awe. It was then I became convinced that this was a job my agile husband could learn, as quickly and easily as he learned to toss and twist pizzas. We could travel together into a world much larger than the one that was squeezing us flat, far, far away from his mother. We could fly.

I am surprised now at my naïveté when I tell this story, though when I was in it I didn't feel naïve. By the last harrumphs of the circus band, I was utterly convinced and felt extremely practical about my new plan. I knew the days of the job at the pizzeria were almost over, and a job on the trapeze in the circus was something I became absolutely convinced my husband could do.

I don't remember how we got from the circus to the pizzeria to where my husband was working the afternoon shift. I do remember the way the sun came in through the colored dark glass in the restaurant as the manager retrieved my husband from the kitchen, and how excited I was about the possibility of the opportunity for a job, something that might engage him, use his dancer skills, and keep everyone in food and clothes. I introduced the acrobat to my husband. They were civil to each other as I explained my notion. As a ripple of tension coursed through all of us, I realized I had made a serious mistake in my assumption of a job possibility. It was my own dream of flying.

After I left the pizza parlor that afternoon, the flying man insisted on accompanying me to my apartment and waited as I put the children down for their naps. I was now confused about his intentions but played the perfect hostess, offered him coffee, water, and food, which he declined. Then he praised my beauty and abruptly asked me to leave with him immediately for Corsica. Everything stopped. I considered the sudden shift of events and a story that would shine garishly when displayed next to all the others in my small, rude life. The exhilaration of the force of possibility pinned me there, for a moment, in the slant of the late afternoon sun. This was what I had been waiting for, but it wouldn't fit, and nothing I could do would make it fit into a map that was apparently there, but not there. I told him I couldn't go anywhere, not even Corsica, I had babies. I asked him to leave.

The circus left town that afternoon. My husband did lose his job a few weeks later, as I had predicted. We had to move to another part of town after he found work in another pizza restaurant and his mother followed us. Things got worse, but I eventually flew far from that place, those times, and the story of the flying man.

2000

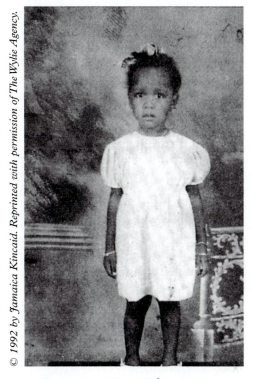

Jamaica Kincaid (B. 1949)

Biography of a Dress

The dress I am wearing in this black-and-white photograph, taken when I was two years old, was a yellow dress made of cotton poplin (a fabric with a slightly unsmooth texture first manufactured in the French town of Avignon and brought to England by the Huguenots, but I could not have known that at the time), and it was made for me by my mother. This shade of yellow, the color of my dress that I am wearing when I was two years old, was the same shade of yellow as boiled cornmeal, a food that my mother was always eager for me to eat in one form (as a porridge) or another (as fongie, the starchy part of my midday meal) because it was cheap and therefore easily available (but I did not know that at the time), and because she thought that foods bearing the colors yellow, green or orange were particularly rich in vitamins and so boiled cornmeal would be particularly good for me. But I was then (not so now) extremely particular about what

I would eat, not knowing then (but I do now) of shortages and abundance, having no consciousness of the idea of rich and poor (but I know now that we were poor then), and would eat only boiled beef (which I required my mother to chew for me first and, after she had made it soft, remove it from her mouth and place it in mine), certain kinds of boiled fish (doctor or angel), hard-boiled eggs (from hens, not ducks), poached calf's liver and the milk from cows, and so would not even look at the boiled cornmeal (porridge or fongie). There was not one single thing that I could isolate and say I did not like about the boiled cornmeal (porridge or fongie) because I could not isolate parts of things then (though I can and do now), but whenever I saw this bowl of trembling yellow substance before me I would grow still and silent I did not cry, that did not make me cry. My mother told me this then (she does not tell me this now, she does not remember this now, she does not remember telling me this now): she knew of a man who had eaten boiled cornmeal at least once a day from the time he was my age then, two years old, and he lived for a very long time, finally dying when he was almost one hundred years old, and when he died he had looked rosy and new, with the springy wrinkles of the newborn, not the slack pleats of skin of the aged; as he lay dead his stomach was cut open, and all his insides were a beautiful shade of yellow, the same shade of yellow as boiled cornmeal. I was powerless then (though not so now) to like or dislike this story; it was beyond me then (though not so now) to understand the span of my lifetime then, two years old, and it was beyond me then (though not so now), the span of time called almost one hundred years old; I did not know then (though I do now) that there was such a thing as an inside to anybody, and that this inside would have a color, and that if the insides were the same shade of yellow as the yellow of boiled cornmeal my mother would want me to know about it.

On a day when it was not raining (that would have been unusual, that would have been out of the ordinary, ruining the fixed form of the day), my mother walked to one of the Harneys stores (there were many Harneys who owned stores, and they sold the same things, but I did not know then and I do not know now if they were all of the same people) and bought one-and-a-half yards of this yellow cotton poplin to make a dress for me, a dress I would wear to have my picture taken on the day I turned two years old. Inside, the store was cool and dark, and this was a good thing because outside was hot and overly bright. Someone named Harney did not wait on my mother, but someone named Miss Verna did and she was very nice still, so nice that she tickled my cheek as she spoke to my mother, and I reached forward as if to kiss her, but when her cheek met my lips I opened my mouth and bit her hard with my small child's teeth. Her cry of surprise did not pierce the air, but she looked at me hard, as if she knew me very, very well; and later, much later, when I was about twelve years old or so and she was always in and out of the crazy house, I would pass her on the street and throw stones at her, and she would turn and look at me hard, but she did not know who I was, she did not know who anyone was at all, not at all. Miss Verna showed my mother five flat thick bolts of cloth, white, blue (sea), blue (sky), yellow and pink, and my mother chose the yellow after holding it up against the rich copper color that my hair was then (it is not so now); she paid for it with a one-pound note that had an engraving of the king George Fifth on it (an ugly man with a cruel, sharp, bony nose, not the kind, soft, fleshy noses I was then used to), and she received change that included crowns, shillings, florins and farthings.

My mother, carrying me and the just-bought piece of yellow poplin wrapped in coarse brown paper in her arms, walked out of Mr. Harney's store, up the street a few doors away, and into a store called Murdoch's (because the family who owned it were the Murdochs), and there my mother bought two skeins of yellow thread, the kind used for embroidering and a shade of yellow almost identical to the yellow poplin. My mother not only took me with her everywhere she went, she carried me, sometimes in her arms, sometimes on her back; for this errand she carried me in her arms; she did not complain, she never complained (but later she refused to do it anymore and never gave an explanation, at least not one that I can remember now); as usual, she spoke to me and sang to me in French patois (but I did not understand French patois then and I do not now and so I can never know what exactly she said to me then). She walked back to our house on Dickenson Bay Street, stopping often to hold conversations with people (men and women) she knew, speaking to them sometimes in English, sometimes in French; and if after they said how beautiful I was (for people would often say that about me then but they do not say that about me now), she would laugh and say that I did not liked to be kissed (and I don't know if that was really true then but it is not so now). And that night after we had eaten our supper (boiled fish in a butter-and-lemon-juice sauce) and her husband (who was not my father but I did not know that at the time, I know that now) had gone for a walk (to the jetty), she removed her yellow poplin from its brown wrapper and folded and made creases in it and with scissors made holes (for the arms and neck) and slashes (for an opening in the back and the shoulders); she then placed it along with some ordinary thread (yellow), the thread for embroidering, the scissors and a needle in a basket that she had brought with her from her home in Dominica when she first left it at sixteen years of age.

For days afterward, my mother, after she had finished her usual chores (clothes washing, dish washing, floor scrubbing, bathing me, her only child, feeding me a teaspoon of cod-liver-oil), sat on the sill of the doorway, half in the sun, half out of the sun, and sewed together the various parts that would make up altogether my dress of yellow poplin; she gathered and hemmed and made tucks; she was just in the early stages of teaching herself how to make smocking and so was confined to making straight stitches (up-cable, down-cable, outline, stem, chain); the bodice of the dress appeared simple, plain, and the detail and pattern can only be seen close up and in real life, not from far away and not in a photograph; and much later, when she grew in confidence with this craft, the bodice of my dresses became overburdened with the stitches, chevron, trellis, diamonds,

Vandyke, and species of birds she had never seen (swan) and species of flowers she had never seen (tulip) and species of animals she had never seen (bear) in real life, only in a picture in a book.

My skin was not the color of cream in the process of spoiling, my hair was not the texture of silk and the color of flax, my eyes did not gleam like blue jewels in a crown, the afternoons in which I sat watching my mother make me this dress were not cool, and verdant lawns and pastures and hills and dales did not stretch out before me; but it was the picture of such a girl at two years old—a girl whose skin was the color of cream in the process of spoiling, whose hair was the texture of silk and the color of flax, a girl whose eyes gleamed like blue jewels in a crown, a girl whose afternoons (and mornings and nights) were cool, and before whom stretched verdant lawns and pastures and hills and dales—that my mother saw, a picture on an almanac advertising a particularly fine and scented soap (a soap she could not afford to buy then but I can now), and this picture of this girl wearing a yellow dress with smocking on the front bodice perhaps created in my mother the desire to have a daughter who looked like that or perhaps created the desire in my mother to try and make the daughter she already had look like that. I do not know now and I did not know then. And who was that girl really? (I did not ask then because I could not ask then but I ask now.) And who made her dress? And this girl would have had a mother; did the mother then have some friends, other women, did they sit together under a tree (or sit somewhere else) and compare strengths of potions used to throw away a child, or weigh the satisfactions to be had from the chaos of revenge or the smooth order of forgiveness; and this girl with skin of cream on its way to spoiling and hair the color of flax, what did her insides look like, what did she eat? (I did not ask then because I could not ask then and I ask now but no one can answer me, really answer me.)

My second birthday was not a major event in anyone's life, certainly not my own (it was not my first and it was not my last, I am now forty-three years old), but my mother, perhaps because of circumstances (I would not have known then and to know now is not a help), perhaps only because of an established custom (but only in her family, other people didn't do this), to mark the occasion of my turning two years old had my ears pierced. One day, at dusk (I would not have called it that then), I was taken to some-one's house (a woman from Dominica, a woman who was as dark as my mother was fair, and yet they were so similar that I am sure now as I was then that they shared the same tongue), and two thorns that had been heated in a fire were pierced through my earlobes. I do not now know (and could not have known then) if the pain I experienced resembled in any way the pain my mother experienced while giving birth to me or even if my mother, in having my ears bored in that way, at that time, meant to express hostility or aggression toward me (but without meaning to and without knowing that it was possible to mean to). For days afterward my earlobes were swollen and covered with a golden crust (which might have glistened in the harsh sunlight, but I can only imagine that now), and the pain of my earlobes must have filled up all that made up my entire being then and the pain of my earlobes must have been unbearable, because it was then that was the first time that I separated myself from myself, and I became two people (two small children then, I was two years old), one having the experience, the other observing the one having the experience. And the observer, perhaps because it was an act of my own will (strong then, but stronger now), my first and only real act of self-invention, is the one of the two I most rely on, the one of the two whose voice I believe to be the true voice; and of course it is the observer who cannot be relied on as the final truth to be believed, for the observer has woven between myself and the person who is having an experience a protective membrane, which allows me to see but only feel as much as I can handle at any given moment. And so . . .

. . . On the day I turned two years old, the twenty-fifth of May 1951, a pair of earrings, small hoops made of gold from British Guiana (it was called that then, it is not called that now), were placed in the bored holes in my earlobes (which by then had healed); a pair of bracelets made of silver from someplace other than British Guiana (and that place too was called one thing then, something else now) was placed one on each wrist; a pair of new shoes bought from Bata's was placed on my feet. That afternoon, I was bathed and powdered, and the dress of yellow poplin, completed, its seams all stitched together with a certainty found only in the natural world (I now realize), was placed over my head, and it is quite possible that this entire act had about it the feeling of being draped in a shroud. My mother, carrying me in her arms (as usual), took me to the studio of a photographer, a man named Mr. Walker, to have my picture taken. As she walked along with me in her arms (not complaining), with the heat of the sun still so overwhelming that it, not gravity, seemed to be the force that kept us pinned to the earth's surface, I placed my lips against one side of her head (the temple) and could feel the rhythm of the blood pulsing through her body; I placed my lips against her throat and could hear her swallow saliva that had collected in her mouth; I placed my face against her neck and inhaled deeply a scent that I could not identify then (how could I, there was nothing to compare it to) and cannot now, because it is not of animal or place or thing, it was (and is) a scent unique to her, and it left a mark of such depth that it eventually became a part of my other senses, and even now (yes, now) that scent is also taste, touch, sight and sound.

And Mr. Walker lived on Church Street in a house that was mysterious to me (then, not now) because it had a veranda (unlike my own house) and it had many rooms (unlike my own house, but really Mr. Walker's house had only four rooms, my own house had one) and the windows were closed (the windows in my house were always open). He spoke to my mother, I did not understand what they said, they did not share the same tongue. I knew Mr. Walker was a man, but how I knew that I cannot say (now, then, sometime to come). It is possible that because he touched his hair often, smoothing down, caressing, the forcibly straightened strands, and because he admired and said that he admired my dress of yellow poplin with its simple smocking (giving to me a false air of delicacy), and because he admired and said that he admired the plaid taffeta ribbon in my hair, I thought that he perhaps wasn't a man at all, I had never seen a man do or say any of those things, 1 had then only seen a woman do or say those things. He (Mr. Walker) stood next to a black box which had a curtain at its back (this was his camera but I did not know that at the time, I only know it now) and he asked my mother to stand me on a table, a small table, a table that made me taller, because the scene in the background, against which I was to be photographed, was so vast, it overwhelmed my two-year-old frame, making me seem a mere figurine, not a child at all; and when my mother picked me up, holding me by the armpits with her hands, her thumb accidentally (it could have been deliberate, how could someone who loved me inflict so much pain just in passing?) pressed deeply into my shoulder, and I cried out and then (and still now) looked up at her face and couldn't find any reason in it, and could find no malice in it, only that her eyes were full of something, a feeling that I thought then (and am convinced now) had nothing to do with me; and of course it is possible that just at that moment she had realized that she was exhausted, not physically, but just exhausted by this whole process, celebrating my second birthday, commemorating an event, my birth, that she may not have wished to occur in the first place and may have tried repeatedly to prevent, and then, finally, in trying to find some beauty in it, ended up with a yard and a half of yellow poplin being shaped into a dress, teaching herself smocking and purchasing gold hoops from places whose names never remained the same and silver bracelets from places whose names never remained the same. And Mr. Walker, who was not at all interested in my mothers ups and downs and would never have dreamed of taking in the haphazard mess of her life (but there was nothing so unusual about that, every life, I now know, is a haphazard mess), looked on for a moment as my mother, belying the look in her eyes, said kind and loving words to me in a kind and loving voice, and he then walked over to a looking glass that hung on a wall and squeezed with two of his fingers a lump the size of a pinch of sand that was on his cheek; the lump had a shiny white surface and it broke, emitting a tiny plap sound, and from it came a long ribbon of thick, yellow pus that curled on Mr. Walker's cheek imitating, almost, the decoration on the birthday cake that awaited me at home, and my birthday cake was decorated with a series of species of flora and fauna my mother had never seen (and still has not seen to this day, she is seventy-three years old).

After that day I never again wore my yellow poplin dress with the smocking my mother had just taught herself to make. It was carefully put aside, saved for me to wear to another special occasion; but by the time another special occasion came (I could say quite clearly then what the special occasion was and can say quite clearly now what the special occasion was but I do not want to), the dress could no longer fit me, I had grown too big for it.

1992

Naomi Shihab Nye (B. 1952)

Three Pokes of a Thistle

Hiding Inside the Good Girl

"She has the devil inside her," said my first report card from first grade. I walked home slowly, holding it out from my body, a thistle, a thorn, to my mother, who read the inside, then the note on the back. She cried mightily, heaves of underground rivers, we stood looking deep into the earth as water rushed by.

I didn't know who he was.

One day I'd smashed John's nose on the pencil sharpener and broken it. Stood in the cloakroom smelling the rust of coats. I said No. No thank you. I already read that and it's not a very good story. Jane doesn't do much. I want the spider who talks. The family of little women and their thousand days. No. What I had for breakfast is a secret. I didn't want to tell them I ate dried apricots. I listened to their lineage of eggs. I listened to the bacon crackle in everyone else's pail. Thank you.

What shall we do, what shall we do? Please, I beg you. Our pajamas were flying from the line, waists pinned, their legs fat with fabulous air. My mother peeled beets, her fingers stained deep red. She was bleeding dinner for us. She was getting up and lying down.

Once I came home from school in the middle of the day in a taxi. School gave me a stomachache. I rode in the front passenger seat. It would be expensive. My mother stood at the screen door peering out, my baby brother perched on her hip. She wore an apron. The taxi pulled up in front of the blue mailbox I viewed as an animal across from our house—his opening mouth. Right before I climbed out, another car hit the taxi hard from behind so my mother saw me fly from the front seat to the back. Her mouth wide open, the baby dangling from her like fringe. She came toward us running. I climbed up onto the ledge inside the back window to examine the wreckage. The taxi driver's visored cap had blown out the window. He was shaking his head side to side as if he had water in his ears.

You, you, look what a stomachache gets you. Whiplash.

The doctor felt my neck.

Later I sat on the front steps staring at the spot where it had happened. What about that other driver? He cried when the policeman arrived. He was an old man coming to mail a letter. I was incidental to the scene, but it couldn't have happened without me. *If you had just stayed where you belonged. . . .* My classmates sealed into their desks laboring over pages of subtraction, while out in the world, cars were banging together. Yellow roses opened slowly on a bush beside my step. I was thinking how everything looked from far away.

Then I was old. A hundred years before I found it, Mark Twain inscribed the front of his first-edition leatherbound book, "BE GOOD—AND YOU WILL BE LONESOME." In black ink, with a flourish. He signed his name. My friend had the book in a box in her attic and did not know. It was from her mother's collection. I carried it down the stairs, trembling. My friend said, "Do you think it is valuable?"

Language Barrier

Basically our father spoke English perfectly, though he still got his *b*s and *p*s mixed up. He had a gentle, deliberate way of choosing words. I could feel him reaching up into the air to find them. At night, he told us whimsical, curling "Joha" stories which hypnotized us to sleep. I especially liked the big cooking pan that gave birth to the little pan. My friend Marcia's father who grew up in the United States hardly talked. He built airplanes. I didn't think I would want to fly in anything he made. When Marcia asked him a question, he grunted a kind of pig sound. He sank his face into the paper. My father spilled out musical lines, a horizon of graceful buildings standing beside one another in a distant city. You could imagine people living inside one of my father's words.

He said a few things to us in Arabic—fragrant syllables after we ate, blessings when he hugged us. He hugged us all the time. He said, "I love you" all the time. But I didn't learn how to say "Thank you" in Arabic till I was fourteen, which struck me, even then, as a preposterous omission.

Marcia's father seemed tired. He had seven children because he was a Catholic, Marcia said. I didn't get it. Marcia's mother threw away the leftovers from their table after dinner. My mother carefully wrapped the last little mound of mashed potato inside waxed paper. We'd eat it later.

I felt comfortable in the world of so many different people. Their voices floated around the neighborhood like pollen. On the next block, French-Canadians made blueberry pie. I wanted a slice. It is true that a girl knocked on our door one day and asked to "see the Arab," but I was not insulted. I was mystified. Who?

Sometimes Marcia and I slept together on our screened-in back porch, or in a big green tent in her yard. She was easy to scare. I said the giant harvest moon was coming to eat her and she hid under her pillow. She told me spider stories. We had fun trading little terrors.

When I was almost ready to move away, Marcia and I stood in Dade Park together one last time. I said good-bye to the swings and benches and wooden seesaws with chipped red paint. Two bigger boys rode up on bicycles and circled us. We'd never seen them before. One of them asked if we knew how to do the F-word. I had no idea what they were talking about. Marcia said she knew, but wouldn't tell me. The boys circled the basketball courts, eyeing us strangely. Walking home with Marcia, I felt almost glad to be moving away from her. She stuck her chest out. She said, "Did you ever wish someone would touch you in a private place?"

I looked in the big dictionary at home. Hundreds of F-words I didn't know reached their hands out so it took a long time. And I asked my mother, whose face was so smooth and beautiful and filled with sadness because nothing was quite as good as it could be.

She didn't know either.

Bra Strap

It felt like a taunt, the elastic strap of Karen's bra visible beneath her white blouse in front of me in fifth grade. I saw it even before Douglas snapped it. Who did she think she was, growing older without me?

I spent the night with her one Saturday. In the bathtub together, we splashed and soaped, jingling our talk of teachers, boys, and holidays. But my eyes were on her chest, the great pale fruits growing there. Already they mounded toward stems.

She caught me looking and said, "So?" Sighing, as if she were already tired. Said, "In my family they grow early." Downstairs her bosomy mother stacked cups in a high old cabinet that smelled of grandmother's hair. I could hear her clinking. In my family they barely grew at all. I had been proud of my mother's boyishness, her lithe trunk and straight legs.

Now I couldn't stop thinking about it: what was there, what wasn't there. The mounds on the fronts of certain dolls with candy-coated names. One by one, watching the backs of my friends' blouses, I saw them all fall under the spell. I begged my mother, who said, "For what? Just to be like everybody else?"

Pausing near the underwear displays at Famous and Barr, I asked to be measured, sizing up boxes. "Training Bra"—what were we in training for?

When Louise fell off her front porch and a stake went all the way through her, I heard teachers whispering, "Hope this doesn't ruin her for the future." We discussed the word "impaled." What future? The mysteries of ovaries had not yet been explained. Little factories for eggs. Little secret nests. On the day we saw the film, I didn't like it. If that was what the future meant, I didn't want it anymore. As I was staring out the window afterwards, my mouth tasted like pennies, my throat closed up. The leaves on the trees blurred together so they could carry me.

I sat on a swivel chair practicing handwritings. The backwards slant, the loopy up-and-down. Who would I ever be? My mother was inside the lawyer's office signing papers about the business. That waiting room, with its dull wooden side tables and gloomy magazines, had absolutely nothing to do with me. Never for a second was I drawn toward the world of the dreary professional. I would be a violinist with the Zurich symphony. I would play percussion in a traveling band. I would bake zucchini muffins in Yarmouth, Nova Scotia.

In the car traveling slowly home under a thick gray sky, I worked up courage. Rain, rain, the intimacy of cars. At a stoplight, staring hard at my mother, I asked, "What really happens between men and women to make babies?"

She jumped as if I'd thrown ice at her.

"Not *that!* Not *now!*" From red to green, the light, the light. "There is *oh so much you do not know.*"

It was all she ever told me. The weight of my ignorance pressed upon us both.

Later she slipped me a book, *Little Me, Big Me.* One of the more incomprehensible documents of any childhood: "When a man and a woman love one another enough, he puts his arms around her and part of him goes into part of her and the greatness of their love for one another causes this to feel pleasurable."

On my twelfth birthday, my father came home with our first tape recorder. My mother produced a bouquet of shiny boxes, including a long, slim one. My Lutheran grandparents sat neatly on the couch as the heavy reels wound up our words. "Do you like it? Is it just what you've been waiting for?"

They wanted me to hold it up to my body, the way I would when I put it on. My mother shushing, "Oh, I guess it's private!"

Later the tape would play someone's giggles in the background. My brother? Or the gangs of little girl angels that congregate around our heads, chanting, "Don't grow up, don't grow up!"

I never liked wearing it as much as I did thinking about it.

1996

Hilda Raz

Looking at Aaron

From *What Becomes You*
by Aaron Raz Link and Hilda Raz

Midnight and Aaron is sitting behind the wheel of our rented car. "So what's this book we're writing?" he asks. His voice is uninflected. We're both exhausted from the day's heat. The night sky is flat black. The car is parked in front of the guest house where I'm staying with my laptop computer, working on our collaborative book.

"I don't know," I say.

He shifts impatiently. As far as I can tell, his part of the book is done. I hope to finish my part now, the mother's part, years after his surgery.

Aaron says he hates everything he's written. His voice is speeding up. He articulates very clearly.

"Who cares about this kind of book?" he asks me. "You don't read books about breast cancer, right Mom?" He's talking fast now. He knows I've been well for twelve years.

"Transformation happens in all lives. We'll tell about ours," I say in a soothing voice.

"Okay," he says. His shoulders relax a little as he leans back in the driver's seat.

I lean forward in the passenger seat. "Okay," I say. "But don't expect me to provide any analysis of our experience. Analysis is beyond me."

"You must want to analyze, since the negative always implies the positive," he says.

I reach underneath the seat, grab and open a fresh bottle of water. We could go into the cool guest house where I'm staying, rest on the beds underneath the ceiling fan, switch it on high. I could say we're both tired, let's talk tomorrow when we're fresh. Instead I say, "Let's begin with the garage sale today. You liked my story about the clothes."

"Okay," says Aaron.

Aaron and I look through the newspaper over breakfast and find neighborhood garage sales. It's going to be a very hot day. The first house, in the back yard, has fabulous stuff. Aaron opens a bag and collects Swarovski crystal beads in amber and black, a broken necklace of dyed onyx beads, with Mexican silver charms, and a designer skirt from the 70s in chrome blue Thai silk. The belt loops on the skirt are made of metallic crimson thread. Seven dollars for the lot. He'll tear the silk on the bias, string it with vintage beads and charms to sell as treasure necklaces. Gorgeous. I find a dusty rack of clothes on the cracked, hot driveway. An Anne Klein bomber jacket in silk embroidery lined with candlelight chiffon, a browned-butter cashmere jacket with a diagonal placket, a candlelight satin under-skirt from the 50s.

"Hooh boy!" I say, "look at this slip."

"Why is it a slip, not a skirt?" asks Aaron who comes over to see.

I show him the elastic waistband stitched to the satin and the pliable hoop attached at the hem ruffle. Exquisite.

"How did you wear it?" he asks, turning up the hem to see the fine stitches. He wants me to tell him a story about my clothes. He knows I'll write down what we say.

I tell him about a pink lace overdress with scallops cut out to show the yellow satin knife pleats, the gray tweed skirt with a tomato suede blouson jacket, the matching cloche hat in suede and tweed. Some favorite clothes in the 60s.

Today Aaron and I are both wearing green shorts and white tee-shirts. He has on canvas basketball shoes, one red, one blue, and I'm wearing tattered sandals. We're about the same height but his shoulders and torso are muscular, his chest flat, his waist slender, his hips flat . . . he's very handsome. The guy with the cash box has been looking and looking. As usual, Aaron is oblivious. The driveway is very hot.

"How did you get these clothes?" he asks. "How did you feel wearing them?" Suddenly I know he's working hard and in subversive ways. He wants my attention off him. He thinks the book will be better if I write about myself. I want to write about him, his extraordinary story. Still, such beautiful clothes. I try to answer.

I tell him that when I was a teenager, these clothes helped cover the space I felt inside. I'd learned that I was a girl and should plan to marry a man of substance and have his children. I could help by dressing well. Like Aaron, I was handsome and I earned the clothes by runway modeling. I wore the samples to appear negotiable, of value and substance. My generous parents bought at discount. And so I wore the peau de soie two-piece in navy with my big hair balanced above a thin neck where the keyhole closure fastened at the throat with a soft bow. The skirt was molded high above the waist and fastened with a tiny zipper, thin and long like a scar. Who was I? Who knew? Such beautiful clothes. And the shoes! Black velvet dance slippers with rhinestone clasps at the instep. Kid flats in gold and another pair in silver gilt for dates with short boys. The small heels in layered wood attached to soft leather in camel, the crisp spectator pumps in navy and white. Delissos. Capezzios.

"That's enough," I tell Aaron. He shrugs, pays for his purchases. I leave the clothes behind.

Next day we move, a vacation from our work on the book. We go to the beach.

It's a cool and rainy evening after a day with Aaron driving, negotiating the scenic but winding back roads. Daire, Aaron's friend, sleeps on the back seat. She's carsick. Last year they celebrated ten years of friendship at the Sylvia Beach Hotel at Nye Beach on the Pacific. This year they've reserved rooms for us all. When we arrive, we unpack, eat dinner and talk. Then Aaron and I put on our parkas, take a walk near the ocean. It's dark and chilly but the sand feels warm. Two boys are running around pushing sparklers into the sand. Then they light them all at once. One jumps into the sparkly circle and the other takes his picture, a tiny flash.

"Hey, nice fire," Aaron calls out to a group sitting around flames in a circle of stones. They call back for us to join them—two youngsters, one a teenager, and their parents from Arizona. The dad says, "These kids just up and moved out here two months ago!" The folks have traveled from Arizona to Oregon in a trailer to bring them their stuff. Aaron talks to the kids. I fall into place beside Ed, the dad. I can hear Aaron saying "If you've got insomnia because of the cloudy weather, try a light box." They're telling the stories about leaving home, new places, adjustments. Aaron says, "We moved to LA, lived there for three years, and then I was done. We moved here."

Over the sound of their voices, Ed tells me that he collects cash registers and he's a school counselor back home. He asks, "How could our kids just up and go?" Alcohol on his breath. I shrug my shoulders. They just do. The mom across the fire smiles at me. We've discovered that we both have little granddaughters, another generation. Then Aaron and I get up, walk away into the mist, call back goodbye, goodbye. At the hotel, we hug each other hard. I rub my cheek against his rough beard and then we return to our chilly, damp and salty rooms.

Daire and Aaron are sitting at breakfast as I join them in the communal dining room. They hold hands, rub each other's necks, look into each other's eyes. Aaron will leave soon to go back to school, in California. Daire will stay behind in their apartment. What shall we do today?

We walk the estuary with a tour group and our affable guide of retirement age. Aaron, a biologist, adds information, answers questions. I take photos of him picking up all available wildlife, naming each, standing in the middle of a crowd of interested kids. He's wearing a black baseball cap. We leave the group, drive to the bay, eat lunch—Aaron's first Dungeness crab, which he orders in black bean sauce, and enjoys a lot. Then we shop—jewelry, glass floats, wood sculptures. So much to buy, and we don't. We all eat ice cream. Later, dinner. Daire goes off to bed.

Aaron and I walk again, this time through the small town. I'm quiet, so glad to listen. We haven't been together for six months. His conversation is fluent, elegant. I know that he's leaving his job as director of a program in art and theater for homeless kids. He's decided to study physical theater. After two years of trying, he's been admitted to a famous school, with a scholarship. A big risk. He talks nonstop about his plans for a theater/dance company when he finishes his studying. One project, in choreography, will use the vocabulary of movement from Parkinson's—his father's disease—and Muscular Dystrophy patients. Another is to make a safe place where multi-cultural homeless youth will meet with macho gym guys, he calls them gangsta guys, to develop performance projects for urban theaters, community centers, and college campuses. He hopes to attract national talent for a board of directors; he has good contacts. His voice is low and steady. He walks fast with his hands in his jacket pockets. Right now he doesn't know what else he wants. He's worried about leaving Daire. They both get migraines, stomachaches, need expensive medicine from the drug store. Maybe their separation will be good.

Then Aaron remembers a secret story from his childhood, something that involved me, something he's never told me he knows. He's going to tell this story no matter what I do. I zip up my jacket. The streets are damp and empty, few lights anywhere and everywhere the sound of the ocean.

Aaron remembers when our family was on the way to visit my old college roommate, Libby. Aaron was still Sarah, and she's probably twelve. The tension among the adults in the car is so great that Sarah is going to refuse to get out of the car until someone tells her what's going on. When we reach a big house in the woods on a pond, the adults and the other kids jump out, race around. Sarah waits in the back seat. After a while, my old college roommate Libby comes out of her house, opens the back door of the car, and suggests Sarah come with her for a walk through the woods. They walk on fallen pine needles, a soft path over gravel. Then Libby takes Sarah's hand and tells her if things had been different, Libby would have been Sarah's father.

I am astonished, and breathless. I wonder if this dialogue is exactly right. The story is so crazy. Aaron and I, walking on the sandy tarmac of the parking lot next to the Pacific Ocean, are walking faster now, through wind. I ask Aaron what he said. Aaron said, "You wouldn't have been my father because I wouldn't have been born."

What do I think? I think that this little person Sarah was my young daughter. What could she have thought? She sounded angry. Certainly she knew that two women don't give birth to a child. Not then. Apparently Sarah also knew that Libby was drunk. Sure enough, she falls in a hole and twists her ankle. She has to lean on Sarah as she limps from the woods. Sarah decides to come into the house since she knows the secret.

I ask Aaron why he hadn't told me this story before. Silence. We walk on, come to the hotel, hug, and separate for the night. I've concealed my distress but later I have flaming dreams. Why didn't I know this story? Where was I? In the house, tending the others. I didn't worry about Sarah. She was so much a tomboy we thought she might be lesbian, like Libby. We were wrong. She was a boy.

The summer after my freshman year of college, shortly after Aaron's father and I married, Libby drove to Newport, Rhode Island with her sisters to wait tables at a grand hotel. We followed, slept on the floor of her room or on the beach, wore swimsuits all summer, walked and drove the winding road along the ocean to see the grand houses of the very rich. Libby, very tall, very thin, very blonde, beautiful and brilliant. My best friend, who had been maid of honor at our wedding. Frilly dresses of embroidered organdy. Who came to live with us after the honeymoon. She and I both eighteen. Best friends.

I wake after a fitful night, finish eating breakfast alone, and wander into the library at the top of the hotel. This place is an old beach house where pictures of authors and copies of their books are backdrop for guests reading and writing, drinking hot tea or coffee. The ocean whispers out the windows. Aaron has gone off to chase a dream. He wants to rent a horse to ride the beach. When he was a child we sent him to horse camp where neighbor kids, Mary Zimmerman, now a Tony winning playwright, and her sister Annie, now mother of triplets in a family that lives in Paris, went each summer. Aaron hated camp. He came home, refused to go back. But he was Sarah then. Now he wants to ride the beach. Daire and Aaron both seemed in good spirits as we started our day but they left breakfast early as I was talking about Aaron's brother, a composer of new music. The guests were talking about the Ernest Bloch festival this weekend, apparently a showcase for new music. Bloch had a summer home here.

Later in the day, the distance between Aaron and me is palpable; then permeable; then dissolves. We sit in adjacent desk chairs on the high narrow balcony that opens from the library over the beach. High tide. Midnight. Dawn has gone to bed. The ocean is loud, the air saturated with salt water. Below us fires flare on the sand, shine on faces. We watch. Aaron is wrapped in a blanket from the library couch. I hold my hands tightly in my sleeves in order not to pat his hair, rub his shoulders, touch his cheek, reach for his hand.

I have no idea what to do. Analysis out of the question. But my grown son Aaron, who was my daughter Sarah, has control of his own life now. His resolve is strong and his powers of analysis are keen. He says that he will try to live in a way that anticipates and avoids future regret. He will treat Daire and his friends with love and respect and try to avoid bitterness and accusation. He'll use lessons from his work with homeless kids, who have learned to live in their extra-large sweatshirts they call hoodies, their only reliable homes.

By now, many hours later, in the top floor library, people still read or doze in easy chairs in front of an ocean at low tide. The room is damp and salty, quiet. The lights are low and flicker. On the balcony with Aaron, I drink coffee with cream, listen, speak. We leave the Sylvia Beach Hotel in the morning. When we get back to the city I have only a few more days before flying home. Already the distance between Aaron's life and my life is increasing. For nine months I will not see him as I write. I feel my limits even as I push to extend them to this young man beside me, my son.

And then we all eat breakfast. Before we pack, we walk Nye Beach one last time, to explore crevices in the rock we've seen filling and emptying from the balconies outside our windows. Anemones in tide pools are both green and beige, their tentacles drift among the snails. Daire gives everything we see a name. We laugh and run. In the car we decide to take the scenic road back, make side excursions to Cape Meares to climb to the lighthouse tower, explore more tide pools. We take pictures, eat, talk, tell jokes. Then we stop at Siletz Bay where Aaron goes missing.

For an hour and a half, Daire and I look for him in the water where the seals sleep on the rocks and on the sidewalks around the bay. The ocean pounds. Last night in the hotel library I'd met a woman writing a book. She'd survived the attack of a serial murderer to testify at his trial. An editor, I was careful to pay attention to her book proposal, not her life—but of course I was scared by the danger she'd survived, and the madness of the serial murderer who had been a professional pilot with a wife and kids; he'd traveled so that his crimes were impossible for the police to connect. And now Aaron is missing, who for his entire life, since he began walking at eighteen months, has disappeared at regular intervals—at playgrounds, shopping centers, in airports and bus stations, and train stations. He always reappears in short order. But now I'm thinking that a transsexual man can attract violence anywhere. Even here, at an Oregon Coast National Wildlife Refuge, where someone wearing a chrome yellow kayak is paddling so close to the seals that they slither away in a group, faster than you imagine huge mammals can move. Foolish man. Aaron is wildlife, like the seals. He is not safe from a crazy man wearing a yellow kayak.

An hour and a half later Daire shouts, "There's Aaron," and sure enough, the little tough guy, as his kids call him, is walking toward us, sopping jeans rolled to the knees, carrying his sneakers and socks, grinning. His face is deeply tanned. His high forehead is shining.

"I've had an adventure," he shouts.

At the dock where you can rent kayaks, Aaron had met a man, with a small child, returning a boat. "You've got a free twenty minutes left," said the man, handing Aaron a paddle, pushing him off into the water. Aaron had paddled to the seal island expecting to see us scanning the horizon. He didn't see us, but we and the seals saw him in the borrowed chrome yellow kayak.

I walk away, buy an ice cream, sit in the sun to eat and calm down. I have been so afraid. I mean my silence to be a gift to him. He has been so happy. I think about insane maternal privilege that has kept me secure in a world that holds our children safe so long as we practice rituals: wear warm clothes in cold weather; tell me where you are at all times; don't cross streets alone, or without looking; never talk to strangers and refuse all rides; be home by dark and sleep in your own clean bed wearing your super-hero pajamas. In this fabricated world, kids always have enough to eat, drink clean water, their bodies are covered with clothes that become them and announce their identity. They will never lie down to sleep in their extra-large hoodies on the streets of cities.

Aaron is in the third decade of a life I grew inside my body. I sit on the sand, look out to sea, watch the steady huge gray rocks on the island in the bay. The largest rock on the island raises its head, turns into a bull elephant seal before my eyes. Aaron has seen this transformation from the yellow kayak. He is waiting to tell me the story. I walk back to the car and get ready to listen.

2007

Leslie Marmon Silko (B. 1948)

Landscape, History, and the Pueblo Imagination

From a High Arid Plateau in New Mexico

You see that after a thing is dead, it dries up. It might take weeks or years, but eventually if you touch the thing, it crumbles under your fingers. It goes back to dust. The soul of the thing has long since departed. With the plants and wild game the soul may have already been borne back into bones and blood or thick green stalk and leaves. Nothing is wasted. What cannot be eaten by people or in some way used must then be left where other living creatures may benefit. What domestic animals or wild scavengers can't eat will be fed to the plants. The plants feed on the dust of these few remains.

The ancient Pueblo people buried the dead in vacant rooms or partially collapsed rooms adjacent to the main living quarters. Sand and clay used to construct the roof make layers many inches deep once the roof has collapsed. The layers of sand and clay make for easy gravedigging. The vacant room fills with cast-off objects and debris. When a vacant room has filled deep enough, a shallow but adequate grave can be scooped in a far corner. Archaeologists have remarked over formal burials complete with elaborate funerary objects excavated in trash middens of abandoned rooms. But the rocks and adobe mortar of collapsed walls were valued by the ancient people. Because each rock had been carefully selected for size and shape, then chiseled to an even face. Even the pink clay adobe melting with each rainstorm had to be prayed over, then dug and carried some distance. Corn cobs and husks, the rinds and stalks and animal bones were not regarded by the ancient people as filth or garbage. The remains were merely resting at a mid-point in their journey back to dust. Human remains are not so different. They should rest with the bones and rinds where they all may benefit living creatures—small rodents and insects—until their return is completed. The remains of things—animals and plants, the clay and the stones—were treated with respect. Because for the ancient people all these things had spirit and being. The antelope merely consents to return home with the hunter. All phases of the hunt are conducted with love. The love the hunter and the people have for the Antelope People. And the love of the antelope who agree to give up their meat and blood so that human beings will not starve. Waste of meat or even the thoughtless handling of bones cooked bare will offend the antelope spirits. Next year the hunters will vainly search the dry plains for antelope. Thus it is necessary to return carefully the bones and hair, and the stalks and leaves to the earth who first created them. The spirits remain close by. They do not leave us.

The dead become dust, and in this becoming they are once more joined with the Mother. The ancient Pueblo People called the earth the Mother Creator of all things in this world. Her sister, the Corn Mother, occasionally merges with her because all succulent green life rises out of the depths of the earth.

Rocks and clay are part of the Mother. They emerge in various forms, but at some time before, they were smaller particles or great boulders. At a later time they may again become what they once were. Dust.

A rock shares this fate with us and with animals and plants as well. A rock has being or spirit, although we may not understand it. The spirit may differ from the spirit we know in animals or plants or in ourselves. In the end we all originate from the depths of the earth. Perhaps this is how all beings share in the spirit of the Creator. We do not know.

From the Emergence Place

Pueblo potters, the creators of petroglyphs and oral narratives, never conceived of removing themselves from the earth and sky. So long as the human consciousness remains within the hills, canyons, cliffs, and the plants, clouds, and sky, the term landscape, as it has entered the English language, is misleading. "A portion of territory the eye can comprehend in a single view" does not correctly describe the relationship between the human being and his or her surroundings. This assumes the viewer is somehow outside or separate from the territory he or she surveys. Viewers are as much a part of the landscape as the boulders they stand on. There is no high mesa edge or mountain peak where one can stand and not immediately be part of all that surrounds. Human identity is linked with all the elements of Creation through the clan: you might belong to the Sun Clan or the Lizard Clan or the Corn Clan or the Clay Clan.[1] Standing deep within the natural world, the ancient Pueblo understood the thing as it was—the squash blossom, grasshopper, or rabbit itself could never be created by the human hand. Ancient Pueblos took the modest view that the thing itself (the landscape) could not be improved upon. The ancients did not presume to tamper with what had already been created. Thus *realism,* as we now recognize it in painting and sculpture, did not catch the imaginations of Pueblo people until recently.

The squash blossom is *one thing:* itself. So the ancient Pueblo potter abstracted what she saw to be the key elements of the squash blossom—the four symmetrical petals, with four symmetrical stamens in the center. These key elements, while suggesting the squash flower, also link it with the four cardinal directions. By representing only its intrinsic form, the squash flower is released from a limited meaning or restricted identity. Even in the most sophisticated abstract form, a squash flower or a cloud or a lightning bolt became intricately connected with a complex system of relationships which the ancient Pueblo people maintained with each other, and with the populous natural world they lived within. A bolt of lightning is itself, but at the same time it may mean much more. It may be a messenger of good fortune when summer rains are needed. It may deliver death, perhaps the result of manipulations by the Gunnadeyahs, destructive necromancers. Lightning may strike down an evil-doer. Or lightning may strike a person of good will. If the person survives, lightning endows him or her with heightened power.

Pictographs and petroglyphs of constellations or elk or antelope draw their magic in part from the process wherein the focus of all prayer and concentration is upon the thing itself, which, in its turn, guides the hunter's hand. Connection with the spirit dimensions requires a figure or form which is all-inclusive. A "lifelike" rendering of an elk is too restrictive. Only the elk *is* itself. A *realistic* rendering of an elk would be only one particular elk anyway. The purpose of the hunt rituals and magic is to make contact with *all* the spirits of the Elk.

---

[1]*Clan*—A social unit composed of families sharing common ancestors who trace their lineage back to the Emergence where their ancestors allied themselves with certain plants or animals or elements. *[Silko's note]*

The land, the sky, and all that is within them—the landscape— includes human beings. Interrelationships in the Pueblo landscape are complex and fragile. The unpredictability of the weather, the aridity and harshness of much of the terrain in the high plateau country explain in large part the relentless attention the ancient Pueblo people gave the sky and the earth around them. Survival depended upon harmony and cooperation not only among human beings, but among all things—the animate and the less animate, since rocks and mountains were known to move, to travel occasionally.

The ancient Pueblos believed the Earth and the Sky were sisters (or sister and brother in the post-Christian version). As long as good family relations are maintained, then the Sky will continue to bless her sister, the Earth, with rain, and the Earth's children will continue to survive. But the old stories recall incidents in which troublesome spirits or beings threaten the earth. In one story, a malicious ka'tsina, called the Gambler, seizes the Shiwana, or Rainclouds, the Sun's beloved children.[2] The Shiwana are snared in magical power late one afternoon on a high mountain top. The Gambler takes the Rainclouds to his mountain stronghold where he locks them in the north room of his house. What was his idea? The Shiwana were beyond value. They brought life to all things on earth. The Gambler wanted a big stake to wager in his games of chance. But such greed, even on the part of only one being, had the effect of threatening the survival of all life on earth. Sun Youth, aided by old Grandmother Spider, outsmarts the Gambler and the rigged game, and the Rainclouds are set free. The drought ends, and once more life thrives on earth.

Through the Stories We Hear Who We Are

All summer the people watch the west horizon, scanning the sky from south to north for rain clouds. Corn must have moisture at the time the tassels form. Otherwise pollination will be incomplete, and the ears will be stunted and shriveled. An inadequate harvest may bring disaster. Stories told at Hopi, Zuni, and at Acoma and Laguna describe drought and starvation as recently as 1900. Precipitation in west-central New Mexico averages fourteen inches annually. The western pueblos are located at altitudes over 5,600 feet above sea level, where winter temperatures at night fall below freezing. Yet evidence of their presence in the high desert plateau country goes back ten thousand years. The ancient Pueblo people not only survived in this environment, but many years they thrived. In A.D. 1100 the people at Chaco Canyon had built cities with apartment buildings of stone five stories high. Their sophistication as sky-watchers was surpassed only by Mayan and Inca astronomers. Yet this vast complex of knowledge and belief, amassed for thousands of years, was never recorded in writing.

Instead, the ancient Pueblo people depended upon collective memory through successive generations to maintain and transmit an entire

---

[2]*Ka'tsina*—Ka'tsinas are spirit beings who roam the earth and who inhabit kachina masks worn in Pueblo ceremonial dances. *[Silko's note]*

culture, a world view complete with proven strategies for survival. The oral narrative, or "story," became the medium in which the complex of Pueblo knowledge and belief was maintained. Whatever the event or the subject, the ancient people perceived the world and themselves within that world as part of an ancient continuous story composed of innumerable bundles of other stories.

The ancient Pueblo vision of the world was inclusive. The impulse was to leave nothing out. Pueblo oral tradition necessarily embraced all levels of human experience. Otherwise, the collective knowledge and beliefs comprising ancient Pueblo culture would have been incomplete. Thus stories about the Creation and Emergence of human beings and animals into this World continue to be retold each year for four days and four nights during the winter solstice. The "humma-hah" stories related events from the time long ago when human beings were still able to communicate with animals and other living things. But, beyond these two preceding categories, the Pueblo oral tradition knew no boundaries. Accounts of the appearance of the first Europeans in Pueblo country or of the tragic encounters between Pueblo people and Apache raiders were no more and no less important than stories about the biggest mule deer ever taken or adulterous couples surprised in cornfields and chicken coops. Whatever happened, the ancient people instinctively sorted events and details into a loose narrative structure. Everything became a story.

Traditionally everyone, from the youngest child to the oldest person, was expected to listen and to be able to recall or tell a portion, if only a small detail, from a narrative account or story. Thus the remembering and retelling were a communal process. Even if a key figure, an elder who knew much more than others, were to die unexpectedly, the system would remain intact. Through the efforts of a great many people, the community was able to piece together valuable accounts and crucial information that might otherwise have died with an individual.

Communal storytelling was a self-correcting process in which listeners were encouraged to speak up if they noted an important fact or detail omitted. The people were happy to listen to two or three different versions of the same event or the same humma-hah story. Even conflicting versions of an incident were welcomed for the entertainment they provided. Defenders of each version might joke and tease one another, but seldom were there any direct confrontations. Implicit in the Pueblo oral tradition was the awareness that loyalties, grudges, and kinship must always influence the narrator's choices as she emphasizes to listeners this is the way *she* has always heard the story told. The ancient Pueblo people sought a communal truth, not an absolute. For them this truth lived somewhere within the web of differing versions, disputes over minor points, outright contradictions tangling with old feuds and village rivalries.

A dinner-table conversation, recalling a deer hunt forty years ago when the largest mule deer ever was taken, inevitably stimulates similar memories in listeners. But hunting stories were not merely after-dinner entertainment. These accounts contained information of critical importance about behavior and migration patterns of mule deer. Hunting stories carefully described key landmarks and locations of fresh water. Thus a deer-hunt story might also serve as a "map." Lost travelers, and lost piñon-nut gatherers, have been saved by sighting a rock formation they recognize only because they once heard a hunting story describing this rock formation.

The importance of cliff formations and water holes does not end with hunting stories. As offspring of the Mother Earth, the ancient Pueblo people could not conceive of themselves within a specific landscape. Location, or "place," nearly always plays a central role in the Pueblo oral narratives. Indeed, stories are most frequently recalled as people are passing by a specific geographical feature or the exact place where a story takes place. The precise date of the incident often is less important than the place or location of the happening. "Long, long ago," "a long time ago," "not too long ago," and "recently" are usually how stories are classified in terms of time. But the places where the stories occur are precisely located, and prominent geographical details recalled, even if the landscape is well-known to listeners. Often because the turning point in the narrative involved a peculiarity or special quality of a rock or tree or plant found only at that place. Thus, in the case of many of the Pueblo narratives, it is impossible to determine which came first: the incident or the geographical feature which begs to be brought alive in a story that features some unusual aspect of this location.

There is a giant sandstone boulder about a mile north of Old Laguna, on the road to Paguate. It is ten feet tall and twenty feet in circumference. When I was a child, and we would pass this boulder driving to Paguate village, someone usually made reference to the story about Kochininako, Yellow Woman, and the Estrucuyo, a monstrous giant who nearly ate her. The Twin Hero Brothers saved Kochininako, who had been out hunting rabbits to take home to feed her mother and sisters. The Hero Brothers had heard her cries just in time. The Estrucuyo had cornered her in a cave too small to fit its monstrous head. Kochininako had already thrown to the Estrucuyo all her rabbits, as well as her moccasins and most of her clothing. Still the creature had not been satisfied. After killing the Estrucuyo with their bows and arrows, the Twin Hero Brothers slit open the Estrucuyo and cut out its heart. They threw the heart as far as they could. The monster's heart landed there, beside the old trail to Paguate village, where the sandstone boulder rests now.

It may be argued that the existence of the boulder precipitated the creation of a story to explain it. But sandstone boulders and sandstone formations of strange shapes abound in the Laguna Pueblo area. Yet most of them do not have stories. Often the crucial element in a narrative is the terrain—some specific detail of the setting.

A high dark mesa rises dramatically from a grassy plain fifteen miles southeast of Laguna, in an area known as Swanee. On the grassy plain one hundred and forty years ago, my great-grandmother's uncle and his brother-in-law were grazing their herd of sheep. Because visibility on the plain extends for over twenty miles, it wasn't until the two sheepherders came near the high dark mesa that the Apaches were able to stalk them. Using the mesa to obscure their approach, the raiders swept around from both ends of the mesa. My great-grandmother's relatives were killed, and the herd lost. The high dark mesa played a critical role: the mesa had compromised the safety which the openness of the plains had seemed to assure. Pueblo and Apache alike relied upon the terrain, the very earth herself, to give them protection and aid. Human activities or needs were maneuvered to fit the existing surroundings and conditions. I imagine the last afternoon of my distant ancestors as warm and sunny for late September. They might have been traveling slowly, bringing the sheep closer to Laguna in preparation for the approach of colder weather. The grass was tall and only beginning to change from green to a yellow which matched the late-afternoon sun shining off it. There might have been comfort in the warmth and the sight of the sheep fattening on good pasture which lulled my ancestors into their fatal inattention. They might have had a rifle whereas the Apaches had only bows and arrows. But there would have been four or five Apache raiders, and the surprise attack would have canceled any advantage the rifles gave them.

Survival in any landscape comes down to making the best use of all available resources. On that particular September afternoon, the raiders made better use of the Swanee terrain than my poor ancestors did. Thus the high dark mesa and the story of the two lost Laguna herders became inextricably linked. The memory of them and their story resides in part with the high black mesa. For as long as the mesa stands, people within the family and clan will be reminded of the story of that afternoon long ago. Thus the continuity and accuracy of the oral narratives are reinforced by the landscape—and the Pueblo interpretation of that landscape is *maintained.*

The Migration Story: An Interior Journey

The Laguna Pueblo migration stories refer to specific places—mesas, springs, or cottonwood trees—not only locations which can be visited still, but also locations which lie directly on the state highway route linking Paguate village with Laguna village. In traveling this road as a child with older Laguna people I first heard a few of the stories from that much larger body of stories linked with the Emergence and Migration.[3] It may be coincidental that Laguna people continue to follow the same route which, according to the Migration story, the ancestors followed south from the Emergence Place. It may be that the route is merely the shortest and best route for car, horse,

---

[3] *The Emergence*—All the human beings, animals, and life which had been created emerged from the four worlds below when the earth became habitable.
The Migration—The Pueblo people emerged into the Fifth World, but they had already been warned they would have to travel and search before they found the place they were meant to live. *[Silko's note]*

or foot traffic between Laguna and Paguate villages. But if the stories about boulders, springs, and hills are actually remnants from a ritual that retraces the creation and emergence of the Laguna Pueblo people as a culture, as the people they became, then continued use of that route creates a unique relationship between the ritual-mythic world and the actual, everyday world. A journey from Paguate to Laguna down the long incline of Paguate Hill retraces the original journey from the Emergence Place, which is located slightly north of the Paguate village. Thus the landscape between Paguate and Laguna takes on a deeper significance: the landscape resonates the spiritual or mythic dimension of the Pueblo world even today.

Although each Pueblo culture designates a specific Emergence Place—usually a small natural spring edged with mossy sandstone and full of cattails and wild watercress—it is clear that they do not agree on any single location or natural spring as the one and only true Emergence Place. Each Pueblo group recounts its own stories about Creation, Emergence, and Migration, although they all believe that all human beings, with all the animals and plants, emerged at the same place and at the same time.[4]

Natural springs are crucial sources of water for all life in the high desert plateau country. So the small spring near Paguate village is literally the source and continuance of life for the people in the area. The spring also functions on a spiritual level, recalling the original Emergence Place and linking the people and the spring water to all other people and to that moment when the Pueblo people became aware of themselves as they are even now. The Emergence was an emergence into a precise cultural identity. Thus the Pueblo stories about the Emergence and Migration are not to be taken as literally as the anthropologists might wish. Prominent geographical features and landmarks which are mentioned in the narratives exist for ritual purposes, not because the Laguna people actually journeyed south for hundreds of years from Chaco Canyon or Mesa Verde, as the archaeologists say, or eight miles from the site of the natural springs at Paguate to the sandstone hilltop at Laguna.

The eight miles, marked with boulders, mesas, springs, and river crossings, are actually a ritual circuit or path which marks the interior journey the Laguna people made: a journey of awareness and imagination in which they emerged from being within the earth and from everything included in earth to the culture and people they became, differentiating themselves for the first time from all that had surrounded them, always aware that interior distances cannot be reckoned in physical miles or in calendar years.

The narratives linked with prominent features of the landscape between Paguate and Laguna delineate the complexities of the relationship which human beings must maintain with the surrounding natural world if they hope to survive in this place. Thus the journey was an interior process of

---

[4]*Creation*—Tse'itsi'nako, Thought Woman, the Spider, thought about it, and everything she thought came into being. First she thought of three sisters for herself, and they helped her think of the rest of the Universe, including the Fifth World and the four worlds below. *The Fifth World* is the world we are living in today. There are four previous worlds below this world. *[Silko's note]*

the imagination, a growing awareness that being human is somehow different from all other life—animal, plant, and inanimate. Yet we are all from the same source: the awareness never deteriorated into Cartesian duality, cutting off the human from the natural world.

The people found the opening into the Fifth World too small to allow them or any of the animals to escape. They had sent a fly out through the small hole to tell them if it was the world which the Mother Creator had promised. It was, but there was the problem of getting out. The antelope tried to butt the opening to enlarge it, but the antelope enlarged it only a little. It was necessary for the badger with her long claws to assist the antelope, and at last the opening was enlarged enough so that all the people and animals were able to emerge up into the Fifth World. The human beings could not have emerged without the aid of antelope and badger. The human beings depended upon the aid and charity of the animals. Only through interdependence could the human beings survive. Families belonged to clans, and it was by clan that the human being joined with the animal and plant world. Life on the high arid plateau became viable when the human beings were able to imagine themselves as sisters and brothers to the badger, antelope, clay, yucca, and sun. Not until they could find a viable relationship to the terrain, the landscape they found themselves in, could they *emerge*. Only at the moment the requisite balance between human and *other* was realized could the Pueblo people become a culture, a distinct group whose population and survival remained stable despite the vicissitudes of climate and terrain.

Landscape thus has similarities with dreams. Both have the power to seize terrifying feelings and deep instincts and translate them into images—visual, aural, tactile—into the concrete where human beings may more readily confront and channel the terrifying instincts or powerful emotions into rituals and narratives which reassure the individual while reaffirming cherished values of the group. The identity of the individual as a part of the group and the greater Whole is strengthened, and the terror of facing the world alone is extinguished.

Even now, the people at Laguna Pueblo spend the greater portion of social occasions recounting recent incidents or events which have occurred in the Laguna area. Nearly always, the discussion will precipitate the retelling of older stories about similar incidents or other stories connected with a specific place. The stories often contain disturbing or provocative material, but are nonetheless told in the presence of children and women. The effect of these inter-family or inter-clan exchanges is the reassurance for each person that she or he will never be separated or apart from the clan, no matter what might happen. Neither the worst blunders or disasters nor the greatest financial prosperity and joy will ever be permitted to isolate anyone from the rest of the group. In the ancient times, cohesiveness was all that stood between extinction and survival, and, while the individual certainly was recognized, it was always as an individual simultaneously bonded to family and clan by a complex bundle of custom and ritual. You are never the first to suffer a grave loss or profound humiliation. You are never the first, and you understand that you will probably not be the last to commit or be victimized by a repugnant act. Your family and clan are able to go on at length about others now passed on, others older or more experienced than you who suffered similar losses.

The wide deep arroyo near the Kings Bar (located across the reservation borderline) has over the years claimed many vehicles. A few years ago, when a Viet Nam veteran's new red Volkswagen rolled backwards into the arroyo while he was inside buying a six-pack of beer, the story of his loss joined the lively and large collection of stories already connected with that big arroyo. I do not know whether the Viet Nam veteran was consoled when he was told the stories about the other cars claimed by the ravenous arroyo. All his savings of combat pay had gone for the red Volkswagen. But this man could not have felt any worse than the man who, some years before, had left his children and mother-in-law in his station wagon with the engine running. When he came out of the liquor store his station wagon was gone. He found it and its passengers upside down in the big arroyo. Broken bones, cuts and bruises, and a total wreck of the car. The big arroyo has a wide mouth. Its existence needs no explanation. People in the area regard the arroyo much as they might regard a living being, which has a certain character and personality. I seldom drive past that wide deep arroyo without feeling a familiarity with and even a strange affection for this arroyo. Because as treacherous as it may be, the arroyo maintains a strong connection between human beings and the earth. The arroyo demands from us the caution and attention that constitute respect. It is this sort of respect the old believers have in mind when they tell us we must respect and love the earth.

Hopi Pueblo elders have said that the austere and, to some eyes, barren plains and hills surrounding their mesa-top villages actually help to nurture the spirituality of the Hopi *way*. The Hopi elders say the Hopi people might have settled in locations far more lush where daily life would not have been so grueling. But there on the high silent sandstone mesas that overlook the sandy arid expanses stretching to all horizons, the Hopi elders say the Hopi people must "live by their prayers" if they are to survive. The Hopi way cherishes the intangible: the riches realized from interaction and inter-relationships with all beings above all else. Great abundances of material things, even food, the Hopi elders believe, tend to lure human attention away from what is most valuable and important. The views of the Hopi elders are not much different from those elders in all the Pueblos.

The bare vastness of the Hopi landscape emphasizes the visual impact of every plant, every rock, every arroyo. Nothing is overlooked or taken for granted. Each ant, each lizard, each lark is imbued with great value simply because the creature is there, simply because the creature is alive in a place where any life at all is precious. Stand on the mesa edge at Walpai and look west over the bare distances toward the pale blue outlines of the San Francisco peaks where the ka'tsina spirits reside. So little lies between you and the sky. So little lies between you and the earth. One look and you know that simply to survive is a great triumph, that every possible resource is needed, every possibly ally—even the most humble insect or reptile. You realize you will be speaking with all of them if you intend to last out the year. Thus it is that the Hopi elders are grateful to the landscape for aiding them in their quest as spiritual people.

1986

Jonathan Swift (1667–1745)

A Modest Proposal[1]

For Preventing the Children of Poor People in Ireland from Being a Burden to Their Parents or Country, and for Making Them Beneficial to the Public

It is a melancholy object to those who walk through this great town[2] or travel in the country, when they see the streets, the roads, and cabin doors, crowded with beggars of the female sex, followed by three, four, or six children, all in rags and importuning every passenger for an alms. These mothers, instead of being able to work for their honest livelihood, are forced to employ all their time in strolling to beg sustenance for their helpless infants, who, as they grow up, either turn thieves for want of work, or leave their dear native country to fight for the Pretender in Spain, or sell themselves to the Barbadoes.[3]

I think it is agreed by all parties that this prodigious number of children in the arms, or on the backs, or at the heels of their mothers, and frequently of their fathers, is in the present deplorable state of the kingdom a very great additional grievance; and therefore whoever could find out a fair, cheap, and easy method of making these children sound, useful members of the commonwealth would deserve so well of the public as to have his statue set up for a preserver of the nation.

---

[1] *A Modest Proposal* is a keen example of Swift's use of irony, a favorite satiric device. Irony pervades the piece, from the very title ("modest" as adjective). The piece uses an extended metaphor: "The English are devouring the Irish." The article expresses Swift's concern for the oppressed, populous and hungry Catholic peasants of Ireland and his anger at English absentee landlords, bleeding the country dry.

[2] Dublin.

[3] James Francis Edward Stuart (1688–1766), the son of James II was claimant ("Pretender") to the throne, but his succession had been barred by the Glorious Revolution.

But my intention is very far from being confined to provide only for the children of professed beggars; it is of a much greater extent, and shall take in the whole number of infants at a certain age who are born of parents in effect as little able to support them as those who demand our charity in the streets.

As to my own part, having turned my thoughts for many years upon this important subject, and maturely weighed the several schemes of other projectors,[4] I have always found them grossly mistaken in their computation. It is true, a child just dropped from its dam may be supported by her milk for a solar year, with little other nourishment; at most not above the value of two shillings, which the mother may certainly get, or the value in scraps, by her lawful occupation of begging; and it is exactly at one year old that I propose to provide for them in such a manner as instead of being a charge upon their parents or the parish, or wanting food and raiment for the rest of their lives, they shall on the contrary contribute to the feeding, and partly to the clothing, of many thousands.

There is likewise another great advantage in my scheme, that it will prevent those voluntary abortions, and that horrid practice of women murdering their bastard children, alas, too frequent among us, sacrificing the poor innocent babes, I doubt, more to avoid the expense than the shame, which would move tears and pity in the most savage and inhuman breast.

The number of souls in this kingdom[5] being usually reckoned one million and a half, of these I calculate there may be about two hundred thousand couples whose wives are breeders; from which number I subtract thirty thousand couples who arc able to maintain their own children, although I apprehend there cannot be so many under the present distresses of the kingdom; but this being granted, there will remain an hundred and seventy thousand breeders. I again subtract fifty thousand for those women who miscarry, or whose children die by accident or disease within the year. There only remain an hundred and twenty thousand children of poor parents annually born. The question therefore is, how this number shall be reared and provided for, which, as I have already said, under the present situation of affairs, is utterly impossible by all the methods hitherto proposed. For we can neither employ them in handicraft or agriculture; we neither build houses (I mean in the country) nor cultivate land. They can very seldom pick up a livelihood by stealing till they arrive at six years old, except where they are of towardly[6] parts; although I confess they learn the rudiments much earlier, during which time they can however be looked upon only as probationers, as I have been informed by a principal gentleman in the county of Cavan, who protested to me that he never knew above

---

[4]Creators of schemes.
[5]Ireland.
[6]Dutiful.

one or two instances under the age of six, even in a part of the kingdom so renowned for the quickest proficiency in that art.

I am assured by our merchants that a boy or a girl before twelve years old is no salable commodity; and even when they come to this age they will not yield above three pounds, or three pounds and half a crown at most on the Exchange; which cannot turn to account either to the parents or the kingdom, the charge of nutriment and rags having been at least four times that value.

I shall now therefore humbly propose my own thoughts, which I hope will not be liable to the least objection.

I have been assured by a very knowing American of my acquaintance in London, that a young healthy child well nursed is at a year old a most delicious, nourishing, and wholesome food, whether stewed, roasted, baked, or boiled; and I make no doubt that it will equally serve in a fricassee or a ragout.[7]

I do therefore humbly offer it to public consideration that of the hundred and twenty thousand children, already computed, twenty thousand may be reserved for breed, whereof only one fourth part to be males, which is more than we allow to sheep, black cattle, or swine; and my reason is that these children are seldom the fruits of marriage, a circumstance not much regarded by our savages, therefore one male will be sufficient to serve four females. That the remaining hundred thousand may at a year old be offered in sale to the persons of quality and fortune through the kingdom, always advising the mother to let them suck plentifully in the last month, so as to render them plump and fat for a good table. A child will make two dishes at an entertainment for friends; and when the family dines alone, the fore or hind quarter will make a reasonable dish, and seasoned with a little pepper or salt will be very good boiled on the fourth day, especially in winter.

I have reckoned upon a medium that a child just born will weigh twelve pounds, and in a solar year if tolerably nursed increaseth to twenty-eight pounds.

I grant this food will be somewhat dear, and therefore very proper for landlords, who, as they have already devoured most of the parents, seem to have the best title to the children.

Infant's flesh will be in season throughout the year, but more plentiful in March, and a little before and after. For we are told by a grave author, an eminent French physician,[8] that fish being a prolific diet, there are more children born in Roman Catholic countries about nine months after Lent than at any other season; therefore, reckoning a year after Lent, the markets will be more glutted than usual, because the number of popish infants is at least three to one in this kingdom; and therefore it will have one other collateral advantage, by lessening the number of Papists among us.

---

[7]Meat stew.
[8]François Rabelais (ca. 1494–1553).

I have already computed the charge of nursing a beggar's child (in which list I reckon all cottagers, laborers, and four fifths of the farmers) to be about two shillings per annum, rags included; and I believe no gentleman would repine to give ten shillings for the carcass of a good fat child, which, as I have said, will make four dishes of excellent nutritive meat, when he hath only some particular friend or his own family to dine with him. Thus the squire will learn to be a good landlord, and grow popular among the tenants; the mother will have eight shillings net profit, and be fit for work till she produces another child.

Those who are more thrifty (as I must confess the times require) may flay the carcass; the skin of which artificially[9] dressed will make admirable gloves for ladies, and summer boots for fine gentlemen.

As to our city of Dublin, shambles[10] may be appointed for this purpose in the most convenient parts of it, and butchers we may be assured will not be wanting; although I rather recommend buying the children alive, and dressing them hot from the knife as we do roasting pigs.

A very worthy person, a true lover of his country, and whose virtues I highly esteem, was lately pleased in discoursing on this matter to offer a refinement upon my scheme. He said that many gentlemen of this kingdom, having of late destroyed their deer, he conceived that the want of venison might be well supplied by the bodies of young lads and maidens, not exceeding fourteen years of age nor under twelve, so great a number of both sexes in every county being now ready to starve for want of work and service; and these to be disposed of by their parents, if alive, or otherwise by their nearest relations. But with due deference to so excellent a friend and so deserving a patriot, I cannot be altogether in his sentiments; for as to the males, my American acquaintance assured me from frequent experience that their flesh was generally tough and lean, like that of our schoolboys, by continual exercise, and their taste disagreeable; and to fatten them would not answer the charge. Then as to the females, it would, I think with humble submission, be a loss to the public, because they soon would become breeders themselves: and besides, it is not improbable that some scrupulous people might be apt to censure such a practice (although indeed very unjustly) as a little bordering upon cruelty; which, I confess, hath always been with me the strongest objection against any project, how well soever intended.

But in order to justify my friend, he confessed that this expedient was put into his head by the famous Psalmanazar,[11] a native of the island Formosa, who came from thence to London above twenty years ago, and in conversation told my friend that in his country when any young person happened to be put to death, the executioner sold the carcass to persons of quality as a prime dainty; and that in his time the body of a plump girl of fifteen, who was crucified for an attempt to poison the emperor, was sold

---

[9]Skillfully.

[10]Slaughterhouses.

[11]George Psalmanazar (ca. 1679–1763), a famous imposter. A Frenchman who wrote a fictitious account of Formosa, in which he described cannibalism and human sacrifice.

to his Imperial Majesty's prime minister of state, and other great mandarins of the court, in joints from the gibbet, at four hundred crowns. Neither indeed can I deny that if the same use were made of several plump young girls in this town, who without one single groat to their fortunes cannot stir abroad without a chair, and appear at the playhouse and assemblies in foreign fineries which they never will pay for, the kingdom would not be the worse.

Some persons of a desponding spirit are in great concern about that vast number of poor people who are aged, diseased, or maimed, and I have been desired to employ my thoughts what course may be taken to ease the nation of so grievous an encumbrance. But I am not in the least pain upon that matter, because it is very well known that they are every day dying and rotting by cold and famine, and filth and vermin, as fast as can be reasonably expected. And as to the younger laborers, they are now in almost as hopeful a condition. They cannot get work, and consequently pine away for want of nourishment to a degree that if at any time they are accidentally hired to common labor, they have not strength to perform it; and thus the country and themselves are happily delivered from the evils to come.

I have too long digressed, and therefore shall return to my subject. I think the advantages by the proposal which I have made are obvious and many, as well as of the highest importance.

For first, as I have already observed, it would greatly lessen the number of Papists, with whom we are yearly overrun, being the principal breeders of the nation as well as our most dangerous enemies; and who stay at home on purpose to deliver the kingdom to the Pretender, hoping to take their advantage by the absence of so many good Protestants, who have chosen rather to leave their country than stay at home and pay tithes against their conscience to an Episcopal curate.

Secondly, the poorer tenants will have something valuable of their own, which by law may be made liable to distress,[12] and help to pay their landlord's rent, their corn and cattle being already seized and money a thing unknown.

Thirdly, whereas the maintenance of an hundred thousand children, from two years old and upwards, cannot be computed at less than ten shillings a piece per annum, the nation's stock will be thereby increased fifty thousand pounds per annum, besides the profit of a new dish introduced to the tables of all gentlemen of fortune in the kingdom who have any refinement in taste. And the money will circulate among ourselves, the goods being entirely of our own growth and manufacture.

Fourthly, the constant breeders, besides the gain of eight shillings sterling per annum by the sale of their children, will be rid of the charge of maintaining them after the first year.

Fifthly, this food would likewise bring great custom to taverns, where the vintners will certainly be so prudent as to procure the best receipts

---

[12]Distraint; legal action to seize property for payment of debts.

for dressing it to perfection, and consequently have their houses frequented by all the fine gentlemen, who justly value themselves upon their knowledge in good eating; and a skillful cook, who understands how to oblige his guests, will contrive to make it as expensive as they please.

Sixthly, this would be a great inducement to marriage, which all wise nations have either encouraged by rewards or enforced by laws and penalties. It would increase the care and tenderness of mothers toward their children, when they were sure of a settlement for life to the poor babes, provided in some sort by the public, to their annual profit instead of expense. We should see an honest emulation among the married women, which of them could bring the fattest child to the market. Men would become as fond of their wives during the time of their pregnancy as they are now of their mares in foal, their cows in calf, or sows when they are ready to farrow; nor offer to beat or kick them (as is too frequent a practice) for fear of a miscarriage.

Many other advantages might be enumerated. For instance, the addition of some thousand carcasses in our exportation of barreled beef, the propagation of swine's flesh, and improvement in the art of making good bacon, so much wanted among us by the great destruction of pigs, too frequent at our tables, which are no way comparable in taste or magnificence to a well-grown, fat, yearling child, which roasted whole will make a considerable figure at a lord mayor's feast or any other public entertainment. But this and many others I omit, being studious of brevity.

Supposing that one thousand families in this city would be constant customers for infants' flesh, besides others who might have it at merry meetings, particularly weddings and christenings, I compute that Dublin would take off annually about twenty thousand carcasses, and the rest of the kingdom (where probably they will be sold somewhat cheaper) the remaining eighty thousand.

I can think of no one objection that will possibly be raised against this proposal, unless it should be urged that the number of people will be thereby much lessened in the kingdom. This I freely own, and it was indeed one principal design in offering it to the world. I desire the reader will observe, that I calculate my remedy for this one individual kingdom of Ireland and for no other that ever was, is, or I think ever can be upon earth. Therefore let no man talk to me of other expedients: of taxing our absentees at five shillings a pound: of using neither clothes nor household furniture except what is of our own growth and manufacture: of utterly rejecting the materials and instruments that promote foreign luxury: of curing the expensiveness of pride, vanity, idleness, and gaming in our women: of introducing a vein of parsimony, prudence, and temperance: of learning to love our country, in the want of which we differ even from Laplanders and the inhabitants of Topinamboo:[13] of

---

[13]Implies that Laplanders love their frozen country and residents of Topinamboo in Brazil love their jungle more than the Anglo-Irish love Ireland.

quitting our animosities and factions, nor acting any longer like the Jews, who were murdering one another at the very moment their city was taken:[14] of being a little cautious not to sell our country and conscience for nothing: of teaching landlords to have at least one degree of mercy toward their tenants: lastly, of putting a spirit of honesty, industry, and skill into our shopkeepers; who, if a resolution could now be taken to buy only our native goods, would immediately unite to cheat and exact upon us in the price, the measure, and the goodness, nor could ever yet be brought to make one fair proposal of just dealing, though often and earnestly invited to it.[15]

Therefore I repeat, let no man talk to me of these and the like expedients, till he hath at least some glimpse of hope that there will ever be some hearty and sincere attempt to put them in practice.

But as to myself, having been wearied out for many years with offering vain, idle, visionary thoughts, and at length utterly despairing of success, I fortunately fell upon this proposal, which, as it is wholly new, so it hath something solid and real, of no expense and little trouble, full in our own power, and whereby we can incur no danger in disobliging England. For this kind of commodity will not bear exportation, the flesh being of too tender a consistence to admit a long continuance in salt, although perhaps I could name a country which would be glad to eat up our whole nation without it.[16]

After all, I am not so violently bent upon my own opinion as to reject any offer proposed by wise men, which shall be found equally innocent, cheap, easy, and effectual. But before something of that kind shall be advanced in contradiction to my scheme, and offering a better, I desire the author or authors will be pleased maturely to consider two points. First, as things now stand, how they will be able to find food and raiment for an hundred thousand useless mouths and backs. And secondly, there being a round million of creatures in human figure throughout this kingdom, whose sole subsistence put into a common stock would leave them in debt two millions of pounds sterling, adding those who are beggars by profession to the bulk of farmers, cottagers, and laborers, with their wives and children who are beggars in effect; I desire those politicians who dislike my overture, and may perhaps be so bold to attempt an answer, that they will first ask the parents of these mortals whether they would not at this day think it a great happiness to have been sold for food at a year old in the manner I prescribe, and thereby have avoided such a perpetual scene of misfortunes as they have since gone through by the oppression of landlords, the impossibility of paying rent without money or trade, the want of common sustenance, with neither house nor clothes to cover them from the

---

[14]Refers to the siege of Jerusalem by the Roman Emperor Titus. He destroyed the city, which was torn by bloody fights between various factions.

[15]Swift had made all of these proposals in various writings. The proposals printed during his lifetime were italicized to indicate that he was no longer being ironic.

[16]Implies England.

inclemencies of the weather, and the most inevitable prospect of entailing the like or greater miseries upon their breed forever.

I profess, in the sincerity of my heart, that I have not the least personal interest in endeavoring to promote this necessary work, having no other motive than the public good of my country, by advancing our trade, providing for infants, relieving the poor, and giving some pleasure to the rich. I have no children by which I can propose to get a single penny; the youngest being nine years old, and my wife past childbearing.

1729

Amy Tan (B. 1952)

Mother Tongue

I am not a scholar of English or literature. I cannot give you much more than personal opinions on the English language and its variations in this country or others.

I am a writer. And by that definition, I am someone who has always loved language. I am fascinated by language in daily life. I spend a great deal of my time thinking about the power of language—the way it can evoke an emotion, a visual image, a complex idea, or a simple truth. Language is the tool of my trade. And I use them all—all the Englishes I grew up with.

Recently, I was made keenly aware of the different Englishes I do use. I was giving a talk to a large group of people, the same talk I had already given to half a dozen other groups. The nature of the talk was about my writing, my life, and my book, *The Joy Luck Club*. The talk was going along well enough, until I remember one major difference that made the whole talk sound wrong. My mother was in the room. And it was perhaps the first time she had heard me give a lengthy speech, using the kind of English I have never used with her. I was saying things like, "The intersection of memory upon imagination" and "There is an aspect of my fiction that relates to thus-and-thus"—a speech filled with carefully wrought grammatical phrases, burdened, it suddenly seemed to me, with nominalized forms, past perfect tenses, conditional phrases, all the forms of standard English that I had learned in school and through books, the forms of English I did not use at home with my mother.

Just last week, I was walking down the street with my mother, and I again found myself conscious of the English I was using, the English I do use with her. We were talking about the price of new and used furniture and I heard myself saying this: "Not waste money that way." My husband was with us as well, and he didn't notice any switch in my English. And then I realized why. It's because over the twenty years we've been together I've often used that same kind of English with him, and sometimes he even uses it with me. It has become our language of intimacy, a different sort of English that relates to family talk, the language I grew up with.

So you'll have some idea of what this family talk I heard sounds like, I'll quote what my mother said during a recent conversation which I video-taped and then transcribed. During this conversation, my mother was talking about a political gangster in Shanghai who had the same last name as her family's, Du, and how the gangster in his early years wanted to be adopted by her family, which was rich by comparison. Later, the gangster became more powerful, far richer than my mother's family, and one day showed up at my mother's wedding to pay his respects. Here's what she said in part:

"Du Yusong having business like fruit stand. Like off the street kind. He is Du like Du Zong—but not Tsung-ming Island people. The local people call putong, the river east side, he belong to that side local people. That man want to ask Du Zong father take him in like become own family. Du Zong father wasn't look down on him, but didn't take seriously, until that man big like become a mafia. Now important person, very hard to inviting him. Chinese way, came only to show respect, don't stay for dinner. Respect for making big celebration, he shows up. Mean give lots of respect. Chinese custom. Chinese social life that way. If too important won't have to stay too long. He come to my wedding. I didn't see, I heard it. I gone to boy's side, they have YMCA dinner. Chinese age I was nineteen."

You should know that my mother's expressive command of English belies how much she actually understands. She reads the *Forbes* report, listens to *Wall Street Week*, converses daily with her stockbroker, reads all of Shirley MacLaine's books with ease—all kinds of things I can't begin to understand. Yet some of my friends tell me they understand 50 percent of what my mother says. Some say they understand 80 to 90 percent. Some say they understand none of it, as if she were speaking pure Chinese. But to me, my mother's English is perfectly clear, perfectly natural. It's my mother tongue. Her language, as I hear it, is vivid, direct, full of observation and imagery. That was the language that helped shape the way I saw things, expressed things, made sense of the world.

Lately, I've been giving more thought to the kind of English my mother speaks. Like others, I have described it to people as "broken" or "fractured" English. But I wince when I say that. It has always bothered me that I can think of no way to describe it other than "broken," as if it were damaged and needed to be fixed, as if it lacked a certain wholeness and soundness. I've heard other terms used, "limited English," for example. But they seem just as bad, as if everything is limited, including people's perceptions of the limited English speaker.

I know this for a fact, because when I was growing up, my mother's "limited" English limited *my* perception of her. I was ashamed of her English. I believed that her English reflected the quality of what she had to say. That is, because she expressed them imperfectly her thoughts were imperfect. And I had plenty of empirical evidence to support me: the fact that people in department stores, at banks, and at restaurants did not take her seriously, did not give her good service, pretended not to understand her, or even acted as if they did not hear her.

My mother has long realized the limitations of her English as well. When I was fifteen, she used to have me call people on the phone to pretend I was she. In this guise, I was forced to ask for information or even to complain and yell at people who had been rude to her. One time it was a call to her stockbroker in New York. She had cashed out her small portfolio and it just happened we were going to go to New York the next week, our very first trip outside California. I had to get on the phone and say in an adolescent voice that was not very convincing, "This is Mrs. Tan."

And my mother was standing in the back whispering loudly, "Why he don't send me check, already two weeks late. So mad he lie to me, losing me money."

And then I said in perfect English, "Yes, I'm getting rather concerned. You had agreed to send the check two weeks ago, but it hasn't arrived."

Then she began to talk more loudly. "What he want, I come to New York tell him front of his boss, you cheating me?" And I was trying to calm her down, make her be quiet, while telling the stockbroker, "I can't tolerate any more excuses. If I don't receive the check immediately, I am going to have to speak to your manager when I'm in New York next week." And sure enough, the following week there we were in front of this astonished stockbroker, and I was sitting there red-faced and quiet, and my mother, the real Mrs. Tan, was shouting at his boss in her impeccable broken English.

We used a similar routine just five days ago, for a situation that was far less humorous. My mother had gone to the hospital for an appointment, to find out about a benign brain tumor a CAT scan had revealed a month ago. She said she had spoken very good English, her best English, no mistakes. Still, she said, the hospital did not apologize when they said they had lost the CAT scan and she had come for nothing. She said they did not seem to have any sympathy when she told them she was anxious to know the exact diagnosis, since her husband and son had both died of brain tumors. She said they would not give her any more information until the next time and she would have to make another appointment for that. So she said she would not leave until the doctor called her daughter. She wouldn't budge. And when the doctor finally called her daughter, me, who spoke in perfect English—lo and behold—we had assurances the CAT scan would be found, promises that a conference call on Monday would be held, and apologies for any suffering my mother had gone through for a most regrettable mistake.

I think my mother's English almost had an effect on limiting my possibilities in life as well. Sociologists and linguists probably will tell you that a person's developing language skills are more influenced by peers. But I do think that the language spoken in the family, especially in immigrant families which are more insular, plays a large role in shaping the language of the child. And I believe that it affected my results on achievement tests,

IQ tests, and the SAT. While my English skills were never judged as poor, compared to math, English could not be considered my strong suit. In grade school I did moderately well, getting perhaps B's, sometimes B-pluses, in English and scoring perhaps in the sixtieth or seventieth percentile on achievement tests. But those scores were not good enough to override the opinion that my true abilities lay in math and science, because in those areas I achieved A's and scored in the ninetieth percentile or higher.

This was understandable. Math is precise; there is only one correct answer. Whereas, for me at least, the answers on English tests were always a judgment call, a matter of opinion and personal experience. Those tests were constructed around items like fill-in-the-blank sentence completion, such as, "Even though Tom was _____. Mary thought he was _____." And the correct answer always seemed to be the most bland combinations of thoughts, for example, "Even though Tom was shy, Mary thought he was charming," with the grammatical structure "even though" limiting the correct answer to some sort of semantic opposites, so you wouldn't get answers like, "Even though Tom was foolish, Mary thought he was ridiculous." Well, according to my mother, there were very few limitations as to what Tom could have been and what Mary might have thought of him. So I never did well on tests like that.

The same was true with word analogies, pairs of words in which you were supposed to find some sort of logical, semantic relationship—for example, "*Sunset* is to *nightfall* as _____ is to ____." And here you would be presented with a list of four possible pairs, one of which showed the same kind of relationship: *red* is to *stoplight*, *bus* is to *arrival*, *chills* is to *fever*, *yawn* is to *boring*. Well, I could never think that way. I knew what the tests were asking, but I could not block out of my mind the images already created by the first pair, "*sunset* is to *nightfall*"—and I would see a burst of colors against a darkening sky, the moon rising, the lowering of a curtain of stars. And all the other pairs of words—red, bus, stoplight, boring—just threw up a mass of confusing images, making it impossible for me to sort out something as logical as saying: "A sunset precedes nightfall" is the same as "a chill precedes a fever." The only way I would have gotten that answer right would have been to imagine an associative situation, for example, my being disobedient and staying out past sunset, catching a chill at night, which turns into feverish pneumonia as punishment, which indeed did happen to me.

I have been thinking about all this lately, about my mother's English, about achievement tests. Because lately I've been asked as a writer, why there are not more Asian Americans represented in American literature. Why are there few Asian Americans enrolled in creative writing programs? Why do so many Chinese students go into engineering? Well, these are broad sociological questions I can't begin to answer. But I have noticed in surveys—in fact, just last week—that Asian students, as a whole, always do significantly better on math achievement tests than in English. And this makes me think that there are other Asian-American students whose

English spoken in the home might also be described as "broken" or "limited." And perhaps they also have teachers who are steering them away from writing and into math and science, which is what happened to me.

Fortunately, I happen to be rebellious in nature and enjoy the challenge of disproving assumptions made about me. I became an English major my first year in college, after being enrolled as pre-med. I started writing nonfiction as a freelancer the week after I was told by my former boss that writing was my worst skill and I should hone my talents toward account management.

But it wasn't until 1985 that I finally began to write fiction. And at first I wrote using what I thought to be wittily crafted sentences, sentences that would finally prove I had mastery over the English language. Here's an example from the first draft of a story that later made its way into *The Joy Luck Club*, but without this line: "That was my mental quandary in its nascent state." A terrible line, which I can barely pronounce.

Fortunately, for reasons I won't get into today. I later decided I should envision a reader for the stories I would write. And the reader I decided upon was my mother, because these were stories about mothers. So with this reader in mind—and in fact she did read my early drafts—I began to write stories using all the Englishes I grew up with: the English I spoke to my mother, which for lack of a better term might be described as "simple"; the English she used with me, which for lack of a better term might be described as "broken"; my translation of her Chinese, which could certainly be described as "watered down"; and what I imagined to be her translation of her Chinese if she could speak in perfect English, her internal language, and for that I sought to preserve the essence, but neither an English nor a Chinese structure. I wanted to capture what language ability tests can never reveal: her intent, her passion, her imagery, the rhythms of her speech and the nature of her thoughts.

Apart from what any critic had to say about my writing, I knew I had succeeded where it counted when my mother finished reading my book and gave me her verdict: "So easy to read."

1990

Diane Thiel (B. 1967)

Crossing the Border

From *The White Horse: A Colombian Journey*

We asked about the boat at least ten times the next morning—at the Torres house, at Rosita's. We also asked some of the children who came to find us each morning, thinking they might be the most likely to know. But everyone had a different answer. Some said it would come in the afternoon. Some said no more boats until after Christmas. The boat had actually been there when we arrived a few days before, but for whatever reason, no one had told us about it. So we kept walking down to the dock to check.

It was a new feeling, this helplessness, a reliance on the whims of the tides and a single boat and its captain. I was still used to Miami time and the way in the States you can get everything you want when you want, provided you have the money. Ana Maria really wanted to be in Colombia for Christmas, and it was already the 23rd. Her friend Ricardo was planning to meet us at the port in Punta Ardita to take us down the coast to his piece of land to stay for a week on the ocean.

In one way, it was a good thing that we missed the boat the day we arrived in Jaqué because we ended up speaking to town officials about the environmental project in Punta Ardita, Colombia, and about how we would like to start a similar program in Jaqué—to improve the water conditions, to promote crafts for sale, to clean up the beaches, and other plans. We were told that the town council allots land and that we should write a request to set up an environmental station there. We wrote it immediately and were told we would find out the response in a few weeks, on our way back. So we saw our delay in Jaqué is a blessing, but we really didn't want to miss the next boat.

To our relief, it finally arrived with the tide in the late morning, and we went to pay, reserve our places, and fill out the paperwork to leave the country. As the officials looked at our papers and heard where we were headed, they began discussing whether the tiny village of Punta Ardita was Panama or Colombia. They were in disagreement as to whether we were actually leaving the country. Jaqué and Jurado were the two border towns, but Punta Ardita and Ricardo's place sat somewhere between them.

"*Ardita es Colombia*," said the older official.

"No, I think it's Panama." said the younger.

"Are you going anywhere else?" they asked.

"To visit an indigenous village up the river from Jurado," Ana Maria said.

"Now Jurado, that's Colombia," a third man piped in. "Terrible town. Dirty. Are you sure you want to go to Jurado?"

"Well, we're not really going to Jurado," Ana Maria answered. "Just around it."

One official pulled out a map, and the three men leaned into it, noting where *la frontera* actually was. The older one ran a thick finger down a dotted line to the ocean, hesitated, and then made his decision: "*Ardita es Colombia*," he proclaimed.

At first, I thought it strange that they did not know where one country ended and the other one began. But then I thought about the imaginary lines that make such demarcations and the fact that Panama was part of Colombia until the turn of the century, when the canal made Panama such valuable territory to foreign interests. This tiny checkpoint suddenly felt like a huge border, a significant frontier rich with history, the edge of the other continent.

They sent our passports into the back room, and after a few moments we were called in. A middle-aged, uniformed man with slicked-back hair sat behind a desk. An oscillating fan sat on a box in the corner, nearly blowing the one decoration, a calendar, off the wall. I noticed what looked like a bullet hole in the wall under the calendar. The hole reappeared each time the fan turned.

"And why are you two going to Colombia?" the slicked-back man asked.

"To spend Christmas with a friend," said Ana Maria. I just smiled.

He had Ana Maria's passport open, admired her picture, and asked flirtatiously if she was married: *"Casada o soltera?"*

"Prometida," she lied, saying that she was engaged.

He motioned at me: "Does she speak Spanish?"

"Sí," I answered.

He smiled. *"Casada o soltera?"* he opened my passport.

"Prometida," I answered, following Ana Maria's lead.

"Too bad," he said. "But you must have crazy fiancés to send you out to the jungle alone. And at Christmas!" He shook his head gravely at the foolishness of our imaginary men. "When are you returning?"

Ana Maria explained that I would be coming back in a few weeks by myself, as she had to remain in Colombia a few weeks longer.

"Well," he said, winking at me, "if you have any problems when you return, just come and see me." He stamped my passport and, before closing it, leafed back to the first page and kissed my picture. "Just come and see me," he said again and showed us out.

The boat that would take us over the *frontera* was a tiny motorboat, almost a dinghy. The captain was a young Colombian boy who introduced himself as Archangel. I was surprised by the name, and when he walked away for a moment, Ana Maria whispered to me that his father, Momento, had named all of his sons for angels and saints. "Let's see," she said, "there's Santo, and Lazaro, and Archangel, and I forget the others right now." We were interrupted by Archangel's return. For some reason, he had seemed unsure that he could take us, but then agreed after a short discussion with some officials.

When the plane from Panama City arrived that afternoon, the children who had been our shadows suddenly disappeared, and a half hour later a party of ten or so arrived to board the boat. The mayor of Jurado, the Colombian village close to Punta Ardita, was in the party with his family and entourage and about fourteen huge bags of Panama City Christmas purchases. There was no way we would all fit in that boat.

We did. Somehow they loaded every bag into the boat and then everybody. We were tightly packed. Ana Maria sat me down next to a young man, whispering to me, "It's the mayor's son, Nigel. Talk to him." She wanted me to tell him about our plans for Punta Ardita, the plans we would be proposing as alternatives to cutting the rain forest for lumber.

The tide had come in, and it was finally high enough to leave Jaqué. The waves were huge, especially when we first headed out into the ocean. The boat climbed up each wave, reached a crest, and then slammed down into the water. My body rose completely off the seat and slammed down with it.

"We're lucky," Nigel yelled over the waves. "It's pretty calm today. It's usually much worse."

I nodded and tried to keep my lunch down. It happened about ten times before we were far enough out in the ocean to be beyond the breaking waves. It was much calmer out there as long as we kept moving, but the wind and the engine still made it hard to hear.

Nigel began asking me questions, which I answered in a rudimentary way, about where we were from, why we were headed to Colombia. I had to ask him to repeat everything three times and still only understood about half. Tired, I finally began resorting to the *"Sí"* and smiling which Ana Maria had warned me about.

"You are a very beautiful woman," Nigel said.

I thanked him, becoming used to the Latin way.

"You know, I've been feeling that I'd like to settle down soon" was another sentence I caught completely.

"It's good to settle down," I agreed innocuously, or so I thought.

There were a few sentences I didn't catch in the wind, so I just smiled and nodded.

Finally, he said something and looked at me so intensely that I knew I had to get him to repeat it.

"I said," he moved close to my ear, "that I've been looking for the right woman to float by." He paused. "I'm so glad you'll be in Jurado tonight for the disco."

I instantly stopped smiling and nodding. I wondered what else I had agreed to.

It was one of several such conversations on the trip. I was speaking to Nigel in a frank, matter-of-fact way. I realized that in his culture my behavior, perhaps my very presence, might be viewed as flirtation or invitation. I quickly began undoing the web I had inadvertently woven on the ride.

I thought about the passport official's personal questions, his kissing my picture, and what my response might have been if such a thing had happened back home. But I wasn't back home. Here, I realized that just being an unescorted woman could cause a great deal of miscommunication. Over the loud engine and with salt spray in my eyes, I found myself declining, as politely as I could, both the disco and, more subtly, marriage.

2004

Henry David Thoreau (1817–1862)

Walking

The West of which I speak is but another name for the Wild; and what I have been preparing to say is, that in Wildness is the preservation of the World. Every tree sends its fibres forth in search of the Wild. The cities import it at any price. Men plough and sail for it. From the forest and wilderness come the tonics and barks which brace mankind. Our ancestors were savages. The story of Romulus and Remus being suckled by a wolf is not a meaningless fable. The founders of every State which has risen to eminence have drawn their nourishment and vigor from a similar wild source. It was because the children of the Empire were not suckled by the wolf that they were conquered and displaced by the children of the Northern forests who were.

I believe in the forest, and in the meadow, and in the night in which the corn grows. We require an infusion of hemlock-spruce or arborvitae in our tea. There is a difference between eating and drinking for strength and from mere gluttony. The Hottentots eagerly devour the marrow of the koodoo and other antelopes raw, as a matter of course. Some of our Northern Indians eat raw the marrow of the Arctic reindeer, as well as various other parts, including the summits of the antlers, as long as they are soft. And herein, perchance, they have stolen a march on the cooks of Paris. They get what usually goes to feed the fire. This is probably better than stall-fed beef and slaughter-house pork to make a man of. Give me a wildness whose glance no civilization can endure,—as if we lived on the marrow of koodoos devoured raw.

There are some intervals which border the strain of the wood-thrush, to which I would migrate,—wild lands where no settler has squatted; to which, methinks, I am already acclimated.

The African hunter Cummings tells us that the skin of the eland, as well as that of most other antelopes just killed, emits the most delicious perfume of trees and grass. I would have every man so much like a wild antelope, so much a part and parcel of Nature, that his very person should thus sweetly advertise our senses of his presence, and remind us of those parts of Nature which he most haunts. I feel no disposition to be satirical, when the trapper's coat emits the odor of musquash even; it is a sweeter scent to me than that which commonly exhales from the merchant's or the scholar's garments. When I go into their wardrobes and handle their vestments, I am reminded of no grassy plains and flowery meads which they have frequented, but of dusty merchants' exchanges and libraries rather.

A tanned skin is something more than respectable, and perhaps olive is a fitter color than white for a man,—a denizen of the woods. "The pale white man!" I do not wonder that the African pitied him. Darwin the naturalist says, "A white man bathing by the side of a Tahitian was like a plant bleached by the gardener's art, compared with a fine, dark green one, grow-ing vigorously in the open fields."

Ben Jonson exclaims,—

"How near to good is what is fair!"

So I would say,—

How near to good is what is *wild!*

Life consists with wildness. The most alive is the wildest. Not yet sub-dued to man, its presence refreshes him. One who pressed forward inces-santly and never rested from his labors, who grew fast and made infinite demands on life, would always find himself in a new country or wilderness, and surrounded by the raw material of life. He would be climbing over the prostrate stems of primitive forest-trees.

Hope and the future for me are not in lawns and cultivated fields, not in towns and cities, but in the impervious and quaking swamps. When, formerly, I have analyzed my partiality for some farm which I had con-templated purchasing, I have frequently found that I was attracted solely by a few square rods of impermeable and unfathomable bog,—a natural sink in one corner of it. That was the jewel which dazzled me. I derive more of my subsistence from the swamps which surround my native town than from the cultivated gardens in the village. There are no richer parterres to my eyes than the dense beds of dwarf andromeda (*Cassandra calyculata*) which cover these tender places on the earth's surface. Botany cannot go farther than tell me the names of the shrubs which grow there,—the high-blueberry, panicled andromeda, lamb-kill, azalea, and rhodora,—all standing in the quaking sphagnum. I often think that I should like to have my house front on this mass of dull red bushes, omitting other flower plots and borders, transplanted spruce and trim box, even gravelled walks,—to have this fertile spot under my windows, not a few imported barrow-fulls of soil only to cover the sand which was thrown out in digging the cellar. Why not put my house, my parlor, behind this plot, instead of behind that meagre assemblage of curiosities, that poor apology for a Nature and Art, which I call my front-yard? It is an effort to clear up and make a decent appearance when the carpenter and mason have departed, though done as much for the passer-by as the dweller within. The most tasteful front-yard fence was never an agreeable object of study to me; the most elabo-rate ornaments, acorn-tops, or what not, soon wearied and disgusted me. Bring your sills up to the very edge of the swamp, then, (though it may not be the best place for a dry cellar), so that there be no access on that side to citizens. Front-yards are not made to walk in, but, at most, through, and you could go in the back way.

Yes, though you may think me perverse, if it were proposed to me to dwell in the neighborhood of the most beautiful garden that ever human art contrived, or else of a Dismal swamp, I should certainly decide for the swamp. How vain, then, have been all your labors, citizens, for me!

My spirits infallibly rise in proportion to the outward dreariness. Give me the ocean, the desert or the wilderness! In the desert, pure air and solitude compensate for want of moisture and fertility. The traveller Burton says of it,—"Your *morale* improves; you become frank and cordial, hospitable and single-minded. . . . In the desert, spirituous liquors excite only disgust. There is a keen enjoyment in a mere animal existence." They who have been travelling long on the steppes of Tartary say,—"On reëntering cultivated lands, the agitation, perplexity, and turmoil of civilization oppressed and suffocated us; the air seemed to fail us, and we felt every moment as if about to die of asphyxia." When I would recreate myself, I seek the darkest wood, the thickest and most interminable, and, to the citizen, most dismal swamp. I enter a swamp as a sacred place,—a *sanctum sanctorum*. There is the strength, the marrow of Nature. The wild-wood covers the virgin mould,—and the same soil is good for men and for trees. A man's health requires as many acres of meadow to his prospect as his farm does loads of muck. There are the strong meats on which he feeds. A town is saved, not more by the righteous men in it than by the woods and swamps that surround it. A township where one primitive forest waves above, while another primitive forest rots below,—such a town is fitted to raise not only corn and potatoes, but poets and philosophers for the coming ages. In such a soil grew Homer and Confucius and the rest, and out of such a wilderness comes the Reformer eating locusts and wild honey.

To preserve wild animals implies generally the creation of a forest for them to dwell in or resort to. So it is with man. A hundred years ago they sold bark in our streets peeled from our own woods. In the very aspect of those primitive and rugged trees, there was, methinks, a tanning principle which hardened and consolidated the fibres of men's thoughts. Ah! already I shudder for these comparatively degenerate days of my native village, when you cannot collect a load of bark of good thickness,—and we no longer produce tar and turpentine.

1862

Anthony Walton (B. 1960)

From *Mississippi: An American Journey*

In search of a true plantation (lamp, slate, whip), I drove thirty minutes through dense, almost tropical kudzu, willow and live oak trees, hanging vines, swamps, cotton, bean fields and pine forests. Sometimes the lush vegetation came right to the edge of the road. I drove north of Natchez to the large white door of Springfield, a working plantation that has been maintained in historically accurate eighteenth-century detail since its establishment in 1786 by Thomas Marston Green. I knocked, and the door was opened by Arthur La Salle, an intense, kind, white-haired preservationist in charge of the maintenance of Springfield's historical artifacts.

The plantation of one thousand acres (once several thousand more) is located in Fayette, roughly fifteen miles outside Natchez. I walked through the great house, a modified Greek Revival structure which, with its original interior, is not nearly as sumptuous as the restored and modernized house at Rosalie. "Most folks don't realize they're not looking at the house as the residents actually lived when they're in Natchez," Mr. La Salle explained with a wry smile. He showed me the yellowed parlor where, in 1791, Thomas Green hosted the notorious wedding of Andrew Jackson and Rachel Robards, who later was found to have been married to another man at the time.

Springfield, like Rosalie, had a second-floor gallery that afforded a tremendous view. This view was quite different, if equally majestic: a stretch of fields of cotton, hay and beans that claimed miles in all directions—the Mississippi's true legacy. In the yard below me were oak and pear trees and, close to the porch, forsythia in bloom. I felt the breeze, stronger here in the country, and heard it skim through the trees.

I went back downstairs and out to the empty barnyard, through a pass gate, then walked a quarter of a mile down a shaded clay road to the last surviving "quarter house"—denoting "slave quarter"—on Springfield. Restored by Mr. La Salle, the house is a ten-foot-square box of boards on bricks and timbers, covered by a tin roof; though the structure is solidly put together, at the same time it seems as though a strong wind would knock it all down. Standing there by the edge of the woods, looking out over the fields back toward the big house, I wondered how much different the physical landscape could have been two hundred years ago. I stepped into the cabin, which had no windows, only doors, and noted how close and cramped it was—and dark, even in bright daylight—and stood for a time in the silence. I had come across this description of slave life by Charles Sydnor:

> The last and lowest link in the chain of the human species . . . was the class of negroes who labored on the great plantations and small farms of the state. . . . Agriculture in Mississippi was built upon the hoe gang and the plow gang. Both of these, together with all other slaves who could be put into the field, were converted into a great army of cotton pickers . . . slaves in the old Southwest, of which Mississippi was the heart, were forced to work harder than slaves to the east and north of this region. They are constantly and steadily driven up to their work, and the stupid, plodding machine-like manner in which they labor, is painful to witness.

Planters expected each slave to produce on the average from five to seven bales of cotton a season, each bale weighing four hundred pounds.

The slavery of Mississippi differed from that of early Greece or Rome in that it was based on skin color and economic motives, rather than following directly from war and conquest. Greek slaves worked alongside their masters and were hard to distinguish from them. Roman slaves could become teachers and philosophers, as did Epictetus. American slaves, by contrast, were robbed of much of their personal and psychic dignity, and the residue of that deprivation marks American society still, as millions of African-Americans have yet to recover the ground their ancestors lost in slavery times. Slavery led to sharecropping, another form of race-based peonage, in which blacks received seeds and supplies on loan from the plantation owner and repaid him out of crop profits that never quite materialized—a system my father experienced as a child and young man. The end of sharecropping led to the migration of millions of blacks to the urban North, where many were, and are, caught in the snags of social disarray. A direct line can be drawn from slave ships and quarter houses to housing projects and killing streets.

Standing in the shadows of the quarter house, I found myself wondering if they, the slaves, might have speculated that life would be better for some of their descendants. If my presence didn't redeem what they had lost, I hoped it at least gave some meaning to that loss. I was what came after, and my present perhaps gave further shape to what had gone before.

I walked around to the back of the shed, along a shallow ridge where traces of the rest of the quarter houses remained, bricks and boards littered with rusty Budweiser cans, plastic bags and empty antifreeze jugs. On my way back to the big house I stopped in the Green family cemetery, a small patch of ground behind the mansion. After several minutes I located the gravestone of Thomas Green, the founder of Springfield. His stone had nearly sunk into the ground. I'd seen a copy of Green's will, recorded in the office of the chancery clerk of Jefferson County, in the room that had been Green's office and which now served as the same for Arthur La Salle. On the fifth of December 1812, Green wrote, "I consign my body to the dust from whence it came to be buried in decent Christian burial and my soul into the hands of Almighty God who gave it. And touching such Goods, and worldly effects as it has pleased heaven to bless me with I dispose of them in the manner following. . . ."

Among those "Goods, and worldly effects" to which Green conveys title are "negro slaves." To his son, Joseph, Green bequeathed "Tallton, Emmanuel, Andrew, together with Peter, Lucy, John and Esther also their increase forever. . . . Also five cows and calves, one yoke of oxen, four head of horses, five head of sheep, one feather bed." To his daughter Eliza, "Quamany, Martin, Rose, Milly and Joe, with their increase." Eliza was also given two feather beds. To son-in-law John Hopkins, "Jack, Charlotte and Jude also three hundred and ninety-seven dollars fifty cents to be paid out and applied to the purchase of a young negro for my Grand Daughter Mary Jane Hopkins. . . ." And so on. "To daughter Mary, four slaves, Charles,

Antoine, Harriet and Rachel, to daughter Jane, four slaves, Jacob, Lewis, Amy and Harry." To daughter Rebecca, "Phil, Cooper, Aley and their infant child and Hager." To daughter Augusta, "Anaka, *Anaka* [separate person], Damon, Sophey, Patti, Little Moses and Tom the son of Harriet also a saddle horse the value of one hundred dollars." And this, to wife, Priscilla: "my mansion house and Springfield Estate, together with all the negroes, stock of horses, cattle &c. belonging to the same except such property as has been hereinbefore disposed of."

Green also requested that his "old faithful and trusty servants" Tom, Amaritta and Philes "be not compelled to labor unless they choose so to do and that they be not suffered to want."

By 1850, Natchez and surrounding Adams County had a population of 18,343: 3,949 white, 14,395 black. The blacks had been, with the exception of those few who were free, captured and hauled halfway across the world to subdue a wilderness.

1996

PART FIVE

Writers About the Art
of Creative Nonfiction

Margaret Atwood (B. 1939)

Nine Beginnings

1. *Why do you write?*
I've begun this piece nine times. I've junked each beginning.

    I hate writing about my writing. I almost never do it. Why am I doing it now? Because I said I would. I got a letter. I wrote back *no.* Then I was at a party and the same person was there. It's harder to refuse in person. Saying *yes* had something to do with being nice, as women are taught to be, and something to do with being helpful, which we are also taught. Being helpful to women, giving a pint of blood. With not claiming the sacred prerogatives, the touch-me-not self-protectiveness of the artist, with not being selfish. With conciliation, with doing your bit, with appeasement. I was well brought up. I have trouble ignoring social obligations. Saying you'll write about your writing is a social obligation. It's not an obligation to the writing.

2. *Why do you write?*
I've junked each of nine beginnings. They seemed beside the point. Too assertive, too pedagogical, too frivolous or belligerent, too falsely wise. As if I had some special self-revelation that would encourage others, or some special knowledge to impart, some pithy saying that would act like a talisman for the driven, the obsessed. But I have no such talismans. If I did, I would not continue, myself, to be so driven and obsessed.

3. *Why do you write?*
I hate writing about my writing because I have nothing to say about it. I have nothing to say about it because I can't remember what goes on when I'm doing it. That time is like small pieces cut out of my brain. It's not time I myself have lived. I can remember the details of the rooms and places where I've written, the circumstances, the other things I did before and after, but not the process itself. Writing about writing requires self-consciousness; writing itself requires the abdication of it.

4. *Why do you write?*
There are a lot of things that can be said about what goes on around the edges of writing. Certain ideas you may have, certain motivations, grand designs that don't get carried out. I can talk about bad reviews, about sexist reactions to my writing, about making an idiot of myself on television shows. I can talk about books that failed, that never got finished, and about why they failed. The one that had too many characters, the one that had too many

257

layers of time, red herrings that diverted me when what I really wanted to get at was something else, a certain corner of the visual world, a certain voice, an inarticulate landscape.

I can talk about the difficulties that women encounter as writers. For instance, if you're a woman writer, sometime, somewhere, you will be asked: *Do you think of yourself as a writer first, or as a woman first?* Look out. Whoever asks this hates and fears both writing and women.

Many of us, in my generation at least, ran into teachers or male writers or other defensive jerks who told us women could not really write because they couldn't be truck drivers or Marines and therefore didn't understand the seamier side of life, which included sex with women. We were told we wrote like housewives, or else we were treated like honorary men, as if to be a good writer was to suppress the female.

Such pronouncements used to be made as if they were the simple truth. Now they're questioned. Some things have changed for the better, but not all. There's a lack of self-confidence that gets instilled very early in many young girls, before writing is even seen as a possibility. You need a certain amount of nerve to be a writer, an almost physical nerve, the kind you need to walk a log across a river. The horse throws you and you get back on the horse. I learned to swim by being dropped into the water. You need to know you can sink, and survive it. Girls should be allowed to play in the mud. They should be released from the obligations of perfection. Some of your writing, at least, should be as evanescent as play.

A ratio of failures is built into the process of writing. The wastebasket has evolved for a reason. Think of it as the altar of the Muse Oblivion, to whom you sacrifice your botched first drafts, the tokens of your human imperfection. She is the tenth Muse, the one without whom none of the others can function. The gift she offers you is the freedom of the second chance. Or as many chances as you'll take.

5. *Why do you write?*
In the mid-eighties I began a sporadic journal. Today I went back through it, looking for something I could dig out and fob off as pertinent, instead of writing this piece about writing. But it was useless. There was nothing in it about the actual composition of anything I've written over the past six years. Instead there are exhortations to myself—to get up earlier, to walk more, to resist lures and distractions. *Drink more water,* I find. *Go to bed earlier.* There were lists of how many pages I'd written per day, how many I'd retyped, how many yet to go. Other than that, there was nothing but descriptions of rooms, accounts of what we'd cooked and/or eaten and with whom, letters written and received, notable sayings of children, birds and animals seen, the weather. What came up

in the garden. Illnesses, my own and those of others. Deaths, births. Nothing about writing.

> January 1, 1984. Blakeny, England. As of today, I have about 130 pp. of the novel done and it's just beginning to take shape & reach the point at which I feel that it exists and can be finished and may be worth it. I work in the bedroom of the big house, and here, in the sitting room, with the wood fire in the fireplace and the coke fire in the dilapidated Roeburn in the kitchen. As usual I'm too cold, which is better than being too hot—today is grey, warm for the time of year, damp. If I got up earlier maybe I would work more, but I might just spend more time procrastinating—as now.

And so on.

6. *Why do you write?*
   You learn to write by reading and writing, writing and reading. As a craft it's acquired through the apprentice system, but you choose your own teachers. Sometimes they're alive, sometimes dead.
   As a vocation, it involves the laying on of hands. You receive your vocation and in your turn you must pass it on. Perhaps you will do this only through your work, perhaps in other ways. Either way, you're part of a community, the community of writers, the community of storytellers that stretches back through time to the beginning of human society.
   As for the particular human society to which you yourself belong—sometimes you'll feel you're speaking for it, sometimes—when it's taken an unjust form—against it, or for that other community, the community of the oppressed, the exploited, the voiceless. Either way, the pressures on you will be intense; in other countries, perhaps fatal. But even here—speak "for women," or for any other group which is feeling the boot, and there will be many at hand, both for and against, to tell you to shut up, or to say what they want you to say, or to say it a different way. Or to save them. The billboard awaits you, but if you succumb to its temptations you'll end up two-dimensional.
   Tell what is yours to tell. Let others tell what is theirs.

7. *Why do you write?*
   Why are we so addicted to causality? *Why do you write?* (Treatise by child psychologist, mapping your formative traumas. Conversely: palm-reading, astrology and genetic studies, pointing to the stars, fate, heredity.) *Why do you write?* (That is, why not do something useful instead?) If you were a doctor, you could tell some acceptable moral tale about how you put Band-Aids on your cats as a child, how you've always longed to cure suffering. No one can argue with that. But writing? What is it *for?*

Some possible answers: *Why does the sun shine? In the face of the absurdity of modern society, why do anything else? Because I'm a writer. Because I want to discover the patterns in the chaos of time. Because I must. Because someone has to bear witness. Why do you read?* (This last is tricky: maybe they don't.) *Because I wish to forge in the smithy of my soul the uncreated conscience of my race. Because I wish to make an axe to break the frozen sea within.* (These have been used, but they're good.)

If at a loss, perfect the shrug. Or say: It's *better than working in a bank.* Or say: *For fun.* If you say this, you won't be believed, or else you'll be dismissed as trivial. Either way, you'll have avoided the question.

8. *Why do you write?*

Not long ago, in the course of clearing some of the excess paper out of my workroom, I opened a filing cabinet drawer I hadn't looked into for years. In it was a bundle of loose sheets, folded, creased, and grubby, tied up with leftover string. It consisted of things I'd written in the late fifties, in high school and the early years of university. There were scrawled, inky poems, about snow, despair, and the Hungarian Revolution. There were short stories dealing with girls who'd had to get married, and dispirited, mousy-haired high-school English teachers—to end up as either was at that time my vision of Hell—typed finger-by-finger on an ancient machine that made all the letters half-red.

There I am, then, back in grade twelve, going through the writers' magazines after I'd finished my French Composition homework, typing out my lugubrious poems and my grit-filled stories. (I was big on grit. I had an eye for lawn-litter and dog turds on sidewalks. In these stories it was usually snowing damply, or raining; at the very least there was slush. If it was summer, the heat and humidity were always wiltingly high and my characters had sweat marks under their arms; if it was spring, wet clay stuck to their feet. Though some would say all this was just normal Toronto weather.)

In the top right-hand corners of some of these, my hopeful seventeen-year-old self had typed, "First North American Rights Only." I was not sure what "First North American Rights" were; I put it in because the writing magazines said you should. I was at that time an aficionado of writing magazines, having no one else to turn to for professional advice.

If I were an archeologist, digging through the layers of old paper that mark the eras in my life as a writer, I'd have found, at the lowest or Stone Age level—say around ages five to seven—a few poems and stories, unremarkable precursors of all my frenetic later scribbling. (Many children write at that age, just as many children draw. The strange thing is that so few of them go on to become writers or painters.) After that there's a great blank. For eight years, I simply didn't write. Then, suddenly, and with no missing links in between, there's a wad of manuscripts. One week I wasn't a writer, the next I was.

Who did I think I was, to be able to get away with this? What did I think I was doing? How did I get that way? To these questions I still have no answers.

9. *Why do you write?*

There's the blank page, and the thing that obsesses you. There's the story that wants to take you over and there's your resistance to it. There's your longing to get out of this, this servitude, to play hooky, to do anything else: wash the laundry, see a movie. There are words and their inertias, their biases, their insufficiencies, their glories. There are the risks you take and your loss of nerve, and the help that comes when you're least expecting it. There's the laborious revision, the scrawled-over, crumpled-up pages that drift across the floor like spilled litter. There's the one sentence you know you will save.

Next day there's the blank page. You give yourself up to it like a sleepwalker. Something goes on that you can't remember afterwards. You look at what you've done. It's hopeless.

You begin again. It never gets any easier.

1990

Lee Gutkind (B. 1947)

The Creative Nonfiction Police

I am giving a reading at St. Edwards University in Austin, Texas. It is a Thursday evening after a day of meeting classes and answering questions about essay writing, but now, in the auditorium, the audience is sparse, perhaps 60 or so in a space that seats nearly 250. My host is embarrassed; she informs me that a popular Latino poet is reading on campus at the same time, so the potential audience is divided. I have a feeling that I am the lesser of the two. This is a city with a high percentage of Mexican-American residents. And poetry is written to be read aloud, unlike nonfiction, which is factual and informative and which, students might assume, can be tedious and boring.

Of course, I am a *creative* nonfiction writer, "creative" being indicative of the style in which the nonfiction is written so as to make it more dramatic and compelling. We embrace many of the techniques of the fiction writer, including dialogue, description, plot, intimacy of detail, characterization, point of view; except, because it is nonfiction—and this is the difference—it is true.

Writing nonfiction so that it reads like fiction is challenging and, some critics say, virtually impossible unless the author takes liberties in style and content, which may corrupt the nonfiction—making it untrue, or partially true, or shading the meaning and misleading readers. A comment from John Berendt, author of *Midnight in the Garden of Good and Evil,* is frequently cited as indicative of the danger inherent in the form. Berendt made up transitions in order to move from scene to scene in his book. Creative nonfiction writers aren't supposed to make up anything in the scenes or between the scenes, including transitions, but Berendt said he was making the experience easier for himself and more enjoyable for his readers, a process he called "rounding the corners."

This then is the subject we are discussing in the auditorium after my reading—what writers can do or can't do in walking that thin blurred line between fiction and nonfiction. After all, if you are encouraged to use "literary techniques," straying from the literal truth for the sake of the narrative can be easy. The questions pile up, one after another; the audience is engaged. "How can you be certain that the dialogue you are recreating from an incident that occurred months ago is accurate?" asks one audience member. Another demands, "How can you look through the eyes of your characters if you are not inside their heads?"

I am answering as best I can, but as I try repeatedly to explain, such questions have a lot to do with the believability of your narrative and a writer's ethical and moral boundaries. After a while, I throw up my hands and say, "Listen! I am not the creative nonfiction police."

There is a woman in the audience—someone I had noticed earlier during my reading. She is in the front row—hard to miss—older than most of the undergraduates, blonde, attractive, in her late 30s maybe. She has the alert yet composed look of a nurse, a person only semi-relaxed, always ready to act or react. She has taken her shoes off and propped her feet on the stage; I remember how her toes wiggled as she laughed at the essay I had been reading. But when I say, "I am not the creative nonfiction police," although many people chuckle, this woman suddenly jumps to her feet, whips out a badge, and points in my direction. "Well I am," she announces. "Someone has to be. And you are under arrest." Then she scoops up her shoes and storms barefooted from the room. The Q and A ends and I rush into the hallway, but she is gone. My host says the woman is a stranger. No one knows her. She is a mystery to everyone, especially me.

The bigger mystery, however, then and now, is the set of parameters that govern or define creative nonfiction—the concepts writers must consider while laboring in or struggling with what we call the literature of reality, beginning with the difference between fiction and nonfiction, which is truth, or at least a measure of truth, because most fiction, on some level, is true. But how is the truth in nonfiction determined? Who is the final arbiter of truth? The line between fiction and nonfiction is often debated, but is there a single dividing point or an all-encompassing truth to tell?

Historians and journalists rely on sources—documents and interviews—but how do they know if the documents are accurate or the witnesses' perceptions valid? Witnesses in court will usually tell what they see as the truth—but how many innocent people have been convicted based on testimony of a sincere and objective bystander? In *All the President's Men,* Woodward and Bernstein insisted on the corroboration of two sources, but who is to say two sources are enough? A good historian exhausts the available sources, but sooner or later has to make decisions about which to accept and reject.

And why, I wonder, are we always questioning the ethics of nonfiction writers? Are there no ethical boundaries in poetry and fiction? Are we more deceived by Truman Capote, who did not take notes and relied on memory to retell the horrible story of the murder of the Clutter family in *In Cold Blood,* or Michael Chabon who disguised real characters and situations in his novel, *Wonder Boys?* Many writers in Pittsburgh knew the story as intimately as Chabon, but considered it improper and potentially hurtful to the characters and their families to write about it. David Leavitt's career was significantly damaged when, in his novel, *While England Sleeps,* he described the esteemed poet Sir Stephen Spender, masked by another name and body, in a way that endangered his reputation. Spender triggered litigation to halt the distribution of Leavitt's book. The ethical boundaries of the narrative are not, however, a new dilemma or debate. Henry David Thoreau lived for two years on Walden Pond while documenting only one year. Which part of the two years did he choose and how often, in his painstaking process of revision, did he combine two or three days—or even four weeks—into one?

This technique that Thoreau evidently employed, by the way, is called "compression"—meaning that multiple incidents or situations combined or compressed in order to flesh out the narrative, allowing a writer to build a more compelling, fully executed three-dimensional story.

In her book about Geoffrey Masson, *In the Freud Archives,* Janet Malcolm combined a series of conversations about the same subject or incident into one. Malcolm did not admit to altering facts of the conversations—only when and how the conversations occurred. Does this violate some sort of ethical or moral bond with the reader or the subject? Probably not, as long as the information is not manufactured—which is the reason that Masson's suit against *The New Yorker* and Malcolm went all the way to the U.S. Supreme Court. Masson was initially contending that Malcolm manufactured quotes; he may not have been aware of the use of compression or would not have been disturbed by it had his attorneys not questioned the technique while investigating information subpoenaed from Malcolm.

Another Janet—Janet Cooke, formerly a reporter for *The Washington Post*—was awarded the Pulitzer Prize for her depiction of an eight-year-old boy dealing drugs on the streets of the nation's capital. But curious reporters searching for the subject of the story eventually forced Cooke to admit that he didn't exist. He was a composite of a number of kids she had met. Cooke lost her job—her reputation was ruined. Unfortunately, others have not learned from her mistakes.

In the past couple of years, a number of journalists have been discovered and disgraced for fudging the truth. In 1997, Stephen Glass admitted to fabricating parts of 27 articles for *The New Republic*, *The New York Times*, *George*, and *Harper's*. He even provided fake supporting material, including self-created Web sites, to outfox his fact-checkers. And a columnist for *The Boston Globe*, Patricia Smith, admitted to fabricating the people and the quotations in four of her columns in 1999. In one case she made up an entire story about a woman dying of cancer.

Ironically, the journalistic community has been unceasingly critical of creative nonfiction while virtually ignoring its own misdeeds. In a 1997 feature in *Vanity Fair* magazine, "Me, Myself and I," James Wolcott boiled all creative nonfiction down into what he called "confessional writing" and took to task as "navel gazers" nearly any writer who had been the least bit self-revelatory in their work. Wolcott zeroed in on the memoir and made it seem as if that was the creative nonfiction genre in its totality, while ignoring the significant information-oriented work done by John McPhee, Annie Dillard, Tracy Kidder, Gay Talese, and many others.

Wolcott reserved an especially interesting title and role for me as "the godfather behind creative nonfiction." He abhorred the fact that I traveled and talked about creative nonfiction all over the world, wrote books about creative nonfiction, published a journal (*Creative Nonfiction*), directed a creative nonfiction writers' conference, and taught creative nonfiction. He called me a "human octopus."

Wolcott's observation that memoirists are overly self-obsessed was not new or particularly enlightening. This criticism has been pouring forth from dozens of directions since publication of *The Kiss*, in which Kathryn Harrison relates the details of her affair with the Presbyterian minister who is her father. Many people objected to this book because they found the subject morally indefensible—a separate or moot point. Or because they simply didn't want to know all the sordid details of the relationship; this was something personal and private—something that ought to have been fictionalized. Which it was in two of Harrison's novels, neither of which readers paid any attention to. So Harrison tried the same story in nonfiction—and achieved fame and, perhaps, fortune.

I don't find *The Kiss* particularly skillful or memorable, but I don't object to the story. My major problems concern the innocent victims of Harrison's quest to unload her anxieties. While I don't justify her father's actions, I wonder about the toll this will take on her children when they are old enough to read the book or when the parents of their classmates discuss Harrison in front of their children—an incident that could lead to embarrassment and continued distress. And what of her father's new family, his wife and children—and his congregation? Is he to be punished without being permitted to defend or explain himself?

The Perfect Storm, although not a memoir, is another popular book whose author Sebastian Junger has been accused of victimizing characters. Ray Leonard, a retired forest service ecologist, is depicted as curled on his bunk, "sullen and silent, sneaking gulps off a whiskey bottle" while his sailboat, *The Satori,* is sinking. The incident was never verified and, in fact, *The Satori* was found on a beach, intact, a few days later. It never went down. It is hard to know whether Leonard was a coward—but he is presented as one. Junger never contacted Leonard because the rest of his story and the fate of *The Satori* was irrelevant to the narrative, he said.

The Kiss and *The Perfect Storm* are troubling examples of how an author's need to write the perfect narrative or to share the pain and anxiety of a traumatic life can create innocent victims who may or may not be guilty of corruption, brutality, indecency, cowardice, or responsibility, but who will hardly ever have the opportunity to have their day in court. I understand that writing from memory is often unverifiable, but I believe that memoirists don't go far enough to confront and try to satisfy their own moral and ethical landscape.

I said at the beginning that I wasn't the creative nonfiction police or the literary judiciary. But I am "the godfather behind creative nonfiction," after all, according to *Vanity Fair.* The real point is that I have been doing this for a long time—more than a dozen published books and 25 years of teaching; I may be the first person to teach creative nonfiction on a full-time basis—anywhere. So I would like to recommend a code for creative nonaction writers—kind of a checklist. The word "checklist" is carefully chosen. There are no rules, laws, specific prescriptions relating to what to do and not to do as a creative nonfiction writer. The gospel according to Lee Gutkind or anyone else doesn't and shouldn't exist. It's more a question of doing the right thing, being fair, following the golden rule. Treating others with courtesy and respect and using common sense.

First, strive for the truth. Be certain that everything you write is as accurate and honest as you can make it. I don't mean that everyone who has shared the experience you are writing about should agree that your account is true. As I said, everyone has his or her own very precious, private, and shifting truth. But be certain your narrative is as true to your memory as possible.

Second, recognize the important distinction between recollected conversation and fabricated dialogue. Don't make anything up and don't tell your readers what you think your characters are thinking during the time about which you are writing. If you want to know how or what people are or were thinking, then ask them. Don't assume or guess.

Third, don't round corners—or compress situations or characters—unnecessarily. Not that rounding corners or compressing characters or incidents are absolutely wrong, but if you do experiment with these techniques, make certain you have a good reason. Making literary decisions based on good narrative principles is often legitimate—you are, after all, writers. But stop to consider the people about whom you are writing. Unleash your venom on the guilty parties; punish them as they deserve. But also ask yourself: who are the innocent victims? How have I protected them? Adults can file suits against you, but are you violating the privacy or endangering the emotional stability of children? Are you being fair to the aged or infirm?

Fourth, one way to protect the characters in your book, article, or essay is to allow them to defend themselves—or at least to read what you have written about them. Few writers do this because they are afraid of litigation or ashamed or embarrassed about the intimacies they have revealed. But sharing your narrative with the people about whom you are writing doesn't mean that you have to change what you say about them; rather, it only means that you are being responsible to your characters and the stories that you are revealing. I understand why you would not want to share your narrative; it could be dangerous. It could ruin your friendship, your marriage, your future. But by the same token so too could the publication of your book. And this is the kind of responsible action you might appreciate if the shoe were on the other foot.

I have on occasion shared parts of books with characters I have written about—with positive results. First, my characters corrected my mistakes. But, more importantly, when you come face to face with a character, you are able to communicate on a different and deeper level. When you show them what you think, they think and feel—when they read what you have written—they may get angry—an action in itself which is interesting to observe and write about.

Or they may feel obliged to provide their side of their situation—a side that you have been hesitant to listen to or interpret. With the text in the middle, as a filter, it is possible to discuss personal history as a story somewhat disconnected from the reality you are experiencing. It provides a way to communicate as an exercise in writing—it filters and distances the debate. Moreover, it defines and cements your own character. The people about whom you have written may not like what you have said—and may in fact despise you for saying it—but they can only respect and admire the forthright way in which you have approached them. No laws govern the scope of good taste and personal integrity.

More than in any other literary genre, the creative nonfiction writer must rely on his or her own conscience and sensitivity to others and display a higher morality and a healthy respect for fairness and justice. We all harbor resentments, hatreds, and prejudices, but that doesn't necessarily mean, because we are writers, that we are being given special dispensation to behave in a way that is unbecoming to ourselves and hurtful to others. This sounds so simple—yet it is so difficult. The moral and ethical responsibility of the creative nonfiction writer is to practice the golden rule and to be as fair and truthful as possible—to write both for art's sake and for humanity's sake. In other words, we police ourselves.

By saying this, I do not feel that I am being overly simplistic. As writers we intend to make a difference, to affect someone's life over and above our own. To say something that matters—this is why we write. To impact upon society, to put a personal stamp on history. Remember that art and literature are our legacies to other generations. We will be forgotten, but our books and essays, our stories and poems will always, somewhere, have a life.

Wherever you draw the line between fiction and nonfiction remember the basic rules of good citizenship: Do not recreate incidents and characters who never existed; do not write to do harm to innocent victims; do not forget your own story, but while considering your struggle and the heights of your achievements, think repeatedly about how your story will impact on and relate to your reader. Over and above the creation of a seamless narrative, you are seeking to touch and affect someone else's life— which is the goal creative nonfiction writers share with novelists and poets. We all want to connect with another human being—as many people as possible—in such a way that they will remember us and share our legacy with others.

Someday, I hope to connect with the woman with the badge and the bare feet face-to-face. The truth is, I have never forgotten her. She has, in some strange way, become an accouterment to my conscience, standing over me as I write, forcing me to ask the questions about my work that I have recommended to you. Perhaps she is here today, as I am proofreading this essay—somewhere. But from this point on I am hoping you too will feel her shadow over your shoulders each time you sit down, address your keyboard, and begin to write.

2001

Tracy Kidder (B. 1945)

Making the Truth Believable

When I started writing nonfiction a couple of decades ago there was an idea in the air, which for me had the force of a revelation: that all journalism was inevitably subjective. I was in my 20s then, and although my behavior was somewhat worse than it has been recently, I was quite a moralist. I decided that writers of nonfiction had a moral obligation to write in the first person—really write in the first person, making themselves characters on the page. In this way, I would disclose my biases. I would not hide the truth from the reader. I would proclaim that what I wrote was just my own impression of events. In retrospect it seems clear that this prescription for honesty often served as a license for self-absorption on the page. I was too young and self-absorbed to realize what should have been obvious: that

I was less likely to write honestly about myself than about anyone else on earth.

I wrote a book about a murder case in a swashbuckling first person. After it was published and disappeared without a trace, I went back to writing nonfiction articles for the *Atlantic Monthly,* under the tutelage of Richard Todd, then a young editor there. For about 5 years, during which I didn't dare attempt another book, I worked on creating what many writer friends of mine call "voice." I didn't do this consciously. If I had, I probably wouldn't have gotten anywhere. But gradually, I think, I found a writing voice, the voice of a person who was informed, fair-minded, and always temperate—the voice, not of the person I was, but of the person I wanted to be. Then I went back to writing books, and discovered other points of view besides the first person.

Choosing a point of view is a matter of finding the best place to stand, from which to tell a story. The process shouldn't be determined by theory, but driven by immersion in the material itself. The choice of point of view, I've come to think, has nothing to do with morality. It's a choice among tools. On the other hand, the wrong choice can lead to dishonesty. Point of view is primary; it affects everything else, including voice. I've made my choices by instinct sometimes and sometimes by experiment. Most of my memories of time spent writing have merged together in a blur, but I remember vividly my first attempts to find a way to write *Among Schoolchildren,* a book about an inner-city teacher. I had spent a year inside her classroom. I intended, vaguely, to fold into my account of events I'd witnessed there a great deal about the lives of particular children and about the problems of education in America. I tried every point of view that I'd used in previous books, and every page I wrote felt lifeless and remote. Finally, I hit on a restricted third-person narration.

That approach seemed to work. The world of that classroom seemed to come alive when the view of it was restricted mainly to observations of the teacher and to accounts of what the teacher saw and heard and smelled and felt. This choice narrowed my options. I ended up writing something less comprehensive than I'd planned. The book became essentially an account of a year in the emotional life of a schoolteacher.

My choice of the restricted third person also obliged me to write parts of the book as if from within the teacher's mind. I wrote many sentences that contained the phrase "she thought." I felt I could do so because the teacher had told me how she felt and what she thought about almost everything that happened in her classroom. And her descriptions of her thoughts and feeling never seemed self-serving. Believing in them myself, I thought that I could make them believable on the page.

For me, part of the pleasure of reading comes from the awareness that an author stands behind the scenes adroitly pulling the strings. But the pleasure quickly palls at painful reminders of that presence—the times when, for instance, I sense that the author strains to produce yet another clever metaphor. Then I stop believing in what I read, and usually stop reading. Belief is what a reader offers an author, what Coleridge famously called

"That willing suspension of disbelief for the moment, which constitutes poetic faith." All writers have to find ways to do their work without disappointing readers into withdrawing belief.

In fiction, believability may have nothing to do with reality or even plausibility. In nonfiction, it has everything to do with those things.

I think that the nonfiction writer's fundamental job is to make what is true believable. But for some writers lately the job has clearly become more varied: to make believable what the writer thinks is true (if the writer wants to be scrupulous); to make believable what the writer wishes were true (if the writer isn't interested in scrupulosity); or to make believable what the writer thinks might be true (if the writer couldn't get the story and had to make it up).

I figure that if I call a piece of my own writing nonfiction it ought to be about real people, with their real names attached whenever possible, who say and do in print nothing that they didn't actually say and do. On the cover page of my new book I put a note that reads, "This is a work of nonfiction," and I listed the several names that I was obliged to change in the text. I feared that a longer note would stand between the reader and the spell that I wanted to create, inviting the reader into the world of a nursing home. But the definition of "nonfiction" has become so slippery that I wonder if I shouldn't have written more. So now I'll take this opportunity to explain that I spent a year doing research, that the name of the place I wrote about is its real name, that I didn't change the names of any major characters, and that I didn't invent dialogue or put any thoughts in characters' minds that the characters themselves didn't confess to.

I no longer care what rules other writers set for themselves. If I don't like what someone has written, I can stop reading, which is, after all, the worst punishment a writer can suffer. But the expanded definitions of "nonfiction" have created problems for those writers who define the term narrowly. Many readers now view with suspicion every narrative that claims to be nonfiction. But not all writers make up their stories or the details in them. In fact, scores of very good writers do not—writers such as John McPhee *(Coming into the Country)*, Jane Kramer *(The Last Cowboy)*, J. Anthony Lukas *(Common Ground)*. There are also special cases, which confound categories and all attempts to lay down rules for narrative. I have in mind especially Norman Mailer's *Executioner's Song,* a hybrid of fact and fiction, labeled as such, which I loved reading.

Most writers lack Mailer's powers of invention. Some nonfiction writers do not lack his willingness to invent, but the candor to admit it. Some writers proceed by trying to discover the truth about a situation, and then invent the facts as necessary. Even in these suspicious times, a writer can get away with this. Often no one will know, and the subjects of the story may not care. They may approve. They may not notice. But the writer always knows. I believe in immersion in the events of a story. I take it on faith that the truth lies in the events somewhere, and that immersion in those real events will yield glimpses of that truth. I try to hew to a narrow definition of nonfiction partly in that faith and partly out of fear. I'm afraid that if I started making things up in a story that purported to be about real events and people, I'd stop believing it myself. And I imagine that such a loss of conviction would infect every sentence and make each one unbelievable.

I don't mean to imply that all a person has to do to write good nonfiction is to take accurate notes and reproduce them. The kind of nonfiction I like to read is at bottom storytelling, as gracefully accomplished as good fiction. I don't think any technique should be ruled out to achieve it well. For myself, I rule out only invention. But I don't think that honesty and artifice are contradictory. They work together in good writing of every sort. Artfulness and an author's justified belief in a story can produce the most believable nonfiction.

1993

Bret Lott (B. 1958)

Toward a Definition of Creative Nonfiction

The Reverend Francis Kilvert, an English curate in the Welsh Border region, kept a journal of his life—where he went, what he did, what he dreamt, who he knew, and what he thought—from 1870 to 1879. In the journal he wrote, "Why do I keep this voluminous journal! I can hardly tell. Partly because life appears to me such a curious and wonderful thing that it almost seems a pity that even such a humble and uneventful life as mine should pass altogether away without some record such as this." *Kilvert's Diary,* published in 1941 and reprinted in 1960, serves as a beautiful, moving, and genuine glimpse into country life of that time nonetheless. All well and good, but how does it help define what creative nonfiction is?

That passage serves, I hold, to illuminate as best as any passage from any piece of literature I can find the longing each of us carries, or ought to carry, in our hearts as human beings first, and as writers second. Creative nonfiction is, in one form or another, for better and worse, in triumph and failure, the attempt to keep from passing altogether away the lives we have lived.

And though that may sound like a definitive pronouncement on what creative nonfiction is, I mean what I say in giving this essay the title it has: *Toward* a Definition of Creative Nonfiction. We aren't going to arrive anywhere here. We can no more understand what creative nonfiction is by trying to define it than we can learn how to ride a bike by looking at a bicycle tire, a set of handlebars, the bicycle chain itself. Sure, we'll have something of an idea, maybe a glimpse into the importance of finding your balance when we look at how narrow those tires are. But until we get on that thing and try to steer it with this weirdly twisted metal tube and actually try to synchronize pushing down on the pedals and pushing forward at the same time, we won't have a clue.

Any definition of true worth to you as a writer will and must come to you experientially. What creative nonfiction is will reveal itself to you only at the back end of things, once you have written it. Kilvert wrote his journal in the midst of his life, looking back at what had happened that day, trying to piece together the meaning of his life from the shards of it, however exquisitely beautiful or sharply painful they were. It was the piecing together of it that mattered, and that matters to us here, today.

And because we are human beings, as such we are pattern makers, a species desirous of order, no matter how much we as "artists" may masquerade otherwise. Yet looking back at our lives to find that order—and here is the sticky part—must *not* be an effort to reorder our lives as we want them to be seen; rather, we are after, in creative nonfiction, an understanding of what it is that has happened, and in that way to see order, however chaotic it may be.

Frank O'Connor, arguably the most important and influential short story writer of this century, wrote in a letter to a friend, ". . . there are occasions when we all feel guilt and remorse; we all want to turn back time. But even if we were able, things would go in precisely the same way, because the mistakes we make are not in our judgments but in our natures. It is only when we do violence to our natures that we are justified in our regrets . . . We are what we are, and within our limitations we have made our own efforts. They seem puny in the light of eternity, but they didn't at the time, and they weren't."

It is in creative nonfiction we try to divine from what we have done, who we have known, what we have dreamt and how we have failed, an order to our lives. "The test of a first-rate intelligence," F. Scott Fitzgerald wrote in his landmark essay "The Crack-Up," "is the ability to hold two opposed ideas in the mind at the same time, and still retain the ability to function." The two opposed ideas of creative nonfiction are finding order in chaos without reforming chaos into order; retaining the ability to function is the act of writing all this down for someone else to understand.

So let's begin with just that much: a desire not to let slip altogether away our lives as we have known them, and to put an order—again, for better and worse—to our days.

Creative nonfiction can take any form, from the letter to the list, from the biography to the memoir, from the journal to the obituary. When I say we are trying to find order in what has happened, I do *not* mean creative nonfiction is simply writing about what happened to me. Rather, it is writing about oneself *in relation to* the subject at hand. A book review is creative nonfiction in that it is a written record of the reviewer *in relation to* the book in question; Jon Krakauer's fantastic book *Into the Wild* is a biography of an idealistic young man, Chris McCandless, who upon graduation from college disappeared into the wild, his decomposed body found four months later in an abandoned bus in the Alaskan wilderness. The biography becomes creative nonfiction as the author increasingly identifies himself with the young man, increasingly recognizing in the stupidity of the boy's folly his own reckless self—Krakauer sees himself *in relation to* the subject at hand: the death of Chris McCandless. This essay itself is a form of creative nonfiction in that it is my attempt at defining an abstract through the smallest of apertures: my own experience *in relation to* creative nonfiction. So creative nonfiction is not solely, What happened to me today, and why is it important?

Creative nonfiction can be and often is a euphemism for the personal essay, and my earlier assertion that creative nonfiction's being understood only through its being written is borne out rather handily in the meaning of the word *essay* itself.

The French word *essai* means to attempt something, to give something a trial run, to test. Michel de Montaigne, considered the writer who identified if not invented the form, was the first to use the word *essai* to describe his writings, the first collection of which was entitled strangely enough *Essais*, and which was written between 1572 and 1574. This notion of the attempt, of testing one's words lined up in an order one deems close enough to reveal a personal understanding so that all may have that same understanding is, and will always be, only an attempt. The essay as trial run is inherent to any definition of creative nonfiction; you will only come to know this form by running your own tests.

Montaigne, a landowner and lawyer from a nominally wealthy family in the Perigord region of France, wrote out of his own interests, but wrote convinced that it was his own interest as a human being in a matter or topic at hand that made his attempts universal: "Each man bears the entire form of man's estate," he wrote, and therefore, he reasoned, what he was attempting to render in words might make his attempts of interest to all. Phillip Lopate, in his indispensable anthology *The Art of the Personal Essay*, writes, "What Montaigne tells us about himself is peculiarly, charmingly specific and daily: he is on the short side, has a loud, abrasive voice, suffers from painful kidney stones, scratches his ears a lot (the insides itch), loves sauces, is not sure radishes agree with him, does his best thinking on horseback, prefers glass to metal cups, moves his bowels regularly in the morning, and so on. It is as if the self were a new continent, and Montaigne its first explorer."

The self as continent, and you its first explorer: another definition of creative nonfiction. For self, however at the center of what you are writing or however tangential, must inform the heart of the tale you are telling. It is indeed *self* that is the *creative* element of creative nonfiction. Without you and who you are, a piece of writing that tells what happened is simply nonfiction: a police report. But when I begin to incorporate the sad and glorious fact that the way I see it shapes and forms what it is to be seen, I end up with creative nonfiction.

As a kind of sidebar, I'd like to interject here the fact that one doesn't have to have had a bizarre life before that life becomes worthy of writing about. Contrary to popular belief, that belief borne out by even the most cursory look at the lineup of victim-authors on afternoon and morning TV talk shows and evening newsmagazines, one's life needn't have been wracked by incest or murder or poorly executed plastic surgery to be worthy of examination. Which is, of course, not to say that those lives are not worth writing about. They most certainly are. But E. B. White's words from the introduction to his *Letters of E. B. White* speak as eloquently as I have seen to this matter of whether or not one's life has been miserable enough to record: "If an unhappy childhood is indispensable for a writer, I am ill-equipped: I missed out on all that and was neither deprived nor unloved. It would be inaccurate, however, to say that my childhood was untroubled. The normal fears and worries of every child were in me developed to a high degree; every day was an awesome prospect. I was uneasy about practically everything: the uncertainty of the future, the dark of the attic, the panoply and discipline of school, the transitoriness of life, the mystery of the church and of God, the frailty of the body, the sadness of afternoon, the shadow of sex, the distant challenge of love and marriage, the far-off problem of a livelihood."

These normal fears, if we have been paying the least bit of attention to our lives, inform us all; and if E. B. White, who is the greatest American essayist of this century, found in that uneasiness the material for a lifetime, we too have all we need.

But *how* do we look at ourselves in order best to inform our readers that who we are matters, and is worthy of their attention? In the Tyndale commentary on the Book of Proverbs, Derek Kidner writes that the sayings and aphorisms of King Solomon, and to a lesser degree Lemuel and Agur, constitute "not a portrait album of a book of manners: [the Book of Proverbs] offers a key to life. The samples of behavior which it holds up to view are all assessed by one criterion, which could be summed up in the question, 'Is this wisdom, or is this folly?'" I believe that this same criterion is one that helps define creative nonfiction as well. In examining the self as continent, in seeing the way self shades and informs the meaning of what has happened, the writer must be inquiring of himself, Is this wisdom, or is this folly? The self as inquisitor of self is integral to an examination of one's life; it calls for a kind of ruthlessness about seeing oneself in relation to others: Why did I do that? What was I thinking? Who was I trying to kid? What did I hope to achieve? These questions must be asked, and asked with all the candor and courage and objectivity one can muster, though objectivity is an abstract to be hoped for, and not to be achieved; it is, after all, *you* who is writing about you.

Which brings me to another major point on our way toward a definition: creative nonfiction cannot at any time be self-serving. There is no room here for grandstanding of oneself. To my way of thinking—and this is me speaking as a follower of Christ, and therefore one well aware of my transgressions, my iniquities, my falling short of the glory of God—ninety-nine times out of a hundred the answer to the question, Is this wisdom, or is this folly? is, Folly. Hands down.

Phillip Lopate writes, "The enemy of the personal essay is self-righteousness, not just because it is tiresome and ugly in itself, but because it slows down the dialectic of self-questioning . . . The essayist is someone who lives with the guilty knowledge that he is 'prejudiced' (Mencken called his essay collections *Prejudices*) and has a strong predisposition for or against certain everyday phenomena. It then becomes his business to attend to these inner signals, these stomach growls, these seemingly indefensible intuitions, and try to analyze what lies underneath them, the better to judge them."

So, our definition thus far: a desire not to let slip altogether away our lives as we have known them; to put an order, for better and worse, to our days; this is only a test; the self as continent, you its first explorer; is this wisdom, or is this folly?; no self-righteousness.

This last point, however, seems at odds with the entire notion of the personal essay, all this business about me: isn't talk about myself in relation to others by definition egotistical? Wasn't I taught in seventh grade never to include 'I' in an essay? Who cares about what I think in the first place?

Thoreau, in answer to this assertion we have had pounded into our heads most of our lives, wrote in the opening of Walden, "In most books the I, or first person, is omitted; in this it will be retained; that, in respect to egotism, is the main difference. We commonly do not remember that it is, after all, always the first person that is speaking." And if one is honestly seeking to understand, circling with a cold eye one's relation to events, places, people—whatever the subject of the essay—then that search's chances of being construed as egotistical will be dismissed. Seventeenth-century English writer Alexander Smith wrote, "The speaking about one self is not necessarily offensive. A modest, truthful man speaks better about himself than about anything else, and on that subject his speech is likely to be most profitable to his hearers . . . If he be without taint of boastfulness, of self-sufficiency, of hungry vanity, the world will not press the charge home."

Another element of any definition of creative nonfiction must include the form's circling bent, its way of looking again and again at itself from all angles in order to see itself most fully. The result is literary triangulation, a finding of the subject in a three-dimensional grid through digression, full-frontal assault, guerrilla tactics and humble servitude, all in an effort, simply, to see. The creative nonfiction form attempts in whatever way it can to grab hold hard and sure its subject in any manner possible. Eudora Welty writes in *One Writer's Beginnings,* "In writing, as in life, the connections of all sorts of relationships and kinds lie in wait of discovery, and give out their signals to the Geiger counter of the charged imagination, once it is drawn into the right field . . . What I do make my stories out of is the whole fund of my feelings, my responses to the real experiences of my own life, to the relationships that formed and changed it, that I have given most of myself to, and so learned my way toward a dramatic counterpart." The dramatic counterpart of which she here writes is, of course, her stories—fiction—but I maintain that this "whole fund" of feelings, the complete range of our responses to our own real experiences, must inform creative nonfiction as well. Only when we use our "whole fund" can we circle our subjects in the most complete way, wringing from our stores of knowledge and wisdom and the attendant recognition of how little we have of both—*the essence of who we are*—then coupling those recognitions with what in fact we do not know altogether, will we find what we have come looking for: ourselves and, by grace and by luck, the larger world perhaps we hadn't seen before.

Lopate writes, "The personal essay is the reverse of that set of Chinese boxes that you keep opening, only to find a smaller one within. Here you start with the small—the package of flaws and limits—and suddenly find a slightly larger container, insulated by the essay's successful articulation and the writer's self-knowledge."

I agree with Lopate in how the essay reveals larger and larger selves in itself, but rather than the Chinese box, the image that comes to my mind is that of the Russian nesting dolls, one person inside another inside another. But instead of finding smaller selves inside the self, the opposite occurs, as with Lopate's boxes: we find nested inside that smallest of selves a larger self, and a larger inside that, until we come to the whole of humanity within our own hearts.

Now back to our definition: a desire not to let slip altogether away our life as we have known it; to put an order, for better and worse, to our days; this is only a test; the self as continent, you its first explorer; is this wisdom, or is this folly?; no self-righteousness, though it is always the first person talking; circle the subject to see it most whole.

I'm saving perhaps the most conundrum-like element for nearly last. What role, we have to ask once all these prior elements are taken into account, does *truth* have here? If you look at the pieces of our definition thus far, each one contains within it the angle of perception: the fact that it is only me who is seeing. That is, I don't want to let slip away my life as I have seen it, but who is to say I am telling the truth? In my attempt to put order to my days, am I deluding myself, inflicting an order that was and is now nowhere to be seen? If this is only a test, who is to say I pass? If I am the explorer of my self as continent, what does my discovery matter—didn't Leif Erikson set up shop in North America 500 years before Columbus discovered the place? Isn't one man's wisdom another man's folly? How do I know if I'm not being self-righteous unless there's somebody outside myself to cut me down to size? In circling my subject, isn't it me who determines my course, my longitude and latitude, and therefore am I, by definition, being the most subjective of anyone on planet earth when it comes to my subject?

The answer to each and every one of these questions is: continue to question. Only through rigorous and ruthless questioning of the self can we hope to arrive at any kind of truth.

If you wish to understand creative nonfiction, hope to find a definition, then it is up to you to embrace die fact that, as Montaigne saw, "Each man bears the entire form of man's estate." Inherent to that form are the eccentricities, egotism, foolishness, and fraud of all mankind; inherent as well are the wisdom and self-recognition, the worth and value and merit available to mankind, once enough scouring of what we know and do not know has taken place. V S. Pritchett, in his memoir *Midnight Oil*, wrote, "The true autobiography of this egotist is exposed in all its intimate foliage in his work. But there is a period when a writer has not yet become one, or, just having become one, is struggling to form his talent, and it is from this period that I have selected most of the scenes and people in this book. It *is* a selection, and it is neither a confession nor a volume of literary reminiscences, but as far as I am able I have put in my 'truth.'"

Pritchett puts the word *truth* in quotation marks; he predicates it with the possessive pronoun *my*. We must recognize that this is the deepest truth we can hope to attain on our own: quotation marks, calling it our own. Only when we have scoured as clean as possible by self-inquiry, even interrogation, what we *perceive*, can we approach calling it *truth;* and even then that crutch of the quotation marks and the assignation of who it belongs to—me—must be acknowledged.

Finally, we have to try and further illuminate *why* we write creative nonfiction. Certainly that first element—a desire not to let slip altogether away our lives as we have known them—is a beginning point, but simply trying to capture our lives before they slip away seems more *reactive* than *proactive*. Writing is, I believe, both, and so any definition must encompass both the reactive and the proactive.

Karen Blixen, AKA Isak Dinesen, in a dinner meeting speech she gave in 1959 at the National Institute of Arts and Letters in New York, addressed the subject, "On Mottoes of My Life." In it she said, "The family of Finch Hatton, of England, have on their crest the device *Je responderay*, 'I will answer' . . . I liked it so much I asked Denys . . . if I might have it for my own. He generously made me a present of it and even had a seal cut for me, with the words carved on it. The device was meaningful and dear to me for many reasons, two in particular. The first . . . was its high evaluation of the idea of the answer in itself. For an answer is a rarer thing than is generally imagined. There are many highly intelligent people who have no answer at all in them . . . . Secondly, I liked the Finch Hatton device for its ethical content. I will answer *for* what I say or do; I will answer *to* the impression I make. I will be responsible."

This is the proactive element of creative nonfiction, and the final element of my *essai* to define creative writing: *our responsibility as human beings to answer for and to our lives.* It is a responsibility that must encompass all the elements laid out in all this talk about definitions; it is a responsibility that must be woven through the recognition of the fleeting nature of this span of days we have been given, woven through our attempt to see order in chaos, through our understanding that we are only attempting this test and through our being the first explorers of the continent of ourselves. This responsibility to answer for and to ourselves must be woven through the interrogation of self as to whether this is folly or wisdom, through the pledge to humility and to avoiding the abyss of self-righteousness, through the recognition that it is always and only me—the first person—talking, and through the relentless circling of the subject to see it most completely. And this responsibility to answer for and to ourselves must be woven through our recognition that the only truth I can hope to approach will finally and always and only be *my truth.*

But if we are rigorous enough, fearless enough, and humble enough to attempt this responsibility, this way of seeing—for creative nonfiction, like fiction, like poetry, is simply and complexly a way of seeing—the rewards we will reap will be great: we will *understand.* To understand, and nothing more, and that is everything.

2000

Gregory Martin (B. 1971)

Other People's Memories

How breaking the conventions of a genre can lead to a richer, more dramatic story

THE WORK: *Mountain City*, a memoir of the life of a town of thirty-three people in remote northeastern Nevada.
THE PROBLEM: A conventional first person point of view is too confining.
THE SOLUTION: The use of multiple points of view heightens drama and allows the memoir to be more about the place and its people and less about the author.

My craft problems in writing *Mountain City* began with the very premise of the book—a memoir of the life of a town of thirty-three people in remote northeastern Nevada. I wanted the book to be a memoir, but I didn't want it to be about me. When I started *Mountain City*, at twenty-five years old, self-awareness was not my strong suit, but I somehow knew better than to write a book of profound reflections about my life up to that point. What I wanted was to make a record of this place I loved and the people who lived there, before it all disappeared.

One solution came early. I chose six main characters: my grandfather and grandmother, my Uncle Mel and Aunt Lou, my cousin Graham, and

Rosella Chambers, a ninety-one-year-old widow and dear friend to me and my family. I would be a minor character, a lens through which my main characters' stories were told. (I wasn't raised in Mountain City; my mother was; I had visited most my life and lived there for a year after college.)

But one story I wanted to tell took place in 1919. How could I write a *memoir* about a time before I was born? Other stories, from the recent past, took place in Mountain City when I wasn't living there. How could I tell these stories in the conventional first person of memoir?

A memory is not a story but a blur out the corner of the mind's eye. To make a story out of memory requires amplification, emphasis, speculation. To make a story out of other people's memories—and call it memoir—is a recipe for trouble. I knew from the start I would be getting all kinds of things "wrong." But I didn't want to write fiction. The people I wanted to write about were real, and I wanted to write about real things that happened to them. These stories were as "true" as nonfiction stories can be—in telling them, I had no intention to deceive.

But even when relying on my own memory, I confronted my limited understanding. How could I say what some event meant to my grandfather? I couldn't have my characters think things I didn't know they thought. I couldn't render them thinking anything, because that would violate the first person point of view.

One solution was to explicitly speculate about what my characters were thinking:

> I wonder if Gramps's feelings for Graham now are a reflection of his own fear, as if Graham were a mirror in which Gramps sees himself in the time to come: blind, dependent, invalided.

But I often balked at this strategy, because I did sometimes know my characters' thoughts. I knew how Gramps felt about the first time he visited Mountain City, in 1919, when he was a six-year-old boy. He told me the story one night in his living room while I watched, and he listened to, a Denver Broncos game on TV. (He had macular degeneration; the screen was a blur of color.) I didn't want to limit my story to his direct dialogue, which I scribbled onto yellow-sticky-pad after yellow-sticky-pad. (I'm no oral historian.) I wanted the freedom to speculate and elaborate upon his memories, not unlike a jazz musician elaborating upon the melody of a standard. I wanted to clothe him, render his gestures and expressions; I wanted to paint the landscape he never described because he knew I could supply it myself. But my reader couldn't. I wanted to incorporate things I understood from knowing him all my life, and apply them to his character as a boy. I wanted more than memories. I wanted a lot more. I wanted access to the thoughts of that six-year-old boy. And so I made two leaps. I wrote the story in the third person. And I granted myself omniscience. At the time, I thought this was *forbidden*. A memoir, told in the third person, limited omniscient? This was six years before James Frey's problems, but still,

I imagined some kind of investigation. Never once did I think, "It's my book, why not just do what I want?" One hears all the time that you have to know the rules before you can break them. Well, all right. But it's also true that you can make your own rules—as long as it's clear to the reader what they are, and as long as you follow them.

> The day begins before dawn. The sky is dark and shadowed with clouds as Oliver takes the bucket to the pump, where he will draw water from the well. He is six. He is small and wiry, his hair blonde and uncombed and curly. He is dressed in patched jeans and shortsleeves, though it is not yet 5 a.m. He knows what cold is like and this is not cold . . . It is the Fourth of July, 1919, and today the Tremewan Family will travel north to Mountain City for the celebration.

Speculation is the engine of all art. Fiction speculates upon the significance of a set of possibilities—imagined characters, imagined places, imagined times. Memoir speculates upon the significance of a set of memories—remembered people, remembered places, remembered times.

I finally decided that, to write the book I wanted to write, I would have to appropriate other people's memories as my own. Which is sometimes the way memory works. My memory of the day I learned to ride a bicycle is a murky amalgam of inarticulate thoughts and sense impressions suffused by memories of my father's stories based on his own memory of that day. To say that this memory is *mine* is to slip into the ambiguity at the heart of language.

I should probably say that writing a memoir from multiple points of view isn't something I recommend lightly. It can work. And for me, the writing that explores and blurs the boundaries of genre and category is the most compelling. But the dangers are many. Confusion. A sense of arbitrariness. A loss of credibility.   *Who's* telling the story, now? Why is it being told *this* way? How does *he* know what they were thinking? The gall! Luckily, no one really warned me, and I didn't learn any of this until I was too far along to turn back.

2006

John McNally (B. 1965)

Humor Incarnate

I'll admit it: my tastes are low-brow. I'm an academic only because I happen to teach at a university.

At an on-campus interview several years ago, I was asked about the humor that runs through my fiction and who my influences were. While

I stared blankly ahead, a few of the professors interviewing me offered up a plethora of literary examples. I suppose I could have agreed with them, and then we all could have moved ahead without the awkward silence. But I didn't. If I'd had any chance at the job, I blew it right there. The thing is, no one they mentioned *had* been an influence. It was, however, a question worth thinking about, even if it meant standing there and looking like an idiot. To my detriment, I'd rather look like an idiot than say something I don't really believe. Hence, years of unemployment.

I hadn't ever given any serious thought to my humor influences before that interview, but the answer—the truth—is that I read virtually nothing the first eighteen years of my life. Instead, I watched (and listened to) endless comedy, in one form or another. I bought 8mm movies of Charlie Chaplin and Laurel and Hardy. Every Saturday at 2:30, I watched Abbott and Costello. I watched the Marx Brothers whenever they were on, or the Three Stooges, or even second-rate comedy teams, like the Ritz Brothers. I bought albums with vaudeville routines on them, typed up the routines, and memorized them. I practiced them in front of my dog. I listened to cassettes of old radio shows with Jack Benny and Edgar Bergen. In the seventh grade, I started writing a book about old-time comedians. I finished it at the end of eighth grade—two hundred pages of prose typed on a cast-iron Royal typewriter. Girls scribbled in my autograph book, "Remember me when you're famous!" *Oh yes,* I thought, *I will.* I wrote to every publisher in New York; no one wanted to see it. But it wasn't just the old-time comedians that interested me. I listened to Cheech and Chong, to George Carlin, to Bill Cosby, to Richard Pryor. I started watching *Saturday Night Live* beginning with their second show. I saw Steve Martin in concert back when he could pack the largest amphitheater in Chicago. He wore an arrow through his head and sang "King Tut." I stole his routine and won second place in my eighth-grade talent contest. Disco dancers won first. I savored everything that was funny or supposed to be funny. I bought a lot of books—the *idea* of book interested me, especially since I had written one—but I read next to nothing, unless it was a book about comedians.

How could I not have internalized all of this comedy? How could I not have picked up a thing or two about the ways in which humor works? Many years later, and only after writing several short stories featuring a narrator named Hank—a good kid in eighth-grade—and his troublemaking friend Ralph, who had failed both third and fifth grades, did I realize that they were a comedy team, a straight man and a comic, and the rhythms of their dialog resembled the rhythms of a vaudeville team. Even the dynamic of their relationship—a con artist and a naïf—looked an awful lot like the template for, say, Abbott and Costello. And so it is my contention that there's much to be learned in the so-called low art.

But it's also my contention that one's sense of humor is innate, and that while you may be able to teach the mechanics of comic writing, you can't conjure up the soul of a comic out of thin air. It's either in the DNA or it isn't.

A few semesters ago, I showed a *Saturday Night Live* clip to my fiction writing class, the point of which is now lost on me. Perhaps I had nothing prepared for the day; I don't remember. Anyway, I showed the clip, and everyone laughed, but one young woman who was laughing did so nervously, and when we began discussing the clip, she admitted that she didn't see what was funny about it. Before anyone could say anything, she added that she didn't understand *any* of the humor on *Saturday Night Live*. This wasn't a comment on the show's declining quality or the fact that Lorne Michaels no longer seems to know when to end a skit; no, it was really an admittance that all humor of this variety escaped her. *All of it.* This, I should note, was a student with a 4.0. She wasn't dumb. But over the two semesters that she took classes with me, I saw time and again the fear in her eyes when classmates started to laugh at one thing or another, and then she would join in nervously, only to say, "What? . . . *What?*"

In addition, I tend to believe (and, I should note, I have no proof for anything I say: I'm an English professor, after all) . . . but I tend to believe that the comic sensibility you are born with is the same one you'll have for the rest of your life. That's not to say that it won't become more sophisticated or more complex. It will. And it's not to say that you won't be able to appreciate other types of humor. You will. But the *sorts* of humor that most appeal to you at two and three years old will appeal to you at forty-three. As much as I admire Dorothy Parker, I would still rather watch Moe poke Curly in the eyes than read Ms. Parker's work. In fact, I never tire of watching Moe poke Curly in the eyes. Consider Moe, if you will: that ball of fury, that tightly-wound epitome of pure rage. We may not want to admit it, but Moe is us, really. He's us every time we talk to a stupid boss; he's us every time one of our colleagues does something that makes us look bad; he's us every time someone cuts us off when we're driving. The difference is this. We do nothing. At most, we may flip someone the bird when they're not looking. But Moe: he does what all of us wish to do. He pokes his cohorts in the eyes. He hits them with a sledgehammer. He picks up a cheese grater and gives them a good scrape across the face. Everything within his reach is a weapon: a flowerpot, a band saw, a vice grip. He's us without restraint. Imagine a world in which we can clonk our boss over the head without consequence. I loved Moe when I was three, but in the intervening years the weight of Moe has accumulated, and I love him anew for the larger things Moe represents, the metaphor of Moe, and for that, he's funnier than he's ever been.

But I digress.

Let me say this: There's nothing funnier than watching someone fall into a manhole. I learned the hard way. Drunk one night and walking across a lawn at a party, I failed to notice the drainage ditch. One minute, my friends were watching me walk toward them; the next, I simply wasn't there. I was stuck—wedged, actually—between two concrete slabs. What does this tell me about the humorous scenario? That it's about *point-of-view.* It's about *perspective.* But it's also about the absurd, to some extent. It's about the unexpected coming to fruition.

Take this story. 100% true. For me, it embodies all that one ever needs to know about the art of humor. Lincoln, Nebraska. Mid-1990s. Football Saturday. Bear in mind, these were the glory years when the Cornhuskers were a powerhouse football team with two National Championships behind them, a third championship looming before them. You could hear it in the streets that season, that word that's not really a word: "three-peat." It became a mantra, an incantation, a riddle, like something spoken by the witches in *Macbeth:* Can last year's *repeat* become this year's *three-peat.* My wife—then-girlfriend—and I had decided to go downtown for pizza and a beer. Our friend—let's call him Ned—came along. It was bone-chillingly cold that day, and we had to park several blocks from the restaurant. Furthermore, the Huskers had lost their game, a rarity in those days, and so the mood of the town was palpably somber. On our way to the bar, we passed three portable outdoor toilets, sometimes called Johnny-on-the-Spots, sometimes Porta-Johns. Our friend, like some kind of wild animal, preferring to do his business outside than inside, had to stop. He chose the middle one. Afterward, we continued on, enjoyed our pizza and beer, and then headed back to the car.

"I need to stop again," Ned said.

"We were just in the bar," my wife said. "Why didn't you just go there?"

"I'd rather go here," he said, and, again, he stepped inside the middle Porta-John.

To escape the ear-numbing wind, my wife and I stepped behind an eye-level billboard that ran along the sidewalk. In the distance, I saw a lonely figure: a young man wearing a cowboy hat and a large belt buckle but no coat. His shirt had pearl buttons and his jeans looked ironed. No doubt he had driven here all the way from Western Nebraska for the game. It's important to note that I normally don't talk to strangers. In fact, I never initiate conversations with strangers. Strangers scare me. This may be because I'm a magnet for every crazy person in a room. I'm the one they'll gravitate toward, the one they want to confess to, so I avoid them. It's also important to note that I am not cheery by nature. (I'm not *not* cheery; I'm just not cheery.) But for some inexplicable reason, I couldn't resist on that particular cold Saturday: Just before the young man from Western Nebraska reached us, I stepped out from behind the billboard and cheerily asked, "Where's your coat?" to which he replied, "Huskers lost!" then pivoted on his heel and kicked the middle Porta-John as hard as he could. He kicked it with the flat of his boot and then continued walking. The Porta-John tilted to the point where we were sure it would fall over, tilting toward the street, but then it started to tilt back the other way. We could hear our friend inside screaming. The Porta-John tilted toward us for a moment before tilting back the other way. Finally, it righted itself, and out came our friend, yelling: "What the HELL?" My wife and I were on the ground, on our knees, bent over and laughing. We couldn't talk; we could barely breathe. I pointed down the street in the direction the cowboy had walked, but no one was there.

Why is this funny? Allow me to get academic here for a moment. By some accounts, there are three theories to humor: the incongruity theory, the superiority theory, and the relief theory. The incongruity theory occurs when the outcome is radically different from the one we had expected. Here, I say, "Where's your coat?" and the boy responds, "Huskers lost!" and tries to kick over the Porta-John with my friend inside. It's the incongruity between what's said and what's done that's funny. The superiority theory is when we laugh at someone else's blunder, foolishness, or (in this instance) bad luck. My friend who was in the Porta-John has never fully appreciated the humor of the situation, but everyone else has—and they have for one reason: we're not him. Furthermore, we're *glad* we're not him. The relief theory occurs when a comic moment—sometimes a funny comment—is inserted into a tension-filled moment. The tension in the story is in whether the Porta-John is going to tip over or not, but the comic moment comes when it finally rights itself and my friend bursts out of it, yelling, "What the HELL?"

These are but three theories on humor and how it works. Study them. Memorize them. But I'm not sure it will matter at the end of the day. Humor is instinctual. You can't teach someone who's not funny how to be funny. If you still don't believe me, I've come up with a formula to *become* funny: "John McNally's Sure-Fire Formula for Becoming Funnier in 30 Days!" Let's take a quick look at Day Seven. Here, I ask you to memorize an old vaudeville routine (i.e., "Who's on First?") and then practice it so as to learn something about the cadence of comic timing and comic rapport. After doing so, watch White House Press Secretary Scott McClellan talk to reporters. Pay special attention to the cadence of his answers and the rhythms of his rapport with the press. My point? If you want to write political satire, you'll want to study vaudeville; if you want to watch vaudeville, turn on C-SPAN. The following exchange between McClellan and the press is real, but it *reads* like satire:

REPORTER: So would the President veto a three-month extension?

MR. McCLELLAN: Well, the President has already made his views known on that—I expressed his views last week—and nothing has changed in terms of our views. That's why it's important for them to go ahead and get this passed now.

REPORTER: So you would veto a three-month extension?

MR. McCLELLAN: I expressed our view last week; nothing has changed.

REPORTER: Can you tell me what that was again?

MR. McCLELLAN: You can see what I expressed last week. You know very well what it was.

REPORTER: Sounds like you're backing down from that.

MR. McCLELLAN: No, nothing has changed in terms of what I said last week.

REPORTER: So just say it. Just say—

REPORTER: Will you use the word "veto"? Why are you not using the word "veto"?

MR. McCLELLAN: I expressed our views on that last week—

REPORTER: But if you still stand by them, why won't you reiterate it?

MR. McCLELLAN: Well, again, what I said last week still stands.

REPORTER: Which is what?

ABBOTT: No. What is on second base.

COSTELLO: I'm not asking you who's on second.

ABBOTT: Who's on first.

COSTELLO: One base at a time!

ABBOTT: Well, don't change the players around.

COSTELLO: I'm not changing nobody!

ABBOTT: Take it easy, buddy.

COSTELLO: I'm only asking you, who's the guy on first base?

ABBOTT: That's right.

COSTELLO: OK.

ABBOTT: All right.

And so I offer to you twenty-nine other sure-fire tips below. If at the end of the month you have not laughed at anything you've watched or read, and if no one has laughed at anything you've written or done, then you're not funny. Sorry.

John McNally's Sure-Fire Formula for Becoming Funnier in 30 Days!

- Day 1: Read Mark Twain. Any Mark Twain will do. Twain pretty much embodies every mode of 19th century humor in America, which pretty much set the stage for every form of humor that followed.

- Day 2: Spend the day watching Charlie Chaplin, Laurel and Hardy, Fatty Arbuckle, Buster Keaton, and Harold Lloyd comedies. Stick to their silent movies. There's much to be learned here about how comedy arises out of situation and pathos.

- Day 3: Read Walter Blair's critical history, *Native American Humor*, which is a book about humor that is native to this country and not, as the title leads you to believe, a book about humor by Native Americans.

- Day 4: Listen to (and memorize) George Carlin's "Seven Words You Can't Say on Television." The content may not be applicable anymore, so pay attention to the order of the words and the rhythm that this order creates, and how quite a bit of the humor grows out of the cadence of the list.

- Day 5: Read Charles Portis' novel *Masters of Atlantis*. Portis may be the least-known but funniest contemporary American writer.

- Day 6: Watch *Triumph: The Insult Comic Dog*. Whether you think this is funny or not is a moot point. Watch it. Learn from it. Otherwise . . . *you suck!*

- Day 7: Memorize an old vaudeville routine (i.e., "Who's on First"). Practice it all day long. See above for relevance.

- Day 8: Read *The Signet Book of American Humor*, edited by Regina Barreca. How could you go wrong with a book that includes work by both Benjamin Franklin *and* Jeff Foxworthy? Also included is funnyman Henry James and laugh-a-minute Sylvia Plath.

- Day 9: Watch *The Best of Johnny Carson*. And then, by contrast (and as evidence that the end is indeed nigh) watch Jay Leno.

- Day 10: Read up on the Algonquin Roundtable then read work by those who were part of it: Dorothy Parker, Robert Benchley, George S. Kaufman, Edna Ferber, etc.

- Day 11: Watch *Saturday Night Live: The Best of Chris Farley*. In particular, watch the skit titled "The Herlihy Boy." If you don't find this funny after the fifth viewing, throw this sheet away and go back to your day job.

- Day 12: Read *Honey, Hush: An Anthology of African American Women's Humor* and *Hokum: An Anthology of African American Humor*. Granted, this is nearly 2,000 pages of reading for the day, but so it goes. One must make sacrifices if one wants to become funny.

- Day 13: Work on an impression of someone you know personally but don't like. Hint: The successful impression is really more about nuance than accuracy of voice. A friend of mine believes that in order to do a really good impression, you need to really love the person you're doing an impression of, or you must really hate the person. There's a good deal of truth in this.

- Day 14: Spend the entire day watching the Three Stooges. Acceptable combinations of Stooges include "Moe, Larry, and Curly" or "Moe, Larry, and Shemp." Do not, under any circumstance, watch "Moe, Larry, and Joe" or the feature films starring "Moe, Larry, and Curly-Joe." These are *not* funny.

- Day 15: Take the Day Off: You may be becoming too funny for your own good. Your less funny friends and neighbors are probably starting to hate you.

- Day 16: Find something in the news and then write a joke about it. This is harder than you think.

- Day 17: Watch an early Marx Brothers movie, preferably one that includes Zeppo. Zeppo wasn't funny, but the films in which Zeppo appeared are the best Marx Brothers movies. (Quiz: If you can name the elusive *fifth* Marx Brother, you're probably already funny.)

- Day 18: Go to a joke shop and buy a squirting flower or a buzzer that fits in your palm, and then try it out on a colleague. Why is this funny? (You may be the only person laughing, but it *is* funny. I mean, really, it *is*.)

- Day 19: Rent old *Laugh-In* DVDs but watch only the skits featuring Lily Tomlin. The rest of it won't make sense unless you're stoned.

- Day 20: Watch numerous Road Runner cartoons. Notice that the humor is amplified the more we empathize with Wile E. Coyote. After watching the cartoons, read Ian Frazier's brilliant short piece "Coyote V. Acme," which is written in the form of a lawsuit, complete with legalese, in which Coyote sues Acme for the damage he sustained while using their products.

- Day 21: Read short stories by Lorrie Moore, George Saunders, T.C. Boyle, and Sherman Alexie. Compare and contrast.

- Day 22: Write a parody of something you see all the time: a personal ad; an author's bio; a memo from work. (Read Ian Frazier's "Coyote V. Acme.")

- Day 23: Time to watch some sit-coms. My recommendations: *The Honeymooners, I Love Lucy, Hogan's Heroes, Sanford and Son, and Seinfeld*. Pay attention to dialogue and characterization. Ask yourself, who's the straight man (or woman) and who's the comic? Is there a formula to the configuration of characters? Is Sergeant Schultz really just another variation on Kramer?

- Day 24: Go up to the top of a building that's at least six stories tall and drop a tomato out the window. Why's that funny? Spend the rest of the day contemplating this.

- Day 25: Read *The Onion*. If you don't know what *The Onion* is, crumple up this sheet and go rent *The Prince of Tides*.

- Day 26: Write a satiric news article in the mode of *The Onion*. Good frickin' luck!

- Day 27: Read James Agee's essay, "Comedy's Greatest Era." (Note: It's not a funny essay.)

- Day 28: Dust off those old Cheech and Chong albums. Make sure they're from the early '70s. Are there any parallels between '70s drug humor and the vaudevillians whose sketches you memorized? (Abbott and Costello are really Cheech and Chong's kindred spirits when you get right down to it.)

- Day 29: Watch the documentary *American Movie*. This movie contains perhaps the funniest moment ever recorded on film. If by the end of the movie you're not sure which moment I'm referring to, then go back to "Day 1" and start over.

- Day 30: Give this list to your least funny friend, wait thirty days, and then see if it works. If it does work, my humor-is-innate-theory is clearly wrong, and I'm sorry I've wasted your time. If it doesn't, well, I rest my case.

2007

Index

Credits

Also by the Author

Crossroads: Creative Writing Exercises in Four Genres (2005)
Open Roads: Exercises in Writing Poetry (2005)
The White Horse: A Colombian Journey (2004)
Resistance Fantasies (2004)
Writing Your Rhythm: Using Nature, Culture, Form and Myth (2001)
Echolocations (Nicholas Roerich Prize, 2000)
Cleft in the Wall (chapbook, 1999)

Music in the Post-9/11 World

Edited by

Jonathan Ritter
University of California, Riverside

J. Martin Daughtry
New York University

Routledge
Taylor & Francis Group
New York   London

Routledge
Taylor & Francis Group
270 Madison Avenue
New York, NY 10016

Routledge
Taylor & Francis Group
2 Park Square
Milton Park, Abingdon
Oxon OX14 4RN

© 2007 by Taylor & Francis Group, LLC
Routledge is an imprint of Taylor & Francis Group, an Informa business

Printed in the United States of America on acid-free paper
10 9 8 7 6 5 4 3 2 1

International Standard Book Number-13: 978-0-415-97807-1 (Softcover) 978-0-415-97806-4 (Hardcover)

Library of Congress Cataloging-in-Publication Data

Music in the post-9/11 world / Jonathan Ritter and J. Martin Daughtry, editors.
    p. cm.
  Includes index.
  ISBN-13: 978-0-415-97806-4
  ISBN-10: 0-415-97806-8
  ISBN-13: 978-0-415-97807-1
  ISBN-10: 0-415-97807-6
  1. Popular music--Political aspects. 2. September 11 Terrorist Attacks,
2001--Songs and music--History and criticism. 3. War on Terrorism, 2001---Songs
and music--History and criticism. I. Ritter, Jonathan. II. Daughtry, J. Martin. III. Title:
Music in the post nine/eleven world.

ML3918.P67M83 2007
780.9'05--dc22   2007007584

Visit the Taylor & Francis Web site at
http://www.taylorandfrancis.com

and the Routledge Web site at
http://www.routledge.com